This book is dedicated, in loving memory, to my grandmothers, Etta Riklan and Minnie Rosen. Both of them showed me tremendous love and support while I was still growing up.

May their spirits and love live on forever.

ACKNOWLEDGEMENTS

When I began to write the acknowledgements for this book, I asked myself: "What has really driven me?"

When I began working on Volume 3 of our *101 Great Ways* series, I realized that I had a difficult task ahead. We already created Volumes 1 and 2, which included what I felt were 202 *really great ways* to improve your life. How could we come up with another 101 Great Ways? What could we do next?

Our team went to work and came up with what I believe are truly another *101 Great Ways to Improve Your Life*.

I'd like to acknowledge each and every author that contributed to this book—in fact, there would *be* no book without the inspiring wisdom and words of each of our contributing authors. Thank you to Ken Blanchard, Mark Victor Hansen, Les Brown, Byron Katie, and the 97 other authors that made this book a powerful tool to help improve our lives.

In addition to all of the contributors to the book, there were three people involved that deserve a very special thanks. Stephanie Anastasio, Kristina Kanaley and Jerry Kimbrough made the creation of this book possible. This three person team worked closely together to create this powerful self-improvement book—and, in many ways, were more responsible for the completion of this book than I was.

I would also like to thank many other members of our self-improvement team. I would like to thank Maryann Matera, one of the newest members of our team. She jumped right into this new project with both energy and focus. Todd Lesser and Jamie Albert provided many hours of valuable feedback and insights which were instrumental in the creation of our "101 Great Ways" book series. Joe De Palma provided staunch support for this project and helped me stay focused on this new endeavor. Adriene Hayes has assisted in countless aspects of our business. Amy Gelsomine, Gary Dong, Douglas Pak and Greg Aronne have all helped to expand our self-improvement message around the world.

There have been many other people that have been a continual source of inspiration for my books, my website and my business. The complete list is to large to include, but some of these key people include: Peggy McColl, Mike Litman, Mike Brescia, Pete Bissonette, Gay Hendricks, Karim Hajee, Vic Johnson,

Scott Martineau, Hale Dwoskin, Kyle Wilson, Bill Harris and Brad Antin. Many other "Self Improvement" experts have provided me with great inspiration including Zig Ziglar, Brian Tracy, Jim Rohn, Denis Waitley, John Gray, Jack Canfield, Richard Carlson, Bob Proctor and Alan Cohen,

Many special thanks are due to my friends and family, who have provided much-needed support and encouragement throughout the process.

Finally, a special thanks to my wife, Michelle, who is a continual source of motivation for everything that I do.

TABLE OF CONTENTS

Contents

Contents

Contents

Contents

xi

Contents

Contents

Contents

Contents

Contents

Contents

INTRODUCTION – BY DAVID RIKLAN

Inspiration. Motivation. Knowledge. They all can enter our lives by means of many different influences. We learn from teachers, family, friends, and even strangers. We can learn something from everyone we encounter, but the real challenge comes in synthesizing this vast array of knowledge into manageable, life altering guidance.

Our third volume of *101 Great Ways to Improve Your Life* does just that. We have gathered wisdom from 101 motivational authors, all eager to share their secrets of happiness and success with you. With this book, this wealth of information is literally at your fingertips.

WHY A THIRD VOLUME?

Over the course of the last year, we published Volumes 1 and 2 of *101 Great Ways to Improve Your Life*. The response was overwhelming. The feedback on the articles was so positive it left our readers asking, "How can I learn more?"

Volume 3 is that "more."

In Volume 3, we expand on the topics covered in the previous two volumes and tackle new areas of our lives that need improvement. Would you like to know new ways to control your finances? Better ways to communicate with your spouse? A faster way to do…something?

Also, in this third installment you will find many different voices answering the same challenges that we all face in our life. We have tried to provide different approaches that will work for a broad range of people. Whether you respond to similar personal experiences, a take charge attitude, or strict discipline, you will be able to find one, if not many, authors who are speaking directly to you. Our goal is to provide you with enough quality information to make some real changes in your life.

One of my personal methods for maintaining my focus and drive is to use other people's words to "motivate me." For years, inspirational quotes have been a part of my life and have helped keep me focused. I also think they are an effective way to learn.

1

Take, for example, one of my favorite quotes from President Calvin Coolidge:

Nothing in this world can take the place of persistence. Talent will not; nothing is more common than unsuccessful men with talent. Genius will not; unrewarded genius is almost a proverb. Education is not; the world is full of educated derelicts. Persistence and determination are omnipotent.

There are 101 authors in this book, each with their own opinions, remedies, and advice which they have lived by in order to make the most out of their lives. Though each author's distinctive voice may speak to you in a different way, they all share a common thread: their persistence was the key to improving their lives, and they want it to become a part of improving yours.

Nothing in this world can take the place of persistence.

Persistence is a virtue attainable through a positive attitude and outlook on life. There are chapters in this book on relationships and healing that will help you manage and focus your energy in the right direction. The path to a happy, successful life is just that: a path. Meeting the right people along the way and connecting with the advice they have is essential to developing a persistent attitude which can help you live a positive and productive life.

Talent will not; nothing is more common than unsuccessful men with talent. Genius will not; unrewarded genius is almost a proverb. Education will not; the world is full of educated derelicts.

There are many chapters in this book which lead you in the direction of finding the tools which best compliment the goals in your life. Focusing your energy and persistence is no easy feat, but learning how to harness your natural abilities can lead you in the right direction.

Do you have a creative inner self waiting to be unleashed? Are you using the most of your communication skills? Do you want to know the secret of feeling good? Can meditation help you achieve clarity in your everyday life? Do you want to know how to live a positive life in a negative world?

The tools to finding the best way to improve your life are dispersed throughout 101 motivational chapters. With topics ranging from strengthening your relationships, time management, and achieving your goals there is something in this book for everyone. The table of contents guides you by topic, title, and author making it easy for you to navigate through the wealth of advice these experts have provided.

Persistence and determination are omnipotent.

Volume 3 continues on the track paved by the previous volumes in the *Great Ways* series. There are so many unique authors who submit material to our self improvement super-site, SelfGrowth.com, that those featured in this book are just the tip of the iceberg. Every topic and every question you can think of regarding personal growth and improvement can be found at SelfGrowth.com. Think of Volume 3 as another pocket companion that compliments all the resources available online.

With persistence and determination, you can fully realize the impact you have on your own life. To reference one of the authors in this compilation, *you are the architect of your own destiny*. Hopefully, you can find the same motivation in these articles as we here at Self Improvement Online, Inc, have. So here you have it: 101 inspirational articles, by very motivational authors, that can help you make the most out of your life.

So, on behalf of everyone here at Self Improvement Online, Inc, I wish you the best of luck. Remember, nothing in the world can take the place of persistence, and we have *101 Great Ways* to help you realize your fullest potential!

1

How to Achieve Your Wildest Dreams in Just 12 Minutes a Day

Wendy Y. Carter

> Faith is taking the first step even when you don't see the whole staircase.
> —Martin Luther King, Jr.

How much would your life change if you knew that achieving your wildest dreams could take as little as 12 minutes a day?

Think of the unlimited possibilities that provides! Most of us believe that we simply do not have time to accomplish the goals we secretly wish to achieve. Instead of setting out to tackle our dreams, we whittle away the minutes complaining that there is just not enough time in the day.

In actuality, you do not need a lot of time to achieve your dreams, and you do not have to take a sabbatical from your busy life to achieve a long-term goal. Anything you wish to achieve—large or small—can be completed in tandem with numerous other important life tasks, such as spending time with family and friends, working a full-time job, maintaining your household, and engaging in the hobbies or activities that you love.

All you need is *persistence,* effective time management . . . and at least 12 minutes a day.

Step 1: Break Down Your Goal into Small, Manageable Tasks

Whether it is learning a new language, losing weight, or writing a book, some goals seem so daunting that you simply do not know where to begin. To get started, break down that huge goal of yours into a to-do list of smaller, more manageable tasks. Create a checklist of every item you will need to complete to take you closer to your goal.

I always advise graduate students to break down their thesis projects into 12- to 15-minute tasks. Something as simple as typing a title page or reading a research article will move them closer to their overall goal. Small tasks are less overwhelming to tackle, and they can easily be accomplished in a day. Presto! You are well on your way!

Step 2: Create Daily, Weekly, and Monthly To-Do Lists

Your checklist of tasks is likely to be lengthy. Try not to overwhelm yourself by dealing with the total list. Instead, focus on a schedule of hourly, daily, or weekly tasks that you would like to complete.

For example, I was determined to run a marathon on my 40th birthday and mapped out a six-month training program to prepare. I posted a weekly schedule on my refrigerator so I could easily refer to what I needed to accomplish each day, for example, running a specific number of minutes or miles. I focused *only* on the accomplishment outlined for the current day and did not look any farther down the road. When the week was over, I posted another schedule for the upcoming week. I knew that if I did exactly what was posted on the refrigerator each day, I would be ready for the marathon when the time came. That removed any fear I might have had of not being able to complete my goal.

Step 3: Make a Commitment to Work Every Day

Clearly, accomplishing goals like writing a thesis, losing weight, or running a marathon takes a significant amount of time and effort. As such, it is critical to keep the momentum going by making a commitment to *work toward your goal every day*. On some days your commitment can be as little as 12 minutes; on other days you may log hours. The point is that every day, you need to take *some time* and *some action . . . even if you do not feel like it*.

Each morning, start your day by asking what action you will take to move toward your goal. Refer often to the checklist you made of all the small items that must be completed in order to make forward progress. Resolve yourself to work on one of those items *each and every day* for a minimum of 12 minutes. No task is too small, and no item is too insignificant; *every* action will move you closer to your goal. End every day by reinforcing your to-do items for the following day.

Step 4: Use Rewards as Motivators

When you meet a deadline or complete a significant accomplishment, reward yourself by doing something you enjoy, such as shopping or sharing coffee with a friend, renting a movie, or indulging in an ice cream. Having a tangible reward, however small, can provide added motivation to get work done.

Tell yourself that you will not allow yourself to enjoy these special "luxuries" until you have completed your daily task. For example, I wrote my dissertation during the NBA finals. I would not watch the game unless I had finished my daily checklist items. This allowed me to write with purpose and afterward watch the game *without a sense of guilt.*

Step 5: Always Have a Backup Plan

It is easy to jump out of bed and accomplish your scheduled task when you are filled with joy and enthusiasm or have nothing else planned for the day. But what about when you are rushed for time or your enthusiasm has waned? For those times it is important to establish routines to help motivate you and also to plan *ahead of time* what type of alternative solutions you can fall back on should conflicts arise.

When I was training for the marathon, there were many days when I did not feel inspired to jump out of bed and into my running shoes at 5:00 A.M. The toughest moment was when the alarm clock sounded; I was always tempted to hit the snooze bar and void my training for the day. Knowing this, I set a routine to make getting out the door easier. Each night, I laid my workout clothes at the end of my bed so that I could reach them as soon as I awoke. After dressing, I called my sister and stayed on the phone all the way to the track. By then, there was no turning back.

Sometimes routines alone will not cut it. There will always be circumstances when the openings you have faithfully scheduled to complete your daily tasks are interrupted, be it by family emergencies, impromptu meetings, or an injury that needs treatment. Despite your best intentions, conflicts such as these can force you to reschedule or abandon your plans.

Take heart: Every day and every 12 minutes provide another opportunity. When you are waiting in the airport, grocery line, or dentist's office, revert to a backup plan. For example, if you are writing a book, carry a tape recorder to record ideas while you wait. The most important thing is to *just do something*.

When lack of motivation is the issue, turn back to your trusty checklist. If your scheduled task was to write a key point for a thesis but you just do not feel up to it today, find and complete another—smaller—task. You do not have to complete *every* item on your checklist every day . . . but in order to be successful, you *do* have to work at least 12 minutes each day and complete at least one thing on your checklist.

Go Achieve Your Dreams!

Following these simple steps means that there is no need to procrastinate pursuing your goals any longer. Come on, you can work for just *12 minutes* a day! So set your watch, cell phone, microwave, or timer and see what you can accomplish in that time frame. Those minutes will eventually add up to the realization of your dreams!

ABOUT THE AUTHOR

Dr. Wendy Carter was raised in a home challenged by poverty, alcoholism, and abuse; the statistics said that she would not graduate high school or attend college. Ignoring those statistics, she earned four postbaccalaureate degrees from Stanford, Carnegie Mellon, and the University of Wisconsin–Madison, even after becoming a single parent. That 50 percent of all graduate students fail to graduate prompted Dr. Carter to develop an interactive CD-ROM, *TADA! Thesis and Dissertation Accomplished*, designed to alleviate the high attrition rate among graduate students. As a motivational speaker, Dr. Carter continues to be an inspiration and invaluable resource to students and educators.

2

Anger: It May Not Be What You Think It Is

Wesley Doherty

Even though you can identify it easily in today's world, anger may not be what you think it is. All you have to do is spend a minute with the headlines and you come in contact with many forms of anger. For many of us it is felt much closer than the anger the headlines report: We feel anger toward others and the anger of others directed at us.

Most of us carry some degree of anger within us. We experience anger anywhere from mild irritation all the way up to seething rage, and we can feel it once a year, once a month, once a week, once a day, once a minute, or even all the time. But even if you only experience mild irritation once a year, you still harbor anger. Carrying anger hurts you much more than it hurts the person you have directed your anger at, so it is in your best interest to be free of anger completely.

For example, imagine that you are happily driving down the highway to work one morning. As you come up to an exit, a motorist blows by you and then dangerously cuts you off in order to make the exit ramp. You gesture wildly and yell at him for being so rude and careless. You think about it all the way to work, where you vigorously tell the story to your coworkers. You think about it often during the day. You drive home with your eye out for the offending driver so you can give him a piece of your mind or maybe even dole out a little payback. Once home, you retell the story to your family.

What has happened is that you have kept your body on high alert all day. You have carried that anger with you all day—starting with when you got cut off and then every time you remembered the event or retold the story—and your body responded to every reenactment with a rush of adrenaline, an increase in stress levels, a contraction of your muscles, and a halt to your digestive and sexual functioning, to name just a few of the body's automatic responses to a threat.

The driver who cut you off, on the other hand, has felt none of these symptoms. He forgot that he cut you off before he reached the light at the end of the exit ramp and went merrily about his day, never thinking about you again. You were the only one to feel the anger directed at him, and you were the only one to pay the price for that anger.

Anger takes many forms, but they fall into two main categories: anger expressed inwardly is felt as depression, and anger expressed outwardly is attack. Whichever category it falls under, your anger hurts you, so it is in your best interest to be completely free of anger.

Here is how most of us believe we get angry: Something external happens that wrongs us (a friend says the wrong thing, a child misbehaves, a driver cuts you off, etc.), and we correctly and justifiably respond with anger. As long as you agree that this is the way anger arises in you, you will be a slave to anger and all of its negative outcomes.

As this is a world of cause and effect, with our thoughts being the cause, to experience anger physically, we first have to hold an angry belief. If you want to be free of anger and its natural outcomes forever, you must first change your beliefs about where anger originates.

As I am writing this, I have been lying in the sun, and occasionally, a hornet will land on me and walk around siphoning off something it finds tasty in my sweat. Once it has had its fill, it harmlessly flies away. These are the same hornets that stung me when I drove over their nest with my lawn mower just the week before. People are the same: We are just going about our day, when someone does something that ticks us off, and we feel attacked by it, so we respond to the attack with righteous anger, knowing full well we were in no way responsible for the attack.

To that I say, "No matter how hard you squeeze a grapefruit, you can't get apple juice." Squeeze a grapefruit with varying degrees of pressure and from a variety of angles, and you can only get out what is already in there: grapefruit juice. People are the same way: No matter how much pressure we are under, only what is already in us can come out of us.

10

When I was a kid, I bit my nails, sometimes to the point of injuring my finger so that it would get cut and filled with pus. The slightest pressure on that finger would cause me great pain, while ten times the pressure on the finger right next to it could hardly be felt. Emotionally, we are the same way: We can withstand great amounts of pressure where we are healed, while small amounts of pressure where we are yet to be healed cause us to writhe in pain and react strongly. So if you feel angry when your spouse misspeaks, your child misbehaves, another driver cuts you off, and so on, it is only because they are putting pressure on a spot where hurt already resides.

There are only two kinds of beliefs: a love-based belief and a fear-based belief. Anger is of fear, so when you are angry, you are actually afraid. As a love-based belief always comes down to "I am enough" and a fear-based belief always comes down to "I am not enough," the original belief that makes you angry is a belief you hold about yourself that you are somehow inadequate, that you are somehow not enough.

When we remember that our thoughts create our realities, we can see that we do not get angry as a response to someone attacking us. We get angry because we hold mistaken beliefs about ourselves as true, and they manifest in such a way that we come face-to-face with a pain we have been trying to disown. When we strike out with anger at the reminder of our mistaken beliefs (whoever or whatever they may be), we reinforce our beliefs in our own victimization and continue the cycle of miserable enslavement to a world that waits to attack. When we instead recognize that our own mistaken beliefs have created this event, we empower ourselves to choose new beliefs and set ourselves, and those around us, completely free.

You will find that over time, by healing your fear-based beliefs about yourself (your emotional sore fingers, if you will), you will respond with anger to fewer and fewer things and with forgiveness and joy to more and more things. And the more forgiveness and joy you experience, the easier your life is!

About the Author

For over 15 years, Wesley Doherty has been helping people redirect their creative powers to work for and not against them in his proven "Lose Weight: Get and Keep Your Ideal Body" and "Freedom from Headaches" programs, his televised lectures, and his book *A Simple Truth for a Peaceful Life*. Visit http://www.AnEasierLife.com today, and sign up for his free "Your Easier Life" e-newsletter. To your easier life!

3

ATTRACTION ACTION

The Nine Strategies to Attract Your Greatest Intentions in Life

Christopher M. Knight

Attraction is an invisible force that moves one object to another. For those who have mastered how to attract whatever they want in life, it feels effortless, and it is a much more fun way to go through life. Anyone can learn the principles of attraction and put them to immediate use.

Following are the nine steps to discovering how to put the power of attraction to work in your own life.

1. Attraction principles or laws are universal and undeniable. You and I did not invent them, yet they exist.

You do not have to agree with the laws of attraction, but you may recognize that you are already attracting what you do and do not want in life by your daily intentions and actions. Focus, and choose your thoughts carefully.

2. Like attracts like. Have you ever noticed that you can never get enough of what you do not want? This is because you are usually focusing on what you do not want to happen, and you keep getting more of what you do not want. Just like you can attract what you want, you can also attract what you do not want.

Attraction as a power does not know good from bad. This is very similar to how your subconscious works. Be very conscious of what specifically you want, and deny yourself the luxury of negative thoughts or thoughts that do not align with what you are intending to attract.

3. Abundance is the natural and normal order of things in this universe. We come into this world preprogrammed by nature to attract whatever it is that we want. Any friction or inability to attract our greatest desires is a learned trait. Therefore immediately assume that your life is filled with abundance, no matter how small.

You have heard the old saying "the rich get richer, and the poor get poorer," right? Can you see why this is true? It is as easy as choosing to be rich because you already are in more ways than you may want to admit.

4. All attraction begins in the formless state of thought or intention. You are already thinking about what you want and do not want all day long. To increase your chances of attracting what you want, you will want to narrow your focus and attention so that a greater percentage of your daily life is spent on activities that pull you toward your highest intentions.

Whatever you focus on expands. You get whatever you think about most. Choose thoughts that move in the same direction as your intentions, and deny yourself the indulgence of negative thoughts. You are the creator of your destiny and experience.

5. Intention without action is a way to guarantee that you will attract what you do not want. Therefore as soon as you have clarity on what you want to attract, find ways to stay in daily massive amounts of action . . . until your intention becomes manifest.

Life rewards action. Here is a fun game to play with yourself: How can you make a higher percentage of your day filled with thoughts and actions that are aligned with your best intentions? You may be surprised to discover how much of your day is not invested in moving toward your intentions. Stop, find out where you are—measure it—and then consciously direct your attention to invest a greater percentage of your time taking action toward your intentions.

6. Attraction only happens in the present moment (never in the past nor in the future); therefore focus on what you can think and do right now in this very moment to move in the direction you want most for yourself, your life, your health, your family, your business, and so on.

The present is perfect. Everything that is is as it is supposed to be. While you cannot always control what happens to you in life, you can control how you respond to life. Start by observing life without judgment, and then move toward becoming an active director in your ideal life experience.

7. Live your passion. Feelings and emotions can amplify and speed up your ability to attract whatever you want in life. Negative emotions can also amplify and speed up the attraction of things you do not want in life.

Begin by choosing to define the experience that you want for this life, and then expect that with massive amounts of action and plenty of faith in yourself, you will attract whatever you want. It is this easy, and you know it is true for you.

8. Become highly aware of what your highest values are so that you can lead a purpose-driven life that is congruent with your own expectations of yourself.

Having intentions that are not consistent with your highest values will result in frustration or, worse, in the successful attraction of a result that does not make you happy on the inside. Intentions that move you toward your goals will always intuitively seem more effortless than ones that feel like a lot of work to attract.

9. Make your intentions extremely specific, yet do not get attached to the outcome. The more clearly you are able to define what you want, the faster it will show up in your life.

Once you have a core set of intentions that you want to manifest for yourself, write them down immediately. Define your dreams, intentions, and goals even further in measurable terms. What gets measured gets managed, and what does not get measured does not get managed. The best way to not get attached to the outcome is to simply believe that you have the ability attract whatever you want in life and that it will show up exactly as it is supposed to. Have faith in yourself.

Conclusion

Whatever you focus your attention on, you will attract more of. Guard your thoughts, and become incredibly aware of which thoughts you are thinking. Do not worry about judging your thoughts as right or wrong, but rather, focus your finite amount of time on this earth on attracting what you want from life. It is the natural order of things that will allow more abundance into life when you choose thoughts and actions that move you toward your greatest values and purpose. You are the creator of your experiences. Choose your thoughts wisely.

ABOUT THE AUTHOR

Christopher Knight is an entrepreneur with a specialty in helping experts in over 300 different business niches to attract high levels of qualified visitors back to their Web sites thanks to quality original article writing and marketing strategies. You can learn more about Chris Knight via his Web site at http://ChrisKnight.com/

4

Be Authentic and True to Yourself

Kiernan Antares

If you have built castles in the air, your work need not be lost;
that is where they should be. Now put foundations under them.
—Henry David Thoreau

No one can make you feel inferior without your consent.
—Eleanor Roosevelt

So many of us spend the majority of our lives trying to please others. Usually, it starts at a very young age through interaction with our parents. We want them to be proud of us, but when we come home with a "B" and they ask why we did not get an "A." our spirits are crushed. The child who is yelled at because he missed scoring the goal or for interrupting a conversation to show something he just created is heartbroken in that moment. I use these as examples, but I think you get the idea.

Our self-worth becomes attached to our performance, whether through academics, athletics, or in our professions. We come to believe that being loved depends on how well we perform, what we look like, how we dress, or what we own.

Somewhere along the way, our light has been extinguished, and we lose sight of the special gifts we brought with us into this world because we have buried them so deep to protect ourselves from being hurt any further.

Abandoning our dreams and desires because they did not fit the so-called normal path, we take jobs because we were conditioned to believe it was the safe and right thing to do. All the while, an ache to return to our true selves resides, and we continue our search to fill the void by looking elsewhere, in relationships, other people, and in our achievements.

We spend years, maybe the rest of our lives, trying to prove our worthiness to our parents, our bosses, our friends, and to others in our lives. Well, guess what? It cannot be done! It is an impossible task because what we are looking for is not outside ourselves.

I will say it again—what we are looking for is not outside ourselves!

My heart goes out to the young girls and women with low self-esteem who are being bombarded with messages that being thin or having large breasts makes them more desirable or acceptable. As a young girl lacking self-confidence in the 1970s, I would starve myself for days or weeks at a time in an attempt to model myself after the women on the hit show *Charlie's Angels*.

It did not stop there: I went from being anorexic to bulimic right up until I was 30 years old. I have suffered some health problems over the years as a result of the damage I did to my body during those years. But thankfully, I survived, and I am now healthy, confident, and strong because I have learned to love, trust, and honor myself and to follow my own path.

The point is that we do stupid things, sometimes detrimental to our health and well-being, to mold ourselves into something we are not meant to be in a vain attempt to search for what is missing. In the process we lose out on realizing our true inner power and what we are meant to do.

The only real source of approval is found in the fountain within. If we want to love and trust ourselves at deeper levels, we must fully accept who we are. This requires acknowledging and accepting our positive qualities as well as the shadow sides.

When we truly know and appreciate every aspect of our beings, then we have the ability to trust our decisions and ourselves. As a result, we will follow our own paths and not ones that others have put upon us.

Are You Self-Accepting?

To help you determine your level of self-acceptance, respond to the following questions by writing down in your journal any thoughts or feelings they stir up.

1. Does my value as a person depend largely on what others think of me?
2. Do I use self-defeating methods as a way to reward myself either for a success or for getting through a rough period? For example, do I overeat, drink too much, or go on shopping sprees when I am already in debt?
3. Do I have difficulties receiving help or compliments with grace?
4. Do I see only flaws when I look at myself in the mirror?
5. Do I beat myself up when I make a mistake?
6. Do I feel that my life would be better if only I were smarter, better looking, or had more money?
7. Do I do things to nurture, strengthen, and relax my body and mind?
8. Am I able to turn to my friends or family for help when I need it?
9. Do I recognize and value my need for solitude or quiet time to reconnect with my Spirit?
10. Am I able to accept and express my vulnerable feelings of sadness, anxiety, or anger?

Take note whether you rely too heavily on other people's opinions and find it difficult to assert or express yourself in your personal or professional life. Check in to see if you are so anxious to please others that you often ignore your own wants and needs, and begin to make changes by including activities to nurture your connection to Spirit.

Learn to be more tolerant of your mistakes if you find you are often self-critical and overly demanding with yourself. It is important to make the time to discover what is important in your life and what gives you the most satisfaction and joy.

If you are patient with yourself, have a well-developed sense of self, and treat yourself with love and respect, congratulations!

Increasing Your Connection to Self

Here are some ideas to improve your sense of self.

- We cannot emphasize enough how life-affirming and empowering journaling can be. So much of our time is spent doing things we "should" do and ignoring our inner calling. Connecting to your Spirit while writing in your journal will allow you to get in touch with your true self, and by listening to what comes up, you will begin to feel safe to explore new ideas or thoughts.

- Practice taking steps every day toward doing things that you value the most in your life, whether it is your health, your personal growth, or your relationships. Your true self will emerge with every small step you take toward recognizing and acting on your personal values.

- Replace self-criticism with kindness. Create a list of qualities you like and admire about yourself, and read it every day to remind yourself what an amazing person you are.

- Learn to celebrate every success, even the ones where you might not have done everything you set out to do. You tried; you gave it an effort, and that is worthy of a reward. Shout to the rooftops, "*Yes!*"

- Respect your newfound dreams or values by not allowing others to disrespect them. If you know someone will ridicule or criticize you, then avoid discussing these new dreams with that person until you develop the confidence in yourself that will keep you protected from negative forces coming toward you.

There is so much life to live. Do not waste another moment trying to live up to other people's expectations. Discover your dreams, speak your truth, and surrender to them. Let the familiar solid ground beneath your feet transform into a fluid unknown force capable of letting you soar to unbelievable heights on the wings of angels. Hold your dreams in your arms, nurture them, and do not let them go. Your soul, your dreams, and your purpose are the reasons you exist.

Excerpted from SAY YES! Discover Your Dreams and Create a Life You Love.

ABOUT THE AUTHOR

Kiernan Antares is an impassioned writer, Reiki Master, life coach, and visionary whose purpose is to inspire people to reconnect with their Spirits and live their dreams. Her work serves to entertain the mind, motivate the spirit, and feed souls that are hungry for possible answers to life's endless questions. Her debut novel, *Phoenix Star—An Adventure of the Spirit*, has been hailed "an inspirational fantasy celebrating the magical potential inside us all. I could not put it down" by Grace Cirocco, author of the best-selling *Take the Step; the Bridge Will Be There*. Kiernan currently lives in Toronto, Canada, where she is writing her next book with her partner, Paul Osland: *SAY YES! Discover Your Passion and Create a Life You Love*, a guide to help readers awaken to their destinies. For more details, visit http://www.kiernanantares.com.

5

The Secrets to Being Unstoppable

Duanna Pang-Dokland

The slogan "press on" has solved and always will solve the problems of the human race.
—Calvin Coolidge, 30th U.S. president

We all start our journey of aspirations with visions, goals, and plans. That seems to be the easy part of the journey. The question is, how do you sustain your inspirational electricity until you get to the finish line? How can you be as unstoppable as the wind? The secret is to keep asking yourself these four questions whenever you feel stuck:

- What conclusion am I making about this person, place, thing, or idea?
- Am I trying to make others fit in with my views, beliefs, and positions?
- Am I designing my environment such that it supports my goals?
- What is my commitment?

Let us look at these questions in a bit more detail.

What conclusion am I making about this person, place, thing, or idea?

As human beings, one rather automatic thing we do is judge and make conclusions about people, places, things, or ideas. An event occurs, and we draw our own conclusions about it. These conclusions then become "reality."

A businesswoman I will call Jane told me her take on why a prospect she had been trying to contact seemed to be avoiding her: "Maybe it's because of my race," Jane said.

I pointed out to Jane that that was just her interpretation of what occurred. Her prospect could be away on vacation or choosing to do business with someone else because he is her boyfriend's cousin. The fact is that people make decisions on whom to do business with for a variety of reasons, some of them as superficial as whether they are even in the mood to buy at a particular time.

The idea is to separate what occurred from one's conclusion about what occurred, and move on.

Am I trying to defend or preserve my views, beliefs, and position about people, places, things, or ideas?

Of all the things that stop people, this is the most common obstacle. We go through life making our minds up about the people, places, things, and ideas around us—we have points of view, beliefs, and positions that we seem to have to defend or preserve, and we will challenge anyone or anything to ensure that those opinions, beliefs, and positions live on.

This is a block that stops us because we either do not want to deal with the people, places, things, or ideas that we perceive as not agreeing with us or because we chase people away when we insist on making our views and beliefs prevail.

A friend I will call John has been married for over 40 years. He lives with his wife, but they hardly talk to each other. The reason? He decided several years ago that she was not "growing" at the rate that he was and that she was not supportive of him and his business. So he set out to find evidence to prove that his opinion was right, and that became the obstacle in their relationship.

I refer to this tendency to be positional as a sneaky benefit because it lets us remain in our comfort zones—we now have an excuse to stop taking risks or reaching out to people. While we are busy "enjoying" this sneaky benefit, we might not realize that it is costing us our joy and our relationship with people. It is also costing us our growth.

The idea is to "unhook" from being positional, and move on.

Am I designing my environment such that it supports my goals?

According to psychologists who study the relationship between our physical environments and our psyches, we usually—consciously or not—choose and arrange our physical spaces to reflect our lives. Conversely, that means that we can intentionally design our environment so that it propels us toward our goals. Then we can rely less on willpower and more on supportive environments to call us into action.

You may have been to a motivational workshop and come back all psyched up, only to lose the high after a few days. Often it was because you did not design your environment to support your new perspective—you were still hanging around the same people, having the same conversations, and living in the same cluttered space, for example.

Thomas Leonard, the founder of the International Coach Federation and CoachVille, defined our environments as constituting nine elements: spiritual, mimetic (ideas, concepts, information), self, relationship, body, physical, financial, network, and nature. This expansive definition unveils many possibilities and points to the fact that we *can* choose the people, places, things, or ideas that inspire rather than drain us. That way, inspiration becomes something real that exists outside our heads.

What is my commitment?

One of the best ways to be unstoppable is by asking the question, what is my commitment? Often we get so caught up in the busy-ness of day-to-day life that we forget what we are committed to and why we do the things we do.

Not only is this question an effective excuse-buster, it is also very useful for making the myriad of decisions we are often confronted with.

As the parent of a four-year-old, my commitment to my son is to ensure that his formative years are spent in a secure, loving, and nurturing environment, where he has direct and constant access to at least one of his parents for part of the day. With this commitment as the backdrop, I could then decide on the kind of business I needed to have, its size, and the rate of growth that was compatible with spending a significant amount of time with my son—in other words, I had to be careful to tame the momentum of my business and not be so carried away that I lost track of my original commitment.

By the same token, if you knew *what* it was you were committed to in your career, business, or relationships, you would not let obstacles stop you. You would keep going.

It is time to start living the life you have imagined. See you at the finish line.

ABOUT THE AUTHOR

Duanna Pang-Dokland is a certified coach who works with entrepreneurs to invent businesses that are a source of growth and fulfillment. Her practice, Igniting Possibility Coaching, designs and delivers programs for business owners that lead to significant and sustainable results, such as increased profits and productivity. A published writer, editor, speaker, and workshop facilitator, her mission is to inspire people to experience the power of coaching. Start igniting possibilities in your life by visiting http://ignitingpossibility.com and signing up for the free report "10 Mistakes That'll Bulldoze Any Business and How to Avoid Them." Get ready for unexpected breakthroughs.

6

BELIEFS

The Scoop on Beliefs

Lesley Cordero

Dear Leslie,

My friend Betty has been battling her weight ever since her last child was born. She still blames him for the 20 to 40 pounds that she has gained and lost repeatedly, and he is now 21. Almost yearly now, she gets her act together, changes her eating behaviors, and tackles the problem once more. She successfully loses a nice chunk of it, gets all kinds of accolades and attention for doing it, and then six months later, starts to gain it back again.

What is Betty's problem? Is it simply lack of discipline? She says that she wants to be a healthy weight, but then she deliberately sabotages herself by reverting back to unhealthy eating habits.

Concerned,
A Friend

Dear Friend,

Betty's problem is not a lack of discipline or willpower. Betty's problem is one of perception. Until Betty is willing to change how she sees herself or change how she perceives the habits that are sabotaging her efforts to lose weight, she is going to continue on this yo-yo forever.

Let me try to explain how perception works: Perception is that delicate balance of selection and interpretation. We are bombarded by the minute with information from our environment. We choose to pay attention to only a small portion of it. What we choose to allow in is then passed through our internal filtering system, and then we interpret what it means to us.

These filters are often beliefs; a belief is simply an interpretation of something that we choose to make true. What you believe, you become. What you have in your head comes true in your life because you will always find evidence to support it. Let us look at how beliefs work.

Belief: I am clumsy.
Supporting evidence:

- My parents told me so repeatedly.
- I have been known to fall even on flat pavement.
- When I was young, they had to reteach me how to walk.
- My "first time in high heels" story is a family classic.

Now, I *could* choose to believe that I am as graceful as a gazelle. What supporting evidence could I find to support that belief?

- I was a good swimmer.
- I love to dance.
- I have gone scuba diving.
- I buy outrageously high heels now and walk in them (albeit for short stints only)!

I choose to believe the first belief, even though it is a limiting belief, as opposed to the second one, which is empowering.

One of my children was having difficulty with tests in college. He had not been overly successful in secondary school, especially with tests, and believed that he simply was not any good at tests and that besides, he was not smart enough. After all, the evidence certainly pointed in that direction. I called attention to the fact that he had avoided courses in school that would have required much if any studying and simply had not acquired the necessary skills. He was passively studying by reading over his textbook and notes. He did not know how to actively study or process the information mentally in order to retain it. I introduced him to active learning. He tried it on his next test and received an 86 percent. With new evidence as to how he does on tests, he was able to eliminate that old belief and adopt the new one.

Getting back to Betty, perhaps she believes that she is not worthy of being healthy or looking great. When I sabotage myself with a sweet treat, I believe that I am pampering myself. "Go ahead," the voice in my head says, "You deserve it, you work so hard!" I perceive eating sweets as pampering myself, therefore my behaviors support that perception, and my results are predictable. In order to lose weight, Betty has to change her perceptions and beliefs about herself in relation to healthy living, and her behavior will fall in line and be reflected in her results.

What do our beliefs actually look like? Think about something that you absolutely believe or hold to be true. Make a picture in your mind that represents that belief. Add as much detail to the picture as you can, include sound and any feelings you may have about it. Now think of something that you doubt is true. Make a picture in your mind to express that. Look at your two pictures, one that expresses something you believe, and one that you doubt is true. What is actually in the two pictures will be different (content), but they will appear different in other ways as well. One picture may be in color and the other in black and white. One may appear to be two-dimensional, while the other has depth. There may be a difference in brightness, focus, or types of sound associated with them. The intensity of one may be different than the other, or perhaps there is a particular temperature associated with one.

Is Betty willing to risk challenging old assumptions and beliefs? How willing is she to change? Let us examine ways to change beliefs that do not really serve us anymore.

1. Change how you picture the belief. Give the belief you want the same structure as the belief you want to get rid of. Follow the exercise above and find out what your belief looks like. Notice that you use language such as "battling," "blame," and "tackles" in your letter. Give the new belief the same properties or structure.
2. Look for supportive evidence to support the new belief that you want to adopt. Remember, when we hold something to be true, we always find evidence in the world to support it. Look for ways to discount the old evidence that supported the old belief.

3. We have a positive intention behind everything we think and do. You have a positive intention for yourself behind everything you choose to believe as well. If you want to change a belief, replace it with a belief that keeps the positive intention of the old one. For example, if I want to change my belief that I am pampering and nurturing myself when I eat junk food, then I need to believe that I am being pampered when I eat healthy food.

4. When you replace a belief, the new belief must be in alignment with your values and how you see yourself (identity) as well as with what you perceive your purpose in life to be.

If your friend Betty selects different information to pay attention to and changes what she believes about her relationship with food, she will be well on her way to finally letting her son off the hook and eliminating those unwanted pounds for good.

ABOUT THE AUTHOR

Lesley Cordero's mission is to guide people through the personal change process by helping them get "Better at Living." She is a public speaker, workshop presenter, author, and the publisher of an Internet Membership Site (http://www.betteratliving.com). Lesley's background is in education. As a professional speaker, she has custom designed and delivered workshops and keynote presentations internationally to colleges and universities, the corporate sector, educational facilities and conferences, and professional associations as well as private groups. She is a Master Practitioner in Neuro-Linguistic Programming (NLP) and a certified Level Two trainer in the True Colors Personality Indicator® & Personality Dimensions® as well as being a trained process consultant. Lesley has coauthored *Expert Women Who Speak . . . Speak Out!* due to be released fall 2006. Subscribe to her free e-zine "Deep Linking" at http://www.LesleyCordero.com and begin to make the changes that are important to you.

7

BREAKING PATTERNS

Breaking the Same Old, Same Old Pattern

Jeannie Campanelli

I don't want to be lonely no more.
I don't want to have to pay for this.
I don't want another lover at my door.
Just another heartache for my list.
—Rob Thomas, "Lonely No More" (2004)

How many of you relate to the words of Rob Thomas' hit single? You want to share your life with someone, really love someone, and yet over and over again, you find yourself in relationships that are not working for you. In your search for Mr. or Ms. Right, how many of you have found that the consequences of your choice have been painful and sometimes even traumatic? Divorce, financial loss, and a decrease in your confidence and self-trust along with emotional scars can all result from choices that were made in good faith.

There are those of you who find that too often, you meet a person who is too busy, so you do not feel as important as that person's work, or even his golf game. Some of you may have a pattern of being with people who are manipulative, passive aggressive, or financially unstable. Or you may unknowingly invite into your life someone emotionally abusive and unstable or with an addiction that is draining and depletes your spirit.

The key to moving out of this pattern or comfort zone (even though it feels uncomfortable, it is familiar) is awareness. Identify your pattern by closely examining all your relationships, particularly those you invite in as potential partners. Take the time to journal. What are their characteristics? How do these characteristics reflect who you are in relationship to yourself? Or how do they reflect a belief that you hold about yourself at a core level? An abusive person may be an indicator of how you abuse yourself with self-criticism and self-doubt. Underlying this may be a belief that you are not good enough or not worthy of the best that life has to offer.

Our outer worlds reflect our inner worlds. Your relationships are a clue to what you are thinking and feeling on the inside. For instance, if you believe that you are unworthy, you vibrate at that frequency and attract others into your life who also vibrate at that frequency, regardless of how confident they appear to be. They may behave differently than you, and yet the core belief from which they operate is the same.

There are important action steps along with increasing your consciousness so you can make different choices. First, own, embrace, and forgive what you see inside yourself. This is vital.

Next, start to envision what you do want to attract into your life and feel deep inside what that would be like for you. Practice coming from a place of love rather than fear. Instead of feeling constricted, your heart will be open and expansive while you are envisioning what you want. You will then create a reality field that will allow positive results. Once you shift at a core level, the flow of people who come into your life will shift as well.

Add in action steps that are grounded in reality. Patrick Carnes, in *The Betrayal Bond*, has many powerful activities. Make a list of your "must-haves" in your relationships, particularly with your partner. Coming from a place of worthiness, be clear about what you want, and commit to following through on this without settling for less. What are the boundaries that you will set for yourself in terms of your behavior? Be specific and concrete. Examples might be the following: I will not try to change or rescue someone; I will not try to talk myself into someone; if my body is telling me that I am unsafe with this person, I will leave. List your relationship goals, which may look like taking 100 percent responsibility for yourself and not making yourself wrong.

Most importantly, what will you do to take care of yourself? Make a list of what you plan to do to address your needs separate from looking to someone else to fulfill you. Think of the metaphor that you are the cake and a relationship is the icing. Audition those who you put into your life from the perspective of what they will add to it.

Shifting out of old comfort zones around how you relate is possible. You can use your past experiences to move forward and create healthy, whole relationships with others because you have created that quality of relationship with yourself—worthy, important, much-appreciated, and valued as you are—and that foundational relationship with yourself will be reflected in all aspects of your life: at home, at work, with your friends, and in your larger community. Enjoy that cake . . . and the special icing on top!

ABOUT THE AUTHOR

Jeannie Campanelli, EdD, CPCC, is a certified professional coach. She has a doctorate in applied psychology from the University of Toronto, with a focus on human development and change. She partners with clients in building relationships, particularly the relationship with self. She is currently authoring a book on inner power and self-confidence titled "At One with Myself." You can visit her Web site at http://www.jeanniecampanelli.com.

8

Real Conversations with the True You: Four Steps to the Life You Want

Bess McCarty

Do you want to break free of old, repeated habits? Have a better life? Lose weight, fear, anger, and loneliness? Then *listen* to what is behind those habits! This simple process can change pain into solutions in minutes. You can do it!

I learned to do this from my own life experiences. I discovered that behind every one of my problems were very real and healthy needs! I found that my pain was simply an unmet need, whether physical, emotional, mental, or spiritual. The solution? I simply found the need and met it in a healthy way!

Here is the process.

1. Look at the behavior you want to change.
2. Allow yourself to feel the uncomfortable emotion that the behavior masks.
3. Let that feeling tell you about the unmet need behind it.
4. Find the means or method to meet that need in a healthy way.

Like a red light on our dashboards, our uncomfortable feelings can clue us in to our unmet needs. Yet our childhood programs of shame and judgment about them may hide our feelings and needs from us. So we need to have the courage, willingness, and compassion to feel our unmet needs. Then we must learn how to meet them!

See if you can find the unmet needs in the following stories.

A man we will call Jerry had a strong compulsion for ice cream one night. "Why so strong?" he wondered. Could eating the ice cream be an escape from uncomfortable feelings inside? He guessed there was an emotional need behind it, but *what was it?* Before getting a great big bowl of ice cream, he sat down for a few minutes with pen and paper because he liked to write. Could he play detective and find his hidden, unmet need?

He focused on his feelings. He was agitated and angry ever since his friend Ian told him that his mother was very ill. Jerry's own mother had been sick when he was a child and eventually died of cancer when he was 10 years old.

Jerry wrote out his feelings that he had buried deep inside as a child. He was angry that she had left, and he missed her. His pen flew across the page as he poured it all out. He cried and gave compassion to that little boy of 10. Then he breathed deeply and was flooded with serenity. Ice cream forgotten, Jerry had met his need for compassion by acknowledging his feelings and comforting his loneliness.

In another story, Ann was tempted to return to a man who had abused her. She discovered her fear and insecurity. "I just want someone to take care of me, to always be there!" she thought. She then knew that her need was to feel secure, to feel confident that she would be okay. She recommitted to deepening her relationship with a Higher Power. Then she worked with the Higher Power to take care of herself, financially and emotionally. Now she is very happy inside and is no longer desperate for a man in her life.

Pam's story involved weight loss. "Why am I gaining weight?" she wondered. "I am active and eat no fat at all. I do crave carbohydrates. I am out of control and scared!" Pam had four children and was very good at being on top of everything—managing details, giving advice, and being a wife and mother. She was super in control of her role as a mother, almost to the point of being overvigilant.

What was out of control was her eating. She found an angry voice inside saying, "I need a break from all this regimen! You have to be perfect, like Mom! You won't let me off the hook! It's too much! I'm rebelling! I've had enough of your control!"

As a child, Pam had a demanding mother. She was the oldest child of five, and she got approval and love for being a capable help to her mother with the younger children. She unknowingly got hooked on that approval early on. Now she had an "inner mother" part of her that kept her on the treadmill. To counter this, there was also an "inner child" that was in control of her appetite!

Pam tearfully agreed that she was ready to let herself off the hook. She realized that peace and health were too great a price to pay for perfection and that she was as valuable as those she cared for.

Whenever she was tempted to micromanage her kids or forego sleep to finish the laundry (while eating chips to stay awake), she learned to take a breath and say to herself, "You don't have to do this. I love you and want you to sleep when you're tired."

She kept a weekly date with her husband. When she felt the need to talk, she walked on the beach with her girlfriend. She spent a little quiet time by herself every day (if only in the bathtub!) to check in with her feelings and needs. She also loves gardening and found a way to make that a family activity. She found that letting her children help was more important than having it done perfectly. So what if the bedspreads were askew? She found out that if she forgot to buy milk at the store, her family survived anyway!

Pam began to feel like a new person. She felt loved and important. Her husband and children liked their new happy wife and mother. They all relaxed more. And with no thought of dieting, Pam dropped 13 pounds over two months. She continues to become slimmer and healthier as her body feels nourished with healthy food that she lovingly eats.

In each of these stories the person became aware of the behavior he or she wanted to change, felt the emotion behind it, found the need under it all, and met that need in a healthy way. This process can transform unwanted behaviors, addictions, and even illness.

Most of us are unfamiliar with the range of our feelings and needs. Here are some lists to help identify them.

Uncomfortable Feelings That Indicate Unmet Needs

- **Sad:** lonely, disheartened, troubled, helpless, gloomy, grief, overwhelmed, distant, despondent, discouraged, distressed
- **Mad:** angry, aggravated, exasperated, frustrated, irritated, agitated, furious, enraged, hostile, bitter, pessimistic, resentful
- **Scared:** fearful, terrified, startled, nervous, panicky, jittery, horrified, anxious, worried, anguished

Healthy Needs

- **Physical:** food, water, air, rest, shelter, exercise, touch, sexual expression, nature
- **Emotional:** love, affection, warmth, compassion, reassurance, support, trust, stability, safety, encouragement, cherishing, play, celebration, emotional expression
- **Mental:** attention, acknowledgment, acceptance, consideration, appreciation, understanding, empathy, respect, honesty, autonomy, competence, learning
- **Spiritual:** divine love, connection with a higher power, guidance, being, harmony, inspiration, order, peace, integrity, authenticity, creativity, meaning, self-worth, renewal, responsibility, to belong, to contribute

Ideas to Meet the Needs

- Visualize your inner parent, Higher Power, or spiritual guide loving your inner child.
- Ask a friend, mate, or group to help you.
- Rewrite your past. Give yourself a new history!
- Learn from functional role models.
- See John Bradshaw's book *Homecoming*, the "Corrective Exercises" chapter.

You, too, can use this process to become free in any area of your life! Try it and see! I would love to hear your results!

ABOUT THE AUTHOR

Bess McCarty, a longtime body/mind therapist, created "Real Conversations™: Four Steps to the Life You Want." Bess coaches individuals, couples and businesses (by phone and in person) and facilitates therapy groups and teleclasses with fast, direct, lasting results. She is a teacher of teachers and a therapist for therapists. Look for her upcoming book series, *Real Conversations for Self-Help, Business, Relationships and Addictions*. Join her free, live teleclasses on Real Conversations™ and enjoy free lessons delivered by e-mail (call 512-986-5288 or subscribe at www.bessmccarty.com).

9

Healing a Broken Heart

Barb Hepperle

As we travel through life, we eventually encounter that most unwelcome of all companions—loss and heartbreak.

There are many kinds of losses: a job, a move that separates us from friends, a death. The loss of a love relationship ranks near the top of stressful life events. It is so devastating because we are hit with so many losses all at once—big and small, tangible and intangible.

If you were embroiled in high conflict, bouncing back can be particularly difficult when the "corpse" from the dead relationship still has the audacity to keep walking around! The lack of closure only adds more agony to the already broken heart.

At the core of all this devastation lies the greatest loss of all—the loss of sense of self.

In reality, *recovery* really means reclaiming your true identity, the golden essence of who you truly are. The good news is that it is a process that has a beginning, a middle, and an end.

In the beginning, nearly everyone is hit, to a greater or lesser degree, with the painful emotions of hurt, anger, guilt, and fear. Where you go from there is up to you. People who successfully navigate through and beyond this stormy transition take this sad, confusing time for inner questioning and deep reflection.

In picking up the pieces they create new hopes and dreams. They learn from their mistakes to create healthier relationships in the future. They get back in touch with what they value and break free from old patterns to redefine who they are.

To successfully rebuild your life, here are eight tips to get you started down the healing path.

1. **Live in the present.** I know, it is tough. You cannot get thoughts of your ex out of your head. Of course it is natural to think about what might have been, could have been, should have been—if only you could do it all over again. But you cannot. That door is closed forever. Choose not to be a victim. Focus on you and your actions, not those of others.

- Where are you avoiding taking responsibility for your life?
- What daily routines, habits, or rituals will help keep you grounded?

2. **Say good-bye to all that you have lost.** Make a list of the good, the bad, the big, the small, the hopes and dreams, the companionships, the house, the security, the favorite picture, and so on. You cannot let go of the past and move on until you know exactly what you are letting go of.

- What do you need to let go of? How can you simplify your life today?

3. **Give yourself lots of time to grieve your loses deeply and fully.** Grief is not something you can get over, around, under, or otherwise avoid. You have to go right through the pain and darkness before you can reach the light on the other side. Allow yourself to cry, then cry some more. It is okay. You will not get stuck here. It is all part of the healing process.

4. **Take really, really good care of yourself.** Grieving is hard work. More than ever right now, you need to be getting lots of rest and quiet time and be eating well and nurturing yourself.

Find activities that will replace all those toxic stress chemicals with more productive, positive ones. You have heard of the "runners' high"? That is sort of what you are looking for. Any physical activity, even walking briskly, will raise your endorphins, those "feel good" chemicals.

Have you ever noticed that you tend to take good care of things that are important to you—things that you care deeply about? Taking care of *you* gives you the message that you are important.

- How can you eat smart and exercise today? How will you nurture and pamper yourself?
- What will you do to have more fun today?

5. **Vent all that rage that is stored up inside you.** If you do not get it out, it will just eat away at you, possibly for years and years. What a waste of a good life! I knew a woman who took up kickboxing following her divorce. You can just imagine the thoughts she had while she was practicing! But she released her rage in a healthy manner and got fit to boot!

- How can you use all that powerful emotional energy to kick you forward and take back control of *your* life?

6. **Take stock of what is left.** No matter how difficult things were, it is likely that something positive came out of your relationship. It is time to consider that good.

- In what ways are you enriched, stronger, better?

7. **Set small, daily goals.** Decide what tasks are most pressing, and then determine how you will get them done.

- What do you want to accomplish today, next week, next month, this year? What is even one tiny action that will move you forward toward your goals today?

8. **Reclaim yourself.** Chances are, you gave up a lot of who you really are by taking care of others in your relationship. The most important person to please is yourself. Learn to say no. You become more authentic when you live according to what is really important to you.

- How can you get back into integrity with yourself? Are you living by your values?

9. **Welcome the future.** Sure, some days look bleak, but the fact remains, there *is* more to life than pain, grief, and frustration. It is not too early to start painting a picture of your new life.

- What do you want your new life to look like? What door has just opened for you? What new opportunities are available, or what have you been putting off that you have no excuse for now?

Yes, this ending has deeply impacted you in so many ways—not only your life as you once knew it, but also, your sense of self has been shattered. You are bound to change in some way.

But things were different in your life a year ago, and things will be different a year from now. This is the next chapter of your life. You get to write the script any way you want it. Is it going to be a third-rate paperback or a best-selling novel full of passion and adventure? Only you can decide.

Your grief is meaningless until you learn how to use it as a stepping stone to your personal power and full potential. When you find some meaning for your pain, when you understand the precious gift of your life lessons, presented to you on this portion of your journey, you will be truly transformed.

Change is inevitable. Why not control it by reinventing yourself and making the changes *you* want?

ABOUT THE AUTHOR

Barb Hepperle, MSc, a divorce coach and family conflict and divorce mediator, has gone through the emotional and physical pain of her own divorce. Barb has created "Healing a Broken Heart—Transforming Your Life," a powerful, life-changing program to help men and women move through and beyond the ending of their love relationship to start rebuilding their dreams. Get her free divorce survival manual "How to Manage Your Divorce" at http://www.edmontondivorcesolutions.com.

10

CAPTURING THE RETIREMENT DREAM

Transitioning into Retirement

Barbara Eubanks

"The only thing constant is change itself," Heraclitus the Greek once said, and so right he was. Our societal lives demand flexibility. The average citizen makes many significant transitions within a lifetime. As sure as life and death, as definite as paying taxes, changes are inevitable. Births, deaths, moves, career changes, marital status, finances, and on and on—with retirement bringing one of the greater transitions—all demand change. Life is liquid, ever moving and ever changing. Along with change, people face fears, new possibilities, and challenges. Any time the status quo is disturbed, a feeling of uncertainty arises. Fears of the unknown haunt like bumps in the night. But for many, flux stirs adrenaline in their souls; a challenge, a new opportunity to start over, produces oxygen for the flames of desire.

People go to work, day after day, year after year, looking forward to weekends, vacation time, or any other break from the mundane work-a-day world, with retirement being the supreme goal. "Then I can do just what I want or do absolutely nothing, as the case may be," think many. Just with so many other great expectations, reaching that goal may turn into supreme disappointment and disillusionment. The difference between a disillusioned retiree and a happy one depends on several factors, three of the major ones being circumstances, preplanning, and attitude. There is little that one can change about some circumstances, but preplanning and attitude are in each individual's control. As with any transition, mapping out a definite strategy can certainly make the journey more pleasant. Some positive steps for making retirement all it can be follow.

1. Start putting money back early in your career. Social security simply will not be adequate for all your wants and needs, nor was it ever intended to be. Often people's needs increase during the retirement years rather than decrease.
2. Do things you have always wanted to but never found time to do. You might start early in life making a list of things you want to achieve or enjoy before your life is finished. When you retire, work down the list.
3. Plan ahead for activities to make your life meaningful: hobbies, a second career, volunteer work, yard work, travel.
4. Stay active in civic and religious activities.
5. Enjoy your freedom from day-to-day responsibilities by doing something spontaneous—unplanned trips, fishing trips, fun things with friends, going for a walk with your mate. Maybe setting the alarm at regular getting up time and having the joy of clicking it off, turning over, and sleeping another hour would be a great exercise of this freedom.
6. Have a plan for each day. (You just do not have to follow it if something better comes along.) If you do not make plans for your time, meaningless activities will absorb it.
7. If taking care of elderly parents is likely to fill some of your retirement time, plan ahead for this, too, as much as possible. (Have a family pow-wow before retirement to divide duties equitably among the siblings. If some live away, make it clear their part may consist of hiring caretakers to take their shifts.) Whatever you do regarding the care of parents, do it with joy; someone will have to do the same for you someday. (The same may apply for taking care of grandchildren.)
8. Make a conscious decision to be happy. Often people who are unhappy before retirement are most likely unhappy afterward simply due to negative attitudes. Circumstances may be out of your control, but your attitude is very much within it.
9. Invest time with younger people. They can benefit from your wisdom, and you can learn from them. Some great avenues for this would be volunteering at school to be a study-buddy, reading to children in the hospital, and yes, volunteering to take care of grandchildren or neighbors' children—at *your* convenience.
10. Start living a healthy lifestyle early and continue it as long as you live. Do not wait until you get older and sicker to start eating a healthy diet and taking regular exercise. It may be too late then. An older man once said, "If I had known I was going to live this long, I would have taken better care of myself."

No, life will not be perfect in retirement, but remember, life was never perfect before retirement. Do not look back and yearn for what is past; look forward to what life opportunities are in store for you at this stage. Be prepared for both joys and sorrows; face all with a positive attitude and a strong sense of spirituality. Enjoy the journey.

ABOUT THE AUTHOR

Barbara Eubanks is a minister's wife, Sunday school teacher, retired high school English teacher (listed in *Who's Who among American Teachers 2002*), mother to three adult sons, and grandmother to eight. She is a Christian humor writer, author, and speaker. Her mission is to promote humor in relation to spiritual, physical, and emotional health. Her books include *Humorous Happenings in Holy Places*, *Whispering in God's Ear*, and *And the Angels Laughed*. Barbara is available for author signings and speaking events nationwide. Visit her at http://www.barbaraeubanks.com.

11

CAREER ANALYSIS

Is Your Career a Dream or a Nightmare?

Carol McClelland

Maria, an employee in a high tech company, thoroughly enjoys what she does in her marketing communications position. However, a recent merger has had a negative impact on the company culture. In fact, the changes are so dramatic that she does not feel she can be herself at work anymore, and she is not sure how much longer she can tolerate it.

John is self-employed and absolutely loves his work as a realtor. The birth of his first child, however, has made him more and more aware that his seven-day-a-week schedule is taking its toll on his personal life. He is torn between the work he loves and the life he sees in front of him.

Claire has created a blended career that works quite well for her. She has a part-time bookkeeping job and runs a cosmetics business. Although the lifestyle is working for her and she feels free to be herself in both of her careers, she is feeling bored.

Although each person enjoys parts of his or her work and lifestyle, each is missing something significant.

Where do you stand?

- Are you able to be yourself at work?
- Does your work or business impinge on your personal life?
- Is your work environment supportive?
- Are you frustrated with what you do each day?

If you are missing one of these elements, it is likely your work is like a bad dream—unsettling and confusing. If you are missing two or more of these elements, it is likely your career is becoming a bit of a nightmare. You are ready to do anything to get your life back.

The trick to creating a lifestyle and career that truly work for you is to discover work that combines who you are, how you live, how you work, and what you do. Now *that* is a dream career.

Describing Your Dream Career in Detail

Building your dream career is like building a dream home. The more time and energy you put into exploring your needs, interests, and desires, the more likely your house (or your career) will be a good match for you.

Use the following questions to create a picture of your ideal vision for yourself and your life.

1. **When left to your own devices, who are you? How do you function best? What do you value? How do you define success?** By understanding your true nature, you can create a career and a life that fully express who you are.

For example, if you like structure, make sure your work environment fulfills this need. If you like freedom and flexibility, create an environment that supports these characteristics. Putting yourself in an environment that is counter to your natural style can have dire consequences.

2. **How do you want to live your life? How do you want to spend your time? With whom do you want to interact?** Although it is easy to think about the ways you would tweak your current lifestyle, I encourage you to broaden your perspective. If you could redesign your lifestyle just the way you want it, what would it look like? How would it feel?

By giving voice to how you would like to live, you put your focus on your ultimate vision.

3. **What work environment makes you most productive and happy?** Think about your entire work arrangement, from your schedule and time off to your pay

and benefits, from your personal work area to your work location, from your work colleagues to your customers and those who manage your work.

By understanding what is important to you in your work environment, you have a much better chance of creating it. Whether you negotiate with your manager or yourself to get what you need to be productive, the changes you make in your work environment can enhance how you feel at work.

4. **What skills do you enjoy using at work? What topics fascinate you? How do you like to help others?** Even if you do not see an immediate way to turn your passions into a cash-producing venture, continue to nurture your interests by using your skills and being involved with others who share your fascination. Keep your mind open to the possibilities. You never know what opportunities will appear that allow you to use your passions.

After you answer these questions, put your notes away for a couple days. When you return to them, verify that you have described your ideal picture.

Taking Action to Create Your Dream Career

Use your vision of your dream career as a point on the horizon to shoot for. Do not be alarmed if you cannot make all your desired changes overnight. The most important thing is to keep taking the actions that move you toward your dream.

Do not worry if you do not see how it is all going to play out. Often taking one step opens up possibilities you could not have seen if you had not taken that original step. Use your intuition to guide you because sometimes the next "logical" step is not the one that is going to create the biggest payoff.

If you are contemplating a significant change to your business or your job, give yourself the opportunity to test the waters before you take the leap. Using what you discover to refocus your plan can save you significant amounts of time, energy, and expense.

As you implement your vision, keep a creative mind-set. If you can only see one or two options, stop yourself and look at your situation from a bigger perspective. If you can, bring in a friend to help you brainstorm an array of options. Someone who is outside the situation will see things that you cannot see.

Here are some ideas for the three people highlighted at the beginning of this article.

- Maria, the marketing communications employee, might explore other companies in her area to see if any have a culture that suits her style better. If the culture she dislikes is endemic to her industry, she might explore the possibility of transferring her skills to another industry that is more consistent with her style.
- John, the realtor who is a new father, might experiment with different schedules to see if he can create an arrangement that melds his family's needs with his professional responsibilities. Another option might be to partner up with another realtor who is also interested in creating a bit more life balance.
- Claire, the bored business owner, might begin by making a list of all the skills and interests she enjoys. With that list in hand, she can discern whether she can reconfigure her current business to incorporate more of her passions, whether she can find a part-time job that is a better fit, or whether her best strategy is to target an entirely new venture.

Sometimes a small change, or a series of small changes over time, can have an unexpectedly large impact on how you feel about yourself, how you work, and how you live. Keep making the choices that move you closer to your dream, and there is no stopping what you can create for yourself!

ABOUT THE AUTHOR

Carol McClelland, PhD, author of *Your Dream Career for Dummies*, the *Career Clarity Program*, and *The Seasons of Change*, is a transition expert. Carol's books and programs provide clients with unique tools, refreshing perspectives, and powerful insights to help them transform their confusion into clarity. In addition to her work with clients, she trains coaches, therapists, and other professionals to build thriving businesses using the *Career Clarity Program* and *The Seasons of Change* in their work with clients. Visit http://www.careerclarityprogram.com/greatwayscareer for your own complimentary copy of the *Dream Career Workbook*.

12

It's a Catastrophe!
The Fine Art of Catastrophizing

Michael Bungay Stanier

Today's common understanding of *catastrophe*—a sudden disaster—is not the word's original meaning. It first meant "a reversal of what is expected," something altogether more broad, more benign, and perhaps more useful (you can see the connection with words like *apostrophe*, the etymology of which means, in effect, a "turning point"). The extension of meaning to "a sudden disaster" was first recorded in 1748, some 200 years after the first use of the word.

The Fine Art of Catastrophizing

Many of us unknowingly invite catastrophe (the modern definition) into our lives on a regular basis. Not that anything bad happens. It is just that we tend to look at a challenge that is facing us and then imagine the very worst thing that could happen. This is what it sounds like for me:

I could never challenge my boss...
... because she might get angry with me
... and then she would put me on nothing but bad projects
... and then I would fail at those projects
... and then I would lose my job
... and then I would not be able to find another job
... and then my wife would leave me
... and then I would have to sell the house
... and then I would start drinking
... and then I would end up on the streets, homeless
... and then I would be dead before I am 40
... and no one will even notice.

It is almost humorous when you see it written down like this. But for many of us, this style of thinking is all too familiar. It paralyzes us. It keeps us small. It keeps us playing safe and not taking chances to do something differently, to explore something new.

This type of thinking has been labeled "catastrophizing" and is symptomatic of a way of seeing the world that sees the bad that happens to you as part of a pervasive and ubiquitous tide of pain and evil that happens to everyone, everywhere. The term was made popular by Dr. Albert Ellis and rational emotive behavior therapy (RBET), a form of cognitive therapy. (Cognitive therapists believe that basically, to get better, you need to start thinking differently. And the bottom line in explaining RBET is "the world is not fair; deal with it.")

Catastrophizing Is Bad for Your Health

Catastrophizing is more than just a limiting way of thinking. It is actually bad for your health. A study in 1998 by psychologist Dr. Christopher Peterson concluded that the tendency to catastrophize was linked to an increased risk of dying before the age of 65. "Males with a tendency to catastrophize were at the highest risk for early death," Professor Christopher Peterson says. "They were 25 percent more likely to die by age 65 than men with other [ways of viewing the world], and they were at especially high risk for deaths by accident or violence."

Breaking the Catastrophizing Cycle

Following are three techniques to break the catastrophizing cycle.

1. **Calculation.** Write down the whole catastrophizing process—like the example I have written out above. Then, for each of the different steps, estimate the odds of that actually happening to you.

For instance, in the example above, "she might be angry with me" might have a 20 percent (0.20) chance of happening, "she would put me on nothing but bad projects" might have a 3 percent (0.03) chance of happening, and so on. You can then estimate the actual chance of the final catastrophe happening by multiplying together the various percentages (for instance, $0.20 \times 0.03 \times ...$).

2. **Personification.** The second approach brings "the voice of doom" to life. That inner voice—which some people call "the inner critic" or "the gremlin"—is not

the truth, it just sounds like it. If you bring it to life, shine on a light on it and give it an appearance, it quickly loses its seeming omnipotence.

So what does your gremlin look like? (Is it big or small? What color is it? Does it look like someone you know—your sister, your father, that terrible teacher from first grade?) Whereabouts does it hang out? (In the back of your head? On your shoulder? In the corner of the room, just out of sight?) What sort of voice does it have? (Loud and shouty? Sly and whispery? Low and muttering?) As soon as you personify the gremlin voice, it is easier to notice it at work—and to realize that it is not as powerful as you have been thinking it is.

3. **Make it absurd.** The final technique is the fastest, and it is one I have borrowed from Benjamin Zander and his book *The Art of Possibility*. Stand up, throw your arms in the air, and declare out loud, "How fascinating!" This is effective because it shifts your physical state, it points to how seriously you are taking everything (and suggests you lighten up!), and it frames the situation as a learning moment.

It Is (Not) the End of the World As We Know It . . .

The most recent research on happiness shows that we imagine the impact of big events (both good and bad) to be greater than, in the end, it actually turns out to be. Our brains are wired in such a way that when those events happen, we reduce their impact and normalize what has happened.

Scientists posit that this is an evolutionary skill, one that has allowed us to more easily adapt to the ups and downs we face. Catastrophizing—so long as you know how to control it—may in fact help with this process as it allows us to imagine the worst and then manage it.

In any case, at the end of the day, it is worth remembering Mark Twain's comment: "I've had a lot of problems in my life and most of them never happened."

Resources for Dealing with Catastrophes

For help in dealing with catastrophes, you can consult the following books: *Get Unstuck & Get Going . . . on the Stuff That Matters* by Michael Bungay Stanier; *Taming Your Gremlin* by Richard Carson; *The Art of Possibility* by Benjamin

Zander and Rosamund Stone Zander; *The 7 Habits of Highly Effective People (Particularly the First Habit)* by Stephen Covey; and *Stumbling into Happiness* by Daniel Gilbert.

ABOUT THE AUTHOR

Michael Bungay Stanier is the principal of Box of Crayons (http://www.BoxOfCrayons.biz), a company that works with organizations, teams, and individuals around the world to help them shift from doing good work to doing great work. Box of Crayons's clients range from AstraZeneca to Xerox in North America and Europe. Michael is the 2006 Canadian Coach of the Year. He was a Rhodes Scholar at Oxford University and holds a master of philosophy degree from Oxford and law and arts degrees from the Australian National University.

He created Get Unstuck & Get Going (http://www.GetUnstuckAndGetGoing.com), a self-coaching tool that is being used around the world, as well as "The Eight Irresistible Principles of Fun" (http://www.EightPrinciples.com), an Internet movie that is been seen in over 125 countries.

13

CHAKRAS' SUCCESS QUALITIES

The Chakras: A Blueprint for Success

David Tomaselli

Throughout history, many Eastern-based ancient cultures, including India and China, have hypothesized the existence of a universal energy that flows through the physical body of all living things. On the basis of spiritual traditions, they believed that a subtle energy body surrounded all living creatures and was responsible for sustaining the life of organs, cells, tissue, and blood and was considered to be the connective flow to their creator. Associated with this idea was the concept of energy centers situated in various locations within the energy body functioning as pumps, regulating the flow of the universal energy. In order to describe the nature of the energy body and energy centers, various energy and spiritual models were developed. One such model, popularized over recent years, is the chakra model. Originating in India, this model recognizes that each energy center, known as a chakra, represents specific physical, psychological, and spiritual functions of a person. The model proposes that if the chakras of a person are healthy and balanced, then that person will be physically, psychologically, and spiritually healthy.

So what does the chakra model have to do with manifesting success in life, whether it is in business, relationships, or some other personal endeavor? If we examine closely the psychological qualities associated with each chakra, we will see that they form an excellent psychological blueprint for success. While it is generally accepted that there are seven chakras, particularly among yoga schools, there are numerous systems that deal with different seven major chakras. Therefore in our discussion we will be looking at psychological functions of eight chakras, including the basic, sex, naval, solar plexus, heart, throat, ajna, and crown. Please note that this is not a definitive list but rather the chakras pertinent to the psychological traits for achieving success.

To start with, the basic chakra, located at the base of the spine, is associated with our ability to survive in the physical world. This means being well grounded and having a practical and realistic approach to life rather than floating off into space. It also means having a good understanding of how the world works, allowing us to exist and operate effectively in today's environment.

The sex chakra, located in the pubic area, is linked with high creativity and capacity to generate ideas. Creativity is an impetus for innovation and can assist us in finding solutions to difficult problems by thinking outside the square. The sex chakra is also associated with the desire to maintain control and power over the external environment, including people and money. Having a positive influence over people is vital for effective leadership and management, while financial wealth allows us make the most of our opportunities.

The navel chakra, located on the naval, is connected to our personal power, that is, our level of self-esteem and self-confidence within ourselves. Naturally, the more belief we have in ourselves and our abilities, the more likely we will be in succeeding. Self-confidence enables us to easily silence the negative voices that arise in our heads, replacing negative statements like "no I cannot" with positive affirmations such as "yes I can!"

The solar plexus chakra, located in the solar plexus, is associated with courage, perseverance, motivation, and the desire to win. Courage and perseverance are keys to overcoming the many obstacles inevitably encountered along the way, such as fear and adversity. Motivation and desire to win serve as the necessary fuel to "fight" on, especially during those critical moments when the challenge appears to be just too great.

The heart chakra, located in the heart, is linked to our ability to love, to feel compassion, to be considerate and act in kindness. Such attributes are very important when it comes to relationships and dealing with people on a personal and professional level. The heart chakra is also the center of our passion. The more passionate we are about our goals and beliefs, the higher the chance of success.

The throat chakra, located on the throat, has an obvious association with our ability to express ourselves and communicate with others via words and actions. Naturally, this is central to achieving mutual understanding in relationships and team environments. The throat chakra is also related to being organized and methodical, that is, our ability to manage tasks and people. Such characteristics are fundamental to the successful management of complex tasks and team-based projects.

The ajna chakra, also known as the Third Eye, is located between the eyebrows. This chakra is related to our intellectual ability, that is, our ability to think logically, comprehend concepts, and solve problems. The benefits of this are obvious. It is also related to our ability to learn from previous experiences, enabling us to make better decisions in the future. Furthermore, it is associated with our level of willpower, stamina, and discipline. Such qualities are typically relied on during the most difficult or tedious parts of a challenge or project.

Finally, the crown chakra, which is located at the top of the head, represents our connection to our soul and creator. It is through this connection that we are able to understand our purpose in life, why we are here. Having a clear vision of the bigger picture means that the goals we will endeavor to achieve will inevitably be far more fulfilling. The crown chakra is also the origin of intuition and inspiration, serving as another useful tool in making decisions and acting quickly on opportunities.

Now if we were to do an honest stock take of ourselves on each these qualities, we would discover, as expected, that we are strong in some areas but not so strong in others. Typically, there are two types of people. There are those that are naturally strong in qualities originating from the lower chakras, that is, the basic, sex, naval, and solar plexus chakras. Such people tend to have the required ability to execute but may lack connection with others or have no sense of purpose and fulfillment. The other group of people tend to be strong in traits found in the higher chakras, including the heart, throat, ajna, and crown. This group may have the required intelligence, a strong sense of purpose, and, in some cases, are highly intuitive, but they lack the capability to execute effectively. What type of person are you?

It is obvious that the key to success is achieving the right balance. Our challenge, if we are to become truly successful in all facets of life, is to develop those qualities that are lacking and continue to enhance further the other traits that come more naturally. Ideally, if we can have our heads in the stars while our feet are firmly planted on the ground, success will inevitably come our way. It is also essential to note that the qualities located in the higher chakras should always exceed those located in the lower chakras; otherwise, we are in danger of being controlled by our lower desires and emotions, such as greed and fear. As the saying goes, "With great power comes great responsibility."

I wish you all the best in the development of your success traits.

ABOUT THE AUTHOR

David Tomaselli is the creator of the self-improvement Web site "The Wholistic Development Exchange" (http://www.wholisticdev.com). His articles are based on 10 years of study and research in creating success driven initially by David's semiprofessional participation in handball followed by his involvement in martial arts, obtaining a black belt in Kung Fu and winning state titles in both disciplines. Recently, David has focused on various energy practices, including Pranic healing, Arhatic Yoga, Chi Kung, meditation, and Tai Chi. In business David has successfully cofounded and sold a start-up software company. He currently consults as a software product development and management specialist.

14

CHANGING ROUTINES

How Breaking Routine and Acts of Kindness Can Energize Your Day

Laurie Hayes

Sometimes life becomes so routine that we do not have to think about a thing we are doing throughout the day. We are programmed to run on automatic. It is important to shake things up every once in a while to get the creative juices flowing, to give us an added boost of energy, or to give us something to concentrate on for a change.

When routine sets in, particularly in relationships, we cannot always see the impact it has until we throw a new ingredient into the mix. This week, I ventured outside of my regular routine and performed a very unexpected act of kindness. The results—terrific!

Northern Ontario, winter 2004: It is Friday morning, snow is falling, there is a nip in the air, and neither my husband nor I want to get out of our toasty, warm bed to get ready for work.

We go through the same exercise every morning. We both wait for the other one to get up first to turn up the furnace, then he heads to his washroom to get ready, and I go into my office to meditate for half an hour.

This morning, however, neither of us would budge. He did not want to get up, shower, make breakfast, and prepare lunch, and I did not want to meditate, go through my agenda for the day, and start prioritizing my long list of outstanding tasks. We were stuck.

I must have been desperate or temporarily insane because I suddenly blurted out, "Hey! You get up and get ready, and *I'll* make you breakfast today!" He was stunned at first and did not say a word, then he started laughing. "Yeah, right. What about your meditation?" For anyone who knows me, there are two things I do not do: cook (unless I am in a real bind) and deviate from my routine.

I insisted I was going to cook for him . . . anything he wanted. Eggs, bacon, you name it! There would be no meditating that day. He hesitantly agreed and headed for his washroom, wondering if his dear partner had been possessed during the night and taken complete leave of her senses. The last time I made him breakfast was, hmmm, let us see . . . when was the last time the Oilers won the cup?

I whipped up a hearty breakfast, and while he ate, he repeatedly commented on how he could not believe I had done so. He thanked me several times.

Once I finished up in the kitchen, it was time for me to start getting ready for my day. I could hear him singing and talking to himself in the kitchen. I called out to him, "You're happy, aren't you?" He answered, "My baby made me breakfast!"

It was amazing how performing a small task for the benefit of someone else made such a *big* impact! My husband was excited and happy, and I felt fantastic for making him feel appreciated and loved.

For the remainder of the day I was a fireball. I joked with everyone I spoke with and had them laughing and feeling great. The day flew by. I accomplished loads of work and had tons of energy left over.

When my husband got home from work, he told me about his great day, how he was zinging off one-liners at the guys and making them laugh, and how good he felt, mentally and physically.

Changing our routine and experiencing an act of kindness elevated both of us mentally, physically, and emotionally. It is no secret that change and giving to others boost our energy levels, but we get so caught up in daily living that we easily forget. We fall into the comfort zone of habit.

Today is a new day. What can *you* do differently? Take a different route to work? Part your hair on the left instead of in the center? Take the stairs instead of the elevator? Whatever it is and no matter how small, change makes a positive impact.

What can *you* do for someone else today, something completely unsolicited and without expectation? If you are going through the drive-thru at the coffee shop, pay for the coffee for the driver behind you. If you see someone struggling with her bags at the grocery store, lend a hand. The simplest act of kindness will reap big rewards for the giver, receiver, and everyone they touch throughout the day.

ABOUT THE AUTHOR

Laurie Hayes is the founder of The HBB Source™, an online resource for home-based business owners, a certified business/executive coach, and author of numerous articles on life balance and business start-ups. Laurie is also the creator of "The Complete 12-Step Guide to Starting a Home-Based Business: How to Transition from Employee to Entrepreneur without Losing Your Mind or Your Shirt," a home study program for aspiring entrepreneurs. For free tips and strategies on starting a home-based business while improving quality of life, go to http://www.thehbbsource.com.

15

CHI

Achieve Balance, Contentment, and Harmony
through Managing Your Chi

Steve Orwin

There are 100 other ways to improve your life in this book. We all have our own needs and aspirations and will be drawn to those chapters we feel most relevant and appropriate for us. I hope this is one of them, for whether you are looking for new skills, ideas, and perspectives or are seeking ways of filling gaps and resolving issues, ultimately, you will only feel contentment if you are balanced.

Contentment is not a languid state of satiation but a vantage point for seeing things as they are and a springboard for taking action, both without stress or hidden agendas. In this state you can be true to yourself and to others.

Balance is also a state in which you have the energies to cope with life's challenges. We lose it when our coping mechanisms fail to meet the demands of the world around us, and in these circumstances, people respond in many self-destructive ways. A more measured response could be to reframe the challenges and focus our efforts more effectively, but learning how to strengthen our inner energies is where real progress can be made because our often-neglected natural source of power responds positively at many levels.

Though Chi is a concept of energy best documented and utilized by traditional Eastern cultures, it is universal in its distribution. Modern life tends to take its functions for granted though, thereby failing to appreciate how to make corrective adjustments when disorder or illness occur.

By increasing your awareness of this energy within, you can improve your sense of health and well-being. There are ways of using massage points, breathing, mental imagery, and meditation to enhance its power and ease of application, which also makes it more accessible for those with physical limitations that preclude more active forms such as Yoga or Tai Chi. Here are some simple examples to get you started.

The first exercise is to breathe out, hold your breath out for a moment, and consider what it would feel like if you never breathed again. Just as it is getting uncomfortable, inhale, and appreciate as you do the life-giving energy that you are drawing into yourself.

Gently stretch your back by raising your hands and pushing them upward, lean from side to side, forward and backward, then slowly twist from the waist to look behind you from side to side.

If you are unable to stand or move your limbs for these exercises, apply their principles as best you can to your circumstances. Because Chi is ultimately moved by your mind, fill in the parts you cannot achieve physically with your thoughts. Imagine your limbs moving and back stretching—it is harder work but will achieve results.

First Mind/Body Exercise

Preferably stand with your knees softened and tailbone tucked in—sit if necessary—hands by your sides. Exhale, and feel your arms extending to pick up energy from under the ground (or floor). Inhale as you scoop the energy up by cupping your hands and slowly lifting them upward, close to your legs and body, to the level of your stomach. Hold for a moment, and then exhale as you lower your arms and release the energy.

Imagine as you do this that you are breathing in energy from the earth. You inhale it through your feet, up your legs, and into your torso. Do not raise it above your stomach.

Some say that exercises like this actually draw energy from the earth, but though I reserve my opinion on this, I feel it is important to believe this occurs in order to communicate your intention effectively to your Chi through visualization. This allows it to respond to your conscious control instead of to the whims of your subconscious.

Acting as though you believe something in order to achieve something you believe in is an interesting state of mind. It allows you to manage your Chi, though almost by proxy, and I can assure you that it holds good to the extent that you can maintain this belief.

Second Mind/Body Exercise

Stand or sit with your feet apart and your arms by your sides. Turn your palms outward, and raise your straight arms out to your sides—lift them until they meet, palms together, above your head. Point your fingers together like a roof, and lower your arms past your face and chest in front of you, hands still touching, as if pressing a balloon downward until your palms flatten by your navel.

Breathe in as you raise your arms and out as you lower them. Feel as though you are slowly pressing your breath down from the top of your head through the center of your body.

Once it has passed your navel, feel it leave through your legs and feet, with a whoosh.

Do these exercises lightly, not straining or concentrating, just with an awareness of your activity. Through the visualization of transporting energy from the air into the ground through your body, you are stimulating the meridians through which Chi flows. Stagnation or imbalance in these channels affects your muscles and organs, and clearing them should make you feel better.

To maintain balance, you must also strive to achieve harmony between your inner and outer selves. Your behavior in the world reflects the essence of your mind, and vice versa, so developing one benefits the other. You must choose to act as you wish to be and be the best that you can. The tensions you may feel while trying to make progress can be eased through meditation, which will also, in itself, help to move you forward.

Breathing circulates Chi, up your spine and over your head on the in breath, down your front from your mouth to your perineum (just behind the genitals) on the out breath. Because it is both unconscious yet controllable at will, breath helps unify the body and mind. Breathing deeply to your abdomen is more powerful than short and rapid breaths and helps calm the nervous system. Be aware of your breathing when it is working well, and bring gentle control to help it when it is not. If you are stressed, angry, hurt, or tired, breathe and imagine your Chi circulating. Also practice this when you are calm, and connect your tongue with the roof of your mouth as a bridge to help the flow.

Chi operates at many levels, from within our cells to across the universe. It is "organizing" energy, so strengthening it or easing its flow can improve not just how our own organs function, but the benefits extend to our personal effectiveness, our relationships, and how we act within organizations. Applying its principles in the workplace is a good way to reduce stress and improve efficiency. Because we all communicate through our energy systems as well as through our words and actions, improving our inner energy benefits others too. So improving your balance and contentment can create the energy to add just a little more harmony to the universe, which is a worthwhile achievement in itself.

ABOUT THE AUTHOR

Steve Orwin is a registered social worker. He has an MA in public and social administration, an MA in management, a diploma in social work, and a diploma in management coaching and mentoring. He is also interested in martial arts and energy therapies. His book, *SoChi*, will be available soon on http://www.lulu.com. Check his Web site for details" http://www.so-chi.co.uk.

16

To Achieve Clarity in Life, Make Meditation Part of Your Day

Keith E. Renninson

I had not been home from Vietnam very long, in 1972, when I met a charismatic man in his mid-forties, with salt and pepper hair and a broad smile. He introduced me to meditation . . . acquiring the creative, sleepy state of mind also known as the alpha state. Thus began a lifelong quest to learn more about and practice meditation.

Over the years I have practiced meditating in the park, on hiking trips in lush forests, in front of a warm fireplace during the winter, in my office at work, when home with the flu, or while sitting in Starbuck's; you can meditate anywhere for any reason and be better for it.

During the 1990s, I traveled to Nepal twice; on the last trip I was able to spend some quality time with Buddhist monks at a monastery deep among the jagged peaks of the towering Himalayas. There I learned how meditation was used in their daily rituals and prayers and how I could use it to improve clarity in my life.

For me, clarity is a goal, a destination, a place of intelligence and knowledge. Self-examination, concentration, discipline, and understanding are all related to clarity. When one has clarity, life becomes easier; goals are achieved more quickly, and one attracts an electrified energy that enables the person to be more creative in all he does.

Meditation is an ancient, elegant tradition that has been practiced worldwide by people who wish to be more in control of their thoughts, their health, and their lives and to connect with higher powers for enlightenment. But, simply put, meditation allows you to calm and quiet your mind from daily chaos, often revealing clarity for troubling issues.

Of the many uses of meditation, some are to rest and reenergize your body, to calm a tense situation, to pray, to solve a problem, to control habits, to plan, to visualize achievement of goals, or to be deliciously quiet.

Back in 1972, I learned a technique that invites the meditative state by softly touching the thumb, forefinger and middle finger of each hand together, while your arms rest at your side or in your lap. The process goes like this:

- Close your eyes, allow your mind to become quiet, and take a deep breath. As you exhale, visualize the number three, three times in your mind's eye (I mentally see the descending numbers you find in elevators as my mind's eye picture).
- Take another deep breath, and as you exhale, visualize the number two, three times.
- Take another deep breath, and as you exhale, visualize the number one, three times. At the conclusion of the third and final deep breath, you will have acquired the alpha or meditative state of mind.
- When you are ready to become alert and active again, simply wiggle your fingers and toes slightly, take a deep breath, open your eyes, smile and be happy.

After only a few meditative sessions using this technique, the brain will make the connection, so from then forward, you can simply touch the three fingers together, take a couple of deep breaths and you will slide into alpha quickly and easily.

Meditation is one of life's free pleasures and only requires slow, concentrated breathing, a quiet place to sit, and about 20 minutes. Obviously, like the monks of Nepal, you may choose to burn a stick of fragrant incense and meditate for hours, but for most of us, 20 minutes is about all it takes to make our days significantly better.

Most every day, I meditate either in the morning, before I begin my day, or around 3:00 P.M., when I feel my energy ebb and need to recharge. Sometimes I have an agenda that I want to explore, trying to open new thoughts to a problem and reveal a solution. Closing your eyes and quieting the mind allows it to function more clearly and more efficiently, often with astounding results.

With this technique, meditation can be combined with other activities, such as Yoga. Yoga is as ancient as meditation, and the two work well together. Enter the meditative state through the process described above, open your eyes, and begin your poses, focusing your mind on your body, individual muscles, or joints and concentrating on your breathing, moving slowly with intent. You will find that your Yoga sessions take on a whole new value when performed this way.

Another place I find this technique to be helpful is in traffic. When traffic is heavy, moving slowly, and I find myself impatient, I will invite an "eyes-open" functional alpha state, calm down, relax, and look for the good in my day, appreciating the sunshine, the air-conditioning, or my solitude and looking forward to something nice later in the day.

You can also apply this usage to a tough day at work: close the door to your office and take a few minutes to quiet your mind and relax before tackling a tough assignment or customer call.

I encourage you to make meditation part of your day—the uses and rewards are many. You will find yourself happier, healthier, and more in control. What more can we ask for?

ABOUT THE AUTHOR

Keith E. Renninson is an energetic entrepreneur, motivational speaker, and coauthor of the popular parenting tool and illustrated storybook *Zooch the Pooch, My Best Friend*, published through Twinkletopia, LLC. Additionally, Keith owns Golden Years Videos, LLC, a film production company dedicated to offering exercise videos for those over 50 or anyone rehabilitating from a serious accident or illness. Now in his late fifties, Renninson regularly competes in bicycle time trials and road races and skis the black diamond runs in Colorado, where he lives. You can contact Keith and view more information on both companies' products at http://www.zoochthepooch.com and http://www.goldenyearsvideo.com.

17

COMMITMENT

Dreams Derailed

Donna Price

I was at a point on the rock face (about 60 feet from the ground) where the next foothold was just out of reach. In order to keep going up, I needed to reach it. I carefully stretched for it but could not make it. I searched for alternatives and tentatively kept retrying for the hold out of grasp. In rock climbing, footholds are often not secure until you put your weight on your foot. With the hold out of reach I could not shift my weight there to test it. The instructor, my belayer (the person holding my safety rope), after patiently waiting for me to explore all options (several times), said, "You have to 'commit to the move,' you have to go for it with everything, without hesitancy, it will be there." Perched on the rock face, I went for it, with everything; I committed, I reached out, put my foot on the hold, boldly shifted my weight, and it was there. I was secure, and I finished the climb.

The lesson for me was commitment: "You have to commit to the move." With each transition I make in my life, that lesson comes back. You cannot change your life with hesitancy. Risk, courage, trust, faith, and commitment are the core values that have guided my life over the past few years—each a lesson learned while changing my life and moving in new and different directions.

Over the years, I have changed careers twice. Each move was risky, and each opened new, unimagined doors. I believe that that is part of risk—not being able to see what is ahead. My lesson was that in taking risks, new opportunities appear. If I sit in the same place and do not move, I do not even see the opportunities. My values of trust, faith, and courage come into play here when taking the risk to move: trusting myself, having faith that all will be well, and moving with courage. And I have to remind myself of these lessons as I move into new territories.

I have created dreams from these values, cycling across the country, changing jobs, learning a whole new industry of outdoor adventure education, and then the biggest dream, creating family through adoption. Over these years, part of what I have tried to do is live intentionally.

Having children was a lifelong dream and one that I waited to take action on until into my late thirties. We quickly figured out that our family was going to be created through adoption, and we jumped through every hoop of paperwork, fingerprinting, background checks, and forms to adopt a beautiful baby from Vietnam. We traveled to Vietnam to finalize our adoption of Jackson and bring him home.

Creating dreams is one of my passions, but with this one we got thrown way off course, and so unexpectedly. On our flight from Hanoi to Ho Chi Minh City, Jackson stopped breathing. A doctor on the flight performed CPR, an ambulance met the flight, but ultimately, he died. We moved through the time in Vietnam before we could bring him home in a daze. Now I realize that the fog that came over me has taken several years to lift. The death of a child is beyond imagination. It changed our lives, forever.

But what do you do when your dream gets derailed in such a major way? We worked, we took every action we could think of to move through our grief and to begin our healing. We sought out help—support groups, grief counseling. We did some of the things that were healing for us—cycling, running, building, gardening—and we cried. Jackson came home, and we had a remembrance service for him. Since no one had met him, we introduced him to our friends and family through stories, memories, and pictures. We buried him at a cemetery near our home. The women at the orphanage in Hanoi said he should be buried with children, so he is in the children's section of the cemetery, and the cemetery is across from the elementary school.

We knew that we were on the right path. We had faith and trust in our desire and dream to parent. We learned from Jackson a total and complete love that we had not experienced before, and that love continued after he was gone. I felt stronger in my conviction that I wanted to parent. Jackson is always in our hearts. My love for him was so complete, and I believe his love for us was deep.

In searching for answers, I met with a Buddhist monk. The monk told me that he thought it was amazing that this soul could call us halfway around the world to come and love him for a week and give him enough love in that week to move on, that he was on a path and it was a good path. I walked, a walking meditation for Jack at the Buddhist monastery and many more in labyrinths, and I found connection with him there and here in our home. I sat in the silence to hear him.

Later that summer, we were able to apply again to Vietnam to adopt a child and within months were traveling to Vietnam to meet her. The rules had changed, and we were required to travel twice, once to file our application and meet the baby, and a second time to pick her up and finalize the adoption.

Again, values came into play. We risked our hearts to adopt another beautiful, perfect baby, this time a girl. We traveled the same path to Vietnam twice, prayed through long flights to get her home, and summoned every ounce of courage. Despite the blow I had taken to trusting in myself, I had to risk and believe that our path was right. Our commitment to family never wavered. As new obstacles appeared, we dealt with them and persevered.

Dreams get derailed every day. Not each derailing is as tragic. Sometimes we derail a dream ourselves with our own fears or limitations. Sometimes other types of changes in our lives or circumstances are the cause. Dreams can be put back on track. With inner strength, determination, commitment, and perseverance you can achieve the dreams you set out to.

I still live my life taking risks, following my heart, and creating dreams. I know that in the midst of them the plan can be totally toppled, and it can be devastating. And I know that I have an inner strength to carry me through. Creating dreams is work; it requires consistent action. Overcoming obstacles, devastations, or whatever else is thrown in the way also requires work, and with intentional work the dream can continue to be realized. For me, having clear core values has helped me to stay on the journey. When I get scared and want to jump ship, I am reminded that I have to totally commit to the move. I have to trust myself and my instincts. I have to take risks to move my dreams forward and have faith that I am on the right path. Throughout it all, I walk with courage to live my dreams.

ABOUT THE AUTHOR

Donna Price, president of Compass Rose Consulting, LLC, loves working with daydreamers that are ready to take action and move into living their dreams. Donna is the author of *Launching Your Dream*, a dream-maker's book filled with tools and ways to help you move your dream into your life. Donna provides individual and group coaching services. She is the parent of three beautiful children. Check out how you are doing on your dream-making efforts at http://www.launchingyourdreams.com/dreamassessment.htm, or contact Donna at dprice@compassroseconsulting.com or at (973) 948–7673.

18

Communication in Relationships: Is There Such a Thing as Bad Communication?

Carl Herkes

Have you been holding on to feelings that bother you? Have you been struggling with whether or not to communicate those feelings to someone whom you care about? This article may help to give you some foresight on whether you should unleash those feelings.

Communication is good, right? Personally, I believe it is next to impossible to have a healthy, rewarding relationship without it. Sure, the level of required communication depends on your level of intimacy with the person you are communicating with. But can open communication ever be destructive, even when the communicator thinks he is providing a helpful message for the recipient? I would say that it all boils down to knowing your audience. Think about what you are about to convey, and then try to predict how your recipient is going to react. Is the message sensitive or volatile enough to destroy the relationship you currently have? If so, it is best to think twice. Sounds simple enough, right?

Take this story, for example. I know a woman who, for her whole life, carried resentment about how her father raised her. This story begins when she was 50 years old and her father was 72. She felt she had not been nurtured and supported as much as she needed when she was growing up. Her father was a hard-liner; we all know the type. A man made mostly of discipline and not enough encouragement, keeping his feelings to himself. Something compelled the woman to spill her guts and write her father a letter. In this letter she described how she felt about her relationship with her father. She pointed out many of the shortcomings in her life and how she felt he was the cause of them because she "didn't get what she needed" from him. She pointed these things out in a very polite manner, obviously assuming that her father would understand and feel compassion for her. What actually happened was quite the contrary. The father was very angry after reading her letter and felt he was being attacked. What was once an acceptable relationship was now broken beyond repair. At the time the daughter wrote the letter she thought it would benefit her to get those things off her chest and did not take time to ponder how her father would deal with such things.

The case above could be considered "bad" communication as it damaged the relationship it was meant to improve. Here are some things you might want to consider before initiating a discussion with someone, especially when your message contains sensitive, blameful, or potentially negative information.

1. What do you expect to accomplish with your message?
2. Try to predict how your audience will respond. Are you prepared for an unexpected outcome?
3. Is it so important for you to get your message across that it is worth the risk of breaking the relationship? In some cases it may be, such as in cases involving a friend or spouse.
4. If you predict that your message may cause undesirable results, you may want to use a good friend or family member as a sounding board so you can clear your head of your thoughts. Even more so, it can be very beneficial for you to write the person a letter but never deliver it. I believe this works better than spilling your guts to a third party.
5. You can ask advice from a trusted friend or family member (especially if he knows the recipient of the message). However, always make the final decision on what to do. Your advisor probably has nothing to lose and may not give you proper advice in the matter.

Relationships are important in everyone's life, whether with friends, family, business associates, or complete strangers. For that reason, care should always be taken when communicating sensitive information. Can communication be a bad thing? I think it always depends on the circumstances. Sometimes you need to choose to hold back or potentially lose the relationship.

ABOUT THE AUTHOR

An entrepreneur and graphic artist, Carl Herkes has an online retail business, Exotic Flames (http://www.exoticflames.com), as well as a photography business called Aapics Digital Studios (http://www.aapics.com). Recently, Carl began writing articles for the fireplace and hearth industry along with articles about relationships. You can reach him at carl@exoticflames.com.

19

CREATIVITY

Unleash Your Creativity

Sheila Dicks

A creative person is generally considered to have talent in painting, drawing, architecture, crafts, and design. Using this narrow definition, many are left believing that they do not have a creative flair. Have you ever thought about your creative ability? Creativity is a talent that we all have and use regularly, whether or not we are aware of it.

If we change how we think about creativity, it will be easier to understand. First, let us get away from the idea that only those who work in creative arts are creative. Being creative is having the ability to create. What we create can be an object that can be seen or a pleasant feeling.

We are all familiar with creating things or objects, and that is how we usually think of creativity. Imagine the areas of your life that cannot be seen or touched but felt only by you. Your feelings are created. You create feelings by first holding beliefs in your mind, which cause you to act in a particular way, bringing reactions from others, producing more beliefs about the situation, and ending in your feelings.

Imagine you go for a job interview believing that you are not as well qualified as others and thinking that the job will most likely go to someone else. When you walk into the interview holding that thought in your mind, you will not sell yourself like you should; your confidence is lacking, and your body language will show it. The interviewer will quickly pick up on your nonverbal cues and adopt your belief that there is a better person for the job. When you get notice that you have not received the job, you say to yourself, "I knew this would happen," leading to a bad feeling. The bad feeling you have created will intensify each time it is created so that the next time you are in a similar situation, you will have beliefs about the situation that will impact what you receive and how you feel about it.

Think of the person who goes into the interview believing that he is fully qualified and deserving of the job. He will be more enthusiastic, giving an air of confidence, which will be picked up by the employer. The employer will believe that this person would be a good hire and will be more likely to offer him the job, resulting in good feelings.

Since we have control over our thoughts (we create them), which influences what we do and how we behave, then ultimately, we have control over and create our feelings. When we do not get what we want, the beliefs we hold about the situation and the thoughts that result will determine whether we have pleasant or unpleasant feelings. For example, you are in a relationship with a person you truly love. A year or so into the relationship, your partner tells you that he is not content in the relationship and wants to move on. This is your opportunity to create a pleasant or unpleasant outcome. We all know how an unpleasant outcome in this situation is created. We get mad and create a fuss and a lot of bad feelings. How do you create a pleasant outcome? It all has to do with how you think about the situation. You can fight it all the way and create bad feelings that will haunt you forever, or you can be understanding of the other person's feelings, knowing that it was not a perfect relationship if both people were not completely happy.

Believing that you have something to look forward to (your new mate is out there) and believing that your life is over will create two totally different feelings and outcomes. You are in the present, and the future is to be made, so neither is true yet; your beliefs will have an impact on how the future unfolds. This situation is similar to the job interview: Your beliefs create your feelings. Your beliefs affect your actions, which affect your results and your feelings about your results.

To unleash your creative talents and get more of what you want, trust that you have the ability to create. You are continuously creating the world around you by choosing beliefs and then acting as if they are true. To become more in tune to your creations, consider what you have already created, and reflect on how it has impacted your feelings and your life.

Decide what you want to create. If, for example, you want to create better health but have always thought of yourself as an out-of-shape, unfit person, then you can start by changing your beliefs about you and your health. Know that your results will follow your beliefs.

Start by making a list of what good health means to you, and be specific. What would you be able to do that you cannot do now? Climb stairs. How would you feel? Energized. How would you look? Toned. How would you feel about yourself? Great. You should be more specific, but this is the general idea. After you have decided what better health means to you, set up a plan of how you will achieve the results, and put that plan into action.

To help your creativity, get rid of negative feelings, and trust that when you change your beliefs, you change your outcomes. Find time to relax, be still, and reflect on your life and your feelings. Going through life in a rush and not stopping to think causes confusion in our minds, giving us little control over what we create. To clear your mind, spend time participating in relaxing activities (yoga, tai chi, meditation) and spend quiet time with yourself, away from the pressures of everyday life.

ABOUT THE AUTHOR

Sheila Dicks is the founder of Dynamic Impressions, an image consulting company committed to helping people feel unstoppable on the inside while looking great on the outside. Through personal development and image workshops Sheila helps men and women transform their wardrobes, lives and self esteem. Visit http://www.sheiladicks.com or http://www.sheilasfashionsense.com.

20

DEATH

Cultivate a Friendship with Death

Tim Ong

> Men fear death as children fear to go in the dark.
> —Bacon

Why We Fear Death

There may be a thousand reasons why we fear death, but most of all, we fear death because we fear the unknown, and death is an unknown entity to most people. We fear that dying may be painful, and we do not know what will happen to us at the point of death.

Some people fear death because they imagine the dying process to be very painful. Death is not painful. In fact, death is often very peaceful and silent, even for those suffering from cancers or other terminal illnesses.

When the physical body is deteriorating day by day from a terminal illness and pain arises from a superficial wound, such as a bed sore, or from deep pain, such as bone or nerve pain, death may even be a welcome relief for the sufferer.

We need to distinguish the pain of the physical body from the process of dying. The dying process is a distinct process that is separate from the deterioration of the physical body. At the point of death, there is no pain.

What happens at death is the cessation of the breath and all other physiological functions. The heart stops pumping, and the blood stops circulating. The body stops generating heat and thus progressively turns cold.

For those who believe that we are more than just physical bodies and that we are in fact spiritual beings, the dying process means much more than just physical death. Death is just a natural process that allows us to discard the physical body as we move into the spiritual realm.

Since our fear of death is due to the fact that we do not know or understand death, it makes sense to familiarize ourselves with it. The more we understand death, the less we fear it. We should therefore cultivate a friendship with death and be totally familiar with it, just as we are familiar with our friends.

We can cultivate a friendship with death in three simple steps.

1. Establish a link with God.
2. Cultivate a habit of acceptance, instead of blame.
3. Be a blessing to others.

Establish a Link with God

By establishing a link with God, we touch base with our own spirituality. God can be whatever you perceive God to be. For Christians, Muslims, and Hindus, that may mean an omnipotent God. For Buddhists, it may mean the Buddha seed within. Atheists may have to come to term with their own spirituality.

Establishing a link with God means regaining your spirituality. It leads you closer to the spiritual aspect of yourself. Whether we accept it or not, we are more than just this physical body. When we die, we leave this physical body behind, and only our spirituality continues on. It is therefore essential for us to be familiar with our own spirituality. It is the only part of us that continues after death. This "fact" is in accordance with all major religions.

Cultivate a Habit of Acceptance

It is funny how when good things come to us, we readily accept them as though we deserve them or have worked hard for them, yet when calamities befall us, we quickly look for an external source to blame.

This is especially so when misfortunes such as a terminal illness befall us. We may blame God and later blame ourselves or people around us. We should cultivate a habit of neutrality, regardless of whether good or bad things come our way. Otherwise, we can become very bitter about life when negative things happen. Looking for someone or something to blame only serves to prolong our own suffering. Death is an enemy when we resist it, but the moment we accept it, it turns into an ally.

However, cultivating a habit of acceptance does not mean not doing anything to correct or improve our conditions. It does not mean, for example, that when we are diagnosed with a terminal illness, we should do nothing about it. It is only sensible to seek treatment, if it is available to us. On the other hand, it also means that we must know and accept when curative treatment is no longer possible. We fear death only when we refuse to face it.

Unfortunately, there are unscrupulous people who would take advantage of our fear of death to sell their "cures." In my experience with the terminally ill I have come across countless stories of dying people being duped into parting with their savings and properties in the hope of achieving a cure.

Be a Blessing to Others

This is our greatest and most reliable ally at the time of death.

Knowing that we have been helpful to others and that we have tried to live blameless lives takes away the fear of death. If our lives have been honest ones, free of any conscious intention to hurt any living beings, we have nothing to fear when death approaches. Our minds will be at peace, undisturbed.

On the other hand, those who lead selfish lives and harm others to get little advantages for themselves find themselves imprisoned in tiny, dark cells when they move to the other side.

Therefore, while we still can, we should give our best to the world and to people around us. Lend a helping hand to others and help to lighten their loads. Bring joy to the joyless and comfort to those in need of comfort. There are many who are less fortunate than us. Count your blessings, and be a blessing to others.

About the Author

Dr. Tim Ong is a medical doctor with a keen interest in self-improvement, mind science, and spirituality. He teaches meditation, gives talks, and works with the local hospice services. He is the author of *From Fear to Love: A Spiritual Journey* and the webmaster of the *Self Improvement Site*. Visit his Web sites at http://fromfeartolove.com and http://theselfimprovementsite.com.

21

DECISION MAKING

What Makes the Best Decisions:
Your Logic or Intuition?

John Ryder

Life is all about decisions. The right choice can catapult you to great success, just as the wrong one can send you spiraling downward. So the question is, how do we take advantage of the power of logical reasoning or intuition to make better decisions?

The worst decisions we make are often impulsive. We give in to an urge, a wish, something suggested by advertising, or even pressure from friends. This type of decision, without reflection, often brings some degree of regret or dissatisfaction. To obtain a sense of fulfillment, we must make an effort to make our own decisions.

Besides flipping a coin, the two most common approaches we all rely on to make decisions are very different—sometimes they are in agreement, but sometimes they can be radically apart. We can learn to develop and improve both these methods. Which system do you rely on more?

The Rational Approach

This is a pragmatic and logical system that we must learn to use. It depends on (1) collecting concrete, objective, detailed information; (2) carefully analyzing and comparing it to previous experience; and (3) ranking or prioritizing the alternatives. This ultimately becomes the basis for a logical, rational judgment of what appears to be the best choice. This is a conscious and deliberate effort to make a decision.

The Intuitive Approach

This is the original human radar system we are all born with. It depends on our subjective impressions that give us a "gut" feeling or some sort of psychic awareness that provides instant knowledge. This awareness cannot be explained logically but creates a strong positive or negative feeling to do something or not. Intuitive knowledge is not learned or intellectual. It is a spontaneous thought or feeling that may arise from the subconscious mind or some sort of internal radar we have to evaluate situations.

These two approaches are the usual ways we prepare to make decisions. The actual process of deciding is a deeper exercise of judgment, creating the intention and initiating the will to do something. Whether you listen to your logic or intuition, the choice you make is the one you trust will get you what you want. Understanding the following factors can give you the edge to make decisions easier.

Predictability. Do you know what will happen? Guessing the consequences of our decisions falls on a continuum, from total uncertainty to great certainty, with a very wide middle zone, the "may be possible" category.

Significance. How big a deal is your decision? Each choice fits on a spectrum from unimportant all the way to extremely important. At the low end, consequences are neutral or reversible; they are just another experience. In the middle, the consequences are important; they may be costly emotionally or materially, with long-term effects, but these may be corrected. Critical decisions are usually life changing and irreversible, with serious consequences for better or worse.

Alternatives. How many different choices can you find? The more alternatives, the greater flexibility for you to find the best choice.

Being clear about what kind of question you are dealing with is the first step to making a better decision. If the intuition is in agreement with the rational approach, the decision is simple. When these two approaches are in conflict, then we have a new problem. Which system is better to follow—the intuitive or rational? The answer depends on the subject matter.

The fact is that neither system is superior all the time. And despite their respective strengths, both methods can be wrong. That means the most rational person, who reviews every detail and comes to a rock solid logical conclusion he feels certain of, can be totally wrong. Similarly, the most intuitive person, who gets the strongest gut feeling about something, can be equally mistaken. If we cannot rely on either approach to be always right, then that suggests we try to use both systems to balance out any weaknesses.

The advantage of having two very different systems is that each is better in different situations. Nobody wants to fly a plane built by intuition, nor should anyone get married based on a list of logical criteria alone. The point is that the rational approach is better for technical, mechanical, or electrical problems— building, designing, organizing, prioritizing agendas, verifying theories, and so on. Logic is excellent to deal with the hard facts, but it does not do as well with softer, human matters. The intuitive approach is better for dealing with the emotional life—relationships, family matters, art, music, career directions, and so on. Intuition is not meant to be analyzed, it just offers a very simple feeling— approach or avoid.

Taking into consideration all the points above, here are some rules for making decisions that help us utilize the power of both approaches. Obviously, if you cannot gather any objective information, you must rely on your intuition. Conversely, if you have no intuitive sense about something, do everything possible to collect the objective facts to make a rational decision. In each case, be mindful of the type of question you are addressing.

When a decision is not important, then the intuitive approach can be relied on first, followed by the rational one. When the consequences of a decision are very important, the rational approach should be relied on first, except if your intuition sends a strong warning, then you should heed the inner advice. However, if the intuitive message urges you to do something that goes against your rational conclusions, do not be impulsive, think long and hard before going forward. When facing significant problems, the rational approach should come first to isolate a few alternatives. Then your intuition can perhaps help you select the best choice. In general, the intuition is better at warning us about things to avoid than advising us about what to approach.

Questions that are impossible to predict are handled better by our intuition because our internal radar may offer valuable subjective information. In matters where the results can be more accurately predicted, it is better to rely on the rational system and collect additional information until a clear answer becomes evident. When the probability is in the middle zone, with lots of possibilities, the best advice is to utilize both systems and perhaps split the difference. The ultimate measuring stick for making good decisions is to ask yourself, can you afford to make this mistake? That is, consider the options and calculate how much trouble might be caused if the choice you are making turns out to be wrong.

Decisions can be tricky. Even if you are comfortable with your choice, it is wise to remain a bit skeptical, ponder the matter, and reflect about the objective facts as well as the intuitive feelings. Prudence in making decisions means not ignoring either source of information and not jumping to conclusions prematurely. However, do not delay making decisions either since it is always better to learn from your own decisions rather than wasting your life in a state of indecision.

ABOUT THE AUTHOR

John Ryder, PhD, is a psychologist and consultant in private practice in New York City (http://www.Ultimategoals.com). He is an author, speaker, and workshop leader, sharing his set of keys to health, happiness, and prosperity that he has collected from around the world for 30 years. His work integrates the ancient wisdom of the East and the science of the West to offer many valuable tools. To see his most recently published books and articles, visit http://www.RaisingYourCQ.com for information.

22

The Antidote to Anger:
How to Calm an Angry Person and
Turn an Adversary into Your Ally

Janet Pfeiffer

We cannot be a world at peace until we are first a people of peace.
—Janet Pfeiffer

I think it is fairly safe to say that at any given moment in our lives we have all encountered an angry individual: someone who may be yelling, threatening, ranting, or raging, someone who is out of control. How do you typically handle that kind of situation? Do you react by allowing yourself to get sucked into the angry person's bad behavior and respond with more yelling? Or do you retreat in fear and avoidance?

Reacting is often your ego responding to a threat. ("Who do you think you are? How dare you speak to me that way!") My ego tells me that if I huff and puff louder, the offender will back down. That will teach him that he is not going to get away with treating me that way.

Retreating is usually fear: a lack of self-confidence in one's ability to be successful when faced with a difficult situation.

Reacting can actually cause the situation to escalate. Retreating may leave one feeling weak and defeated. Neither is an effective strategy. However, there is a proven method that delivers amazing results. With a deeper awareness of the issues and some simple yet profound strategies, anyone can evoke a more positive response and turn conflict into cooperation.

85

Let me start by presenting you with the following scenario: Imagine that you have suffered a serious burn. You do not ignore it, expecting that it will fix itself. And you do not treat it with more heat. (Isn't that what caused the problem in the first place? Too much heat?) The way to soothe the burn and prevent further damage to the skin is to apply the opposite of heat—cold, such as ice. Common sense, right?

What about an allergic reaction? An antihistamine, not more of the allergen, provides relief. In a medical emergency the most effective treatment is very often found in the antithesis.

The same principle applies to an "emotional emergency," such as anger out of control. When someone is hurt, you offer comfort; when he is lonely, friendship; when he is frightened, reassurance. See how that works? Simple, right?

This same concept applies to anger. To respond to an angry person with more anger is both foolish and potentially deadly. Angry people have been known to cause serious harm to others, even death. So what, then, is the antidote to anger? There are four key strategies to consider when trying to calm someone down. They are understanding, boundaries, compassion, and forgiveness.

First, let us look at understanding. It is important to understand that we are all human and that sometimes we act out in an inappropriate manner. Behavior is merely an expression of what is going on inside. It is not a reflection of who a person is (his intrinsic value as a human being). Sometimes our emotions get the better (or should I say the worst) of us. Few people are trained to be fully attuned to their innermost selves, and most likewise have not learned appropriate methods of expressing anger. Also, I would like you to understand that underneath all anger lies either hurt, fear, or frustration. Knowing this, instead of dealing with the individual's anger, assist him in identifying the underlying, or "root," emotion. ("You sound really frustrated. What's going on?" or "I know you've had a lot on your mind lately. Are you worried about your family?" Worry is a form of fear.)

All human beings crave to be understood. Understanding validates, comforts, and connects: "I can now be more understanding of human imperfections because I recognize that I posses them as well."

Second is boundaries. These are critical guidelines (rules and regulations) that we set in all relationships to establish fairness, safety, and mutual respect. Every individual has a right and a responsibility to determine how she wants to be treated as well as what is not acceptable or permissible to her. Boundaries are most effective when established early in the relationship. If someone attacks you verbally, you may firmly (yet politely) inform him that before you can continue, he must calm down. Explain that you are willing to hear what he has to say but only under those conditions. ("I don't work well when I feel like I'm being attacked. If you can calm down, I'd be more than happy to listen to you.") If the person is unwilling or unable to accommodate your request, another rule might be that you will excuse yourself and return when the person has regained composure.

Third is compassion. This word is defined by Webster's as "a sympathetic consciousness of another's distress together with a desire to alleviate it." This concept, sadly, is foreign to so many people today. When I can connect with another's pain and suffering, it brings our relationship to a much deeper level of understanding. My genuine concern for my fellow human being translates into a compassionate and heartfelt response. ("I'm so sorry that things are not going well for you. Is there anything I can do to help?") I can tell you what I know for sure: Kindness and compassion are *key* ingredients for successful relationships on every level. Try adding compassion to your list of skills in dealing with an angry person, and watch what happens. It is almost magic!

And finally, forgiveness. When someone offends me with her behavior or words, it often leaves in my heart and mind a residue of hurt and anger. Forgiveness cleanses that residue. It does not lessen or eradicate the offense. It simply means that (once again) I understand human weakness and imperfection, and I choose to no longer be angry about what has happened in the past. It frees me from resentment, grudges, and thoughts of retaliation. It restores my sense of inner peace and tranquility. It heals the hurt and allows for a healthier relationship with my (now) ally. We all need to forgive, just as we all need to be forgiven (for the times we have acted badly toward others).

I am intelligent enough to know that you *never* pour gasoline on a fire. It only makes it burn longer and hotter. To safely extinguish a fire and prevent further damage, you apply the opposite: water, dirt, or baking soda. I now know that you never respond to anger with more anger. It only causes the situation to escalate and could have deadly consequences. To safely soothe out-of-control anger, you respond with the opposite: understanding, boundaries, compassion, and forgiveness.

ABOUT THE AUTHOR

Janet Pfeiffer, international speaker and award-winning author, is one of the nation's leading authorities on anger management and conflict resolution. She consults with such companies as the U.S. Postal Service, Hoffman La-Roche, Rutgers University, Carnival Cruise Lines, United Way, AT&T, and the New Jersey Education Association. She is also a counselor at a battered women's center. Janet has spoken at the United Nations and Notre Dame University and was highlighted by NBC News. A former host of her own radio talk show, Janet is also listed in the publication *Who's Who in Authors*.

23

DREAM TEAMS

The Secret to Success: Create Dream Teams

Joe Kahler

Teamwork is the ability to work together toward a common vision. The ability to direct individual accomplishments toward organizational objectives. It is the fuel that allows common people to attain uncommon results.
—Andrew Carnegie

I grew up playing sports, particularly baseball and football. I played throughout high school and college. I loved the game; however, what I enjoyed most was working with a group of people toward a specific goal. I enjoyed the thrill of the game, being "in the moment," giving everything I had to help the team win. I really missed sports when I graduated from college and went out into the real world. I was led to believe that I had to do everything on my own in the business world to be successful. I made a good living, worked hard, but missed that special feeling that I had when I was playing sports. I received awards and promotions at work but could never match that "something" I had with sports.

After 20 years of searching, the answer was sitting right in front of me the whole time . . . *teams!* That is what I loved about sports, and it applies to all aspects of life. Teamwork is the essence of success. And like sports, the key to a great team is coaching. A good coach places the players into the best position to help the team accomplish its goals.

After playing sports for years, reading many biographies on successful people in the real world, and experiencing my own failures through my lack of teams, I finally got it. Do not try to do everything myself. Create teams to help me reach my goals. Once I understood this concept, my life changed forever, and my success began to accelerate.

I am excited to give you the keys to creating your own dream teams. You can immediately begin to enjoy life the way you always imagined it should be. Let's get started!

Creating Your Dream Team

The challenge is finding the right people to help you accomplish your goals. Gathering a successful team is not only helpful, but essential. In school you had mentors, advisors, club leaders, fellow students, teachers, and others to help you accomplish your goals of getting good grades and eventually graduating from school. The only difference now is finding the right teammates to match your future goals. You will be looking for bankers, financial planners, health and fitness coaches, or businesspeople associated with your line of work. Have a team for every aspect of your future goals and dreams. You do not have to know everything, you just need to find the right people that do and have them on your team!

1. Look for those individuals that logically fit into the specific team you are forming. For example, if you are going to begin investing in real estate, you would want a banker, real estate agent, and mortgage broker on your team, to name a few. If you are working on your health and fitness, you would look for a nutritionist, workout facility, fitness coach, and so on.
2. Check the prospects' interest level. Personally meet with them and make sure they have the interest and ability to help you as it relates to your goals and direction.
3. *Listen* to the prospects' responses. A response tells you a lot about someone's integrity, character, and skills.
4. Do your homework. Are they successful in their particular fields? Do they understand what you are trying to accomplish, and are they going to support you?
5. Find a successful mentor/coach for each team you form. For example, if you are going to start an Internet business, get information from people who are already successful in that field. Do not ask Uncle Joe if he has no experience with an Internet business. That would be like going to an auto mechanic to ask about the best stock to buy! Ask those individuals who have proven success in your area of interest. You will find they will want to share their success principles, if you *ask*.

The last critical piece of advice is to consistently check for the following key attributes in your new team *and* in yourself. You have to be a great team player as well, so that you can help your team succeed.

Attributes of a Team Player

Now check the following attributes to see how well you stack up as a team player and to learn what to look for in bringing your team together.

1. **Flexible.** Know your goal, but understand that there can be numerous routes to achieve it. Know your strengths and weaknesses.
2. **Dedicated.** Get in the habit of asking what is best for the team. Develop a strong level of commitment. Tie your commitments to your values. No one who ever gave his best regretted it.
3. **Communicator.** Communication is important in the teaming process. Open communication develops trust. Having a hidden agenda or talking behind people's backs hurts team relationships. If you encounter an issue with a teammate, deal with it immediately. Share information. Teammates will be more likely to support you when they are in the loop.
4. **Team minded.** Be a giving person.
5. **Positive.** Think solutions, not problems. Be enthusiastic. All problems can be dealt with. Problems can help you and your team grow . . . or dissolve.
6. **Value your teammates.** Add value: Believe in them, and help bring out their uniqueness. Help them reach their potential.
7. **Endless learner.** Value self-improvement above self-promotion.
8. **Organized.** Be prepared.
9. **Accountable.** Have teammates be responsible for their actions. Do not play the "blame game."
10. **Disciplined.** See the big picture.

Now that you have all the ingredients to create your dream teams, decide what areas in your life would benefit from this team approach. Share your gifts with the team, and enjoy the personal and financial rewards that will follow. As Zig Ziglar says, "You can have everything you want in life if you help enough other people receive what they want." Live your dreams!

ABOUT THE AUTHOR

Joe Kahler is an expert on helping young adults successfully transition from home to being out on their own. His latest works have recently been assembled into his book *Out on My Own . . . Now What? Tips and Insights So You Won't Be Left Hanging in the "Real World"!* (it has already received the 2005 Mom's Choice Award and the Family Choice Award). Joe received his undergraduate degree from Whittier College in social sciences and his master's degree in education from Arizona State University. His experience includes teaching, coaching, running numerous businesses, investing, and enduring numerous lessons in real life training. Joe has done a number of television and radio interviews and is available for additional interviews and speaking engagements. For further information, visit http://www.outonmyown.com.

24

EMOTIONAL BAGGAGE

Travel Lightly My Friends

Stacy Corrigan

Travel lightly my friends. Give up your unconscious pain and habits;
they weigh you down. Accept your birthright to be joyous and free.
—Anonymous

When was the last time you flew on a plane? Have you noticed that the weight limits for baggage have been significantly lowered? I discovered this at the airport recently when taking an international flight. At first it bothered me as I am a person that likes to have as much of my stuff as close to me as possible. Then I discovered that there is a significant cost associated with going over the weight limit, and I asked myself, "Why do I need to carry around so much stuff anyhow?" What am I afraid of not having that I might need?

What we do not realize, or remember, is that we already have everything we need. The universe provides everything we need, right away, all the time. We are the ones who think that we need to bring all of our stuff with us. It is not only our physical belongings that we drag around either. Many of us have been hauling our emotional baggage along with us since childhood. How heavy are your emotional bags? How long have you been carrying the weight of the world on your shoulders? What extra price are you paying for insisting that you continually lug all of your stuff with you?

In actuality, the weight of your "baggage" is only that which you choose to assign to it. I will give you an example. I watched my dad die as a result of a heart attack he had in our swimming pool when I was just four years old. For many years I chose to feel like a victim about that fact. I was defining my experience as negative and chose to play the "poor me" role for a long time. As part of my growth and personal development, I have realized that I can choose to remember this situation differently, and I have the choice to change my beliefs

93

about it. I decided to change the truth I chose to assign to that memory. I now choose to feel grateful to my dad for putting me in a position that has caused me to become the person I am today: a person who is strong, independent, driven, capable, resourceful, and a whole lot more! How could you choose to see your "baggage" differently? Who have you become as a result of what you have had to endure? Are you willing to choose to assign a new truth to those seemingly negative events? Are you ready to lighten your load?

There are many ways to lower your emotional baggage burden. One approach you could start with is to count your blessings. What in life are you grateful for? What have you accomplished that you are proud of? What positive things do others say about you? Noticing, documenting, and appreciating the blessings in your life magnetizes the energy of the universe and reduces your resistance so that you have room for more wonderful experiences, people, and things to be invited into your space. When you rest in a state of positive appreciation, you feel as though more things are possible, and your load becomes lighter.

I encourage you to make your list today of all the blessings in your life and then see how many more you can add each day! I like to call it an Appreciation Log. Some call it a Gratitude Journal. It does not matter what you call it, as long as it feels good to you. I would find, make, or buy some paper or a notebook that makes you feel wonderful. Go to your computer, the office supply store, or a stationery store and create or select something pleasing to you so that it reinforces the positive energy you are putting into your list. Keep your log handy so that it is easily accessible for you to recount your blessings daily. This will ensure that you keep it going for as long as you desire. I suggest trying to maintain your log for at least a month, then try for a quarter, then six months, and finally see if you can keep it going for a year. One time, when I had a series of positive, successful events happening in my life, I noticed that I had been adding something new to my log every day for the previous six months! The blessings kept unfolding and multiplying simply by my noticing them, documenting them, and appreciating them, and the same can happen for you!

The next thing that I do to keep my load light on a daily or weekly basis is to look at my Feel Good Photo Book©. This is a pocket photo album that I purchased and filled with pictures that I took or cut out of a magazine that make me feel wonderful. I put beautiful pictures of nature in it, pictures of my family and closest friends, pictures of people laughing, photos of places I have traveled to that I just love, pictures of my pets, and so on. The key is to not put in pictures that have any sort of negative association in the slightest. There cannot be anything but joy produced by looking at these photos. I keep my Feel Good Photo Book in my car so that it is handy whenever I may need a lift. It takes about 30 seconds to a minute to flip through the book, instantly feel better, and shift the energy of the day.

Another technique I have been using lately to keep my emotional bags light is something I call my Pocket Full of Possibilities. On a recent trip to Asia I acquired a small piece of jade and an antique coin. Each morning, I place them both in my pocket, and I am reminded of their presence throughout the day either by their light jingling when I reach to pay for something or by removing them in the evening. I associate these objects with the building of the Great Wall of China and of how successfully the Japanese have rebuilt their country after being destroyed by atomic bombs. I use these items to inspire me to think that if people could accomplish those incredible things on the other side of the world that long ago, then anything is possible, and what can I do today? What possibilities would you create today if you knew you could do anything? If your load were lighter?

Can you imagine how good you would feel if you did not carry around the load that you have been used to carrying for so long? What would it take for you to be willing to let it go? What are you willing to do today, this minute, to lighten your load? Are you ready to:

1. see your baggage differently and assign a new truth to it?
2. count your blessings?
3. begin an Appreciation Log?
4. create a Feel Good Photo Book?
5. produce a Pocket Full of Possibilities?

We make time for the things that are important to us. Where does your motivation to change fall on your personal scale of importance? Would it not be nice if there was a limit to the amount of emotional baggage we could carry? There is. Your limit is up to you. You get to choose if you want your load to be heavy or light. So then why not travel lightly, my friends?

ABOUT THE AUTHOR

Through the building of her own successful business, Stacy Corrigan has been coaching and inspiring people across the world for over 15 years. With her background as a former corporate accountant, independent consultant, senior sales director, CORE© certified coach, and with her passion for sound financial management, Stacy is determined to teach as many people as she can how to drastically improve their financial health. For more information on how you can receive a *free* financial coaching session and your *free* CORE Personal Financial Balance Profile Report©, please visit http://www.financialfreedomzone.net or call (401) 868–4088 or (877) 318–5378.

25

ENERGY HEALING

Increase Your Vibration . . . Change Your Life!

Peggy Carey

Did you know that you can achieve your dreams using mind power or thought energy enhanced and strengthened with the natural energy of plant extracts, meditation, and affirmations? The life force energy of the blood of the plant can help you focus and amplify the energy of your thoughts to better communicate with your inner self, connecting with the creative power of the Universe. Numerous studies and diagnostic procedures provide scientific validation of the existence of measurable energy radiating from essential oils, thoughts, and emotions.

Physicists have proven that everything in the universe that appears solid is actually composed of swirling molecules. Einstein's equation $E = mc^2$ states that all matter is energy. These molecules are vibrating at different frequencies. Therefore all matter, including our bodies and entire life force, is a standing wave of pulsating energy. The vibrational frequency of this pulsating energy (the number of oscillations per second) is measured in Hertz, named after the nineteenth-century German physicist Heinrich Rudolph Hertz (1857–1894). As a Hertzian wave is generated and travels out from its source, the wave transfers energy to the objects through which it passes. This is one of the reasons that a happy and confident person walking into a room has a positive effect on the people present. His or her high vibration has an uplifting impact on everyone within its reach.

On the basis of the knowledge of the different frequencies of energy that can be measured emanating from the human body, a lot can be determined about our states of health, both physical and emotional. One of the most common diagnostic tools is the electrocardiogram (EKG). The electrical energy coming from the heart can give doctors information about whether the heart is functioning properly. The measurement of the beating heart's electrical energy is actually vibrational medical analysis in its most basic form.

Dr. David Hawkins concluded from a 20-year study of kinesiologic calibrations that a person's mental state can have a profound effect on the condition of his or her body. He created an arbitrary scale that mapped the energy of human consciousness. Any state, attitude, or emotion that causes a person to vibrate at a frequency below 200 on the Hawkins scale weakens the body, and from 200 to 1,000, strengthens it. He determined the lowest emotional vibration rate to be shame. A shameful thought weakens the person. Higher on the scale, but below 200, are guilt, apathy, grief, fear and anxiety, craving, anger, and hate. Love, joy, and peace move up the scale, with enlightenment at the top in the 700 to 1,000 range.

Clearly our objective should be to experience these higher vibrational emotions in order to maintain optimum health and let go of uncomfortable negative emotions and limiting thought patterns. Not only can our mental states affect the conditions of our bodies, they can also affect the achievement of our goals and determine the kind of life experiences we attract. The natural energy surrounding us can be used to change our personal lives, increase our businesses, or attract a soul mate.

When the highest and fastest frequencies replace lower and slower frequencies, they eradicate problems of many kinds. With a little effort you can increase your vibration, transform your emotional state, and change your life. You can create a conscious healing partnership between you, your higher self, divine intelligence, and the creative energy of the Universe.

The concept of vibrational healing utilizes the Universal Life Force to maintain balance within the energy field of the human body. This energy field can be modified, balanced, and enhanced to attract unlimited abundance, prosperity, and inner peace through meditation, affirmations, conscious intention, and the inhalation of pure, therapeutic-grade essential oils.

Clinical research shows that essential oils, containing the life force energy of plants, have the highest frequency of any substance known to man (including food or herbs), creating an environment hostile to disease, bacteria, and viruses. These oils receive their energy from the sun through the process of photosynthesis and have a chemical structure that is similar to that found in human cells and tissues.

Many people have come to depend on oils for their ability to eliminate health concerns, increase vitality, promote a feeling of emotional well-being, expand spiritual horizons, and improve creativity and mental functioning. According to ancient texts, oils were used for every condition from gout to a "broken head," referring to mental illness.

There are many easy methods of application, but two of the most popular involve inhalation or topical techniques, such as massage on the area of concern or the nerve endings on the hands or bottoms of the feet. I always keep a collection of oil bottles in my desk which make up my Energy Tune-Up Kit. If I am having trouble concentrating or am experiencing writer's block, I wave a bottle of cedarwood under my nose. A computer or other stressful problem calls for a whiff of lavender. A drop of peppermint on the back of the neck will zap a headache in seconds. Everyone will develop their own favorites, but I find that frankincense is a good oil to put in a diffuser during meditation, or if I want an uplifting experience for a longer period, I put a drop of rosewood or sandalwood in a diffuser pendant that I conveniently wear around my neck. The pendant is an excellent way to enjoy the benefit of a small amount of oil for longer periods.

Each plant has a unique energetic pattern or vibration and has been used for centuries for its role in natural healing. Clinical research shows that essential oils can quickly raise the frequency of the human body, restoring mental, emotional, and physical well-being. High-vibration pure oils, such as rose (highest frequency of all), helichrysum, and lavender, for instance, enable the user to feel happier and experience thoughts that will attract an abundance of all that is good.

Not only will medicinal essential oils raise your vibration, but because of their effect on the limbic system of the brain, they may help combat depression, reduce stress, and improve your mental clarity and focus. Oils can also help release negative energy that is not in harmony with your highest good. Beware of perfume-quality oils or oils with chemical additives, which can actually lower your vibration and cause physical side effects, such as headaches or skin reactions.

Frequencies that surround us influence our state of well-being and our ability to attract either good or bad experiences. Low-vibration, negative thinking and emotional states (depression, sadness, grief, etc.) promote more of the same, unless some positive change occurs in the person's thinking and perceptions. Like attracts like, and we create our existence with our thoughts.

Remember that with these simple and readily available tools, you have the ability to increase your vibration and access the highest and fastest energies for the purpose of ridding yourself of problems, improving your physical, mental, emotional, and spiritual health, and achieving success in life. You will be amazed at what you can accomplish with a 20-minute meditation and a few drops of essential oil, such as frankincense. Learn this simple technique, and take control of your life!

Bibliography

Gerber, Richard. *Vibrational Medicine for the 21st Century: A Guide to Energy Healing and Spiritual Transformation.* New York: Eagle Brook, 2000.

Hawkins, David. *Power vs. Force: The Hidden Determinants of Human Behavior.* Carlsbad, CA: Hay House, 2002.

Price, Shirley, and Len Price. *Aromatherapy for Health Professionals.* New York: Churchill Livingstone, 1995.

Schnaubelt, Kurt. *Medical Aromatherapy: Healing with Essential Oils.* Berkeley, CA: Frog, 1999.

Worwood, Valerie Ann. *The Complete Book of Essential Oils and Aromatherapy.* San Rafael, CA: New World Library, 1991.

Young, D. Gary. *Essential Oils: Integrative Medical Guide.* Orem, UT: Essential Science Publishing, 2003.

ABOUT THE AUTHOR

Peggy Carey, the "Zest Lady," is pursuing a PhD in parapsychic science and has 11 years experience in the vibrational energy healing field. She is an aromatherapy/wellness consultant, writer, creator of the Quantum Business Building and Life Enrichment Program, a successful network marketing professional, and designer of Zest Lady Aromatherapy Pendants[TM]. Having learned of the dynamics of holistic healing through an experience with a cat companion, she hosted the country's first Natural Pet Care Expo. You can learn more about healing and empowerment with Universal Life Force Energy and how to get your *free* Quantum Business Building and Life Enrichment Guide at http://www.peggycarey.com.

26

EXCELLENCE THROUGH HANDWRITING

Sign Here, Please

Lucy Grace Yaldezian

If you are in business, chances are you have a business card. It is certainly one of the most basic and common business tools, so useful both as an introduction and reminder.

Consider how much information is generally available on a business card: your name, of course; how you can be reached (telephone and fax numbers, e-mail and street address, and Web site); and, depending upon the design and font you have chosen, a business card can speak volumes about your style, approach, and personality.

What if I told you that you have a marketing tool right at your fingertips that is less expensive than a business card and offers tremendous amounts of information about you? That tool is your very own handwriting. "Yeah, right," you might say with great skepticism. "Who even writes anymore?" Well, perhaps by learning a bit about the wealth of possibilities in your handwriting, you will be inspired to take pen in hand and write a note to a business colleague instead of dashing off yet another relatively anonymous email. A hand-addressed envelope is always the first one to be opened, and a hand-written note is always the last one to be tossed away. That fact alone makes your handwriting worth a second look!

Consider that everything you write is a reflection of who you are. Your handwriting is not merely a function of your fingers and arm, or even your toes if that is where the pen is being held during the writing process. Handwriting actually begins in the cerebral cortex of the brain and carries encoded information from your subconscious mind to the subconscious mind of the person reading it. Your handwriting is a diagram of your beliefs and attitudes, of how fluidly you think, whether you react primarily from logic or emotion, how comfortable you are with yourself, and much, much more.

If you have trouble believing this, consider for a moment how many companies are requiring a handwriting analysis of potential employees before making final hiring decisions. The link between handwriting and personality has been recognized and explored for centuries. Just because our computer age is threatening to make handwriting obsolete does not negate its importance, its potential, or its impact. By learning how to maximize the ordinary tool of your very own handwriting, you are creating an extraordinary advantage for yourself in the business world.

Taking a look at your signature is a great place to start. First of all, start thinking of it as an "autograph," just like a celebrity. Who is to say that your autograph will not be worth money someday? To prepare for that outcome, really look at how you sign your name. Is your autograph working for you, or against you? Here are a few specifics to get you thinking in some great new directions.

How large or small is your autograph? The smaller the size of your writing, the more intense the traits, both productive and unproductive. An autograph that is too small may send the message that you are only comfortable in a very small space in this big, wide world. An autograph that is disproportionately large may send the message that you expect to always be at the center of the universe. In handwriting, as in life, balance is key.

Does your autograph match the rest of your writing? If slant, size, or spacing is different, consider that you may be putting on a mask for the world. What is it about your true self (revealed in your day-to-day writing) that you may not be comfortable with? What is it about your autograph (your public self) that feels "safer" for you? Sometimes it is your day-to-day writing that could stand to be changed to match your autograph.

Speaking of slant, how is yours? The more slanted your writing, the more you are ruled by your emotions, rather than logic. If your autograph is leaning like the Tower of Pisa, straightening it up will actually help rewire your brain to respond to life in a more centered and, yes, balanced way.

What about spacing? If the letters of your autograph are crowded together, maybe you need some more "breathing room" in your life. Believe it or not,

102

allowing balanced space between the letters reinforces a greater sense of space in your life. A little alone time is healthy for everyone.

Perhaps you cannot tell what the spacing is between the letters because you cannot tell what the letters are. Could it be that your autograph is nothing more than a squiggle of the pen? An autograph that is not completely legible is like using an unreadable font on your business card. What a waste! And what negative PR. While illegible autographs can signal a tremendous intellect and energy, they are also registering a certain level of detachment, inaccessibility, and, in some cases, even fear—probably not the message you want to be sending to colleagues, employees, or clients! What does it feel like to sign your autograph so that it is completely legible? If you are like most people with unreadable, "thready" autographs, efforts to write it legibly may cause surprising discomfort. If this is the case with you, just notice what the emotions are and keep practicing the legible autograph. Eventually, the new neural pathways you create in the brain will override the discomfort, and you will be amazed at how whole and free you might feel.

If you have never before even considered the possibilities for professional—and personal—excellence through handwriting changes, just try some of these suggestions for 40 days and see if you notice a difference. You may discover that your very own autograph in your very own handwriting is a potential business asset that you can maximize with a little time and attention—a proven mind-body connection for success that is right at your fingertips!

ABOUT THE AUTHOR

Lucy Grace Yaldezian of A Higher Perspective is a certified handwriting consultant, certified hypnotherapist, and creator of Essential Healing™. Specializing in panic, anxiety, and phobia relief, Lucy Grace has been helping individuals and groups make good shift happen in their lives since 1992. Download "Power Relaxation" and "At the Beach" for free from her Web site http://www.ahigherperspective.com. In the meantime, take a deep, deep breath, and just begin to relax . . .

27

Creating a Foundation:
The Dilemma of Human Potential

D. Ostaro

A human being consists of many forces and potentialities. Each individual has many possibilities and limitations endowed by circumstances. A person may be likened to an automobile with a top speed of 100 miles per hour. To start the car, the ignition key has to be inserted. Fail to do this, and the car will never start normally. Next you have to turn the ignition key, start the engine, and then start to accelerate. Finally, you begin to steer, moving in your desired direction within the limits of the local driving code.

Most cars will reach their top speed of 100 miles per hour only rarely because of speed limits imposed by the state. Likewise, if circumstances are not favorable, even the most gifted individual may never realize his or her full potential.

The stage of development where we are when we undertake a project is very important because our priorities and commitments at that stage will demand our attention and determine what concentration of our total focus is available. Wishful thinking alone will not solve a pressing problem and help us complete a project successfully. Dreaming alone is not enough. When backed by personal concerted efforts, dreams transform a warrior into a conqueror.

Zones of Human Potential

If you are between the ages of 21 and 50 (Zone A: high energy) you are in great shape because at this position you have the advantages a very high IQ, a maximum energy level, enthusiasm, an adventurous spirit, and so forth. This position increases the chances of your success in any project by about 90 percent.

However, if you are between the ages of 28 and 50 (Zone B: high energy plus knowledge), you have somewhat more experience, knowledge, sobriety of mind, and contacts. These factors help to temper the qualities of Zone A.

If you are between the ages of 57 and 100 (Zone C: mental maturity and resources), you may not have as much energy, but you do have maturity of mind, resources, and added experience and an increased number of contacts, even though you may not work as hard physically. But you have gathered knowledge, which will be your greatest ally, and patience, another very valuable asset. You are more likely to be careful about where you invest your money, energy, and other valuable resources.

Using Your Potential

It does not suffice to merely have potential. You have to do something with it. Talent alone, however great, will not achieve anything unless it is matched with other pertinent factors. Performance will depend on the demands made by situations and on the level of cooperation of the people in your orbit in fulfilling those demands. Most people, I have found, utilize only a part of their potential because they do not find themselves in conducive circumstances; most of their faculties lie dormant because these people are not compelled by circumstances.

It is not enough just to want to do something, either. What makes us act? Let us take the case of a motorcycle. Some machines start with one kick; others need two or three. We humans are similar. Some of us need merely a hint to react to a situation, while others need to be goaded and get kicked many times before they take action. Why? Different strokes for different folks.

Reaction time varies from person to person, depending on constitution and alertness. The degree to which our bodies cooperate with the mind, plus the commands given by the mind, explains the differing results. When the command given is in contradiction to a higher spiritual principle, a problem will arise, and the results will be delayed or may be unsatisfactory. Those of us who are highly developed souls have no conflict between what the soul wishes—its freedom—and what we wish to attain on the material plane. Sensitive people—those composed of higher vibrations—react quickly to any change in circumstances. But if the flesh is weak, though the spirit is willing, not much will be accomplished.

Laying a Foundation

Before you decide to lay any foundation, review your zone (A, B, or C) and see where you are.

Keep your personal affairs in order. Decide on ways to increase your financial worth. Decide on desired earnings, investments, and savings, and do other necessary financial planning. Decide on personal aims, desires, and motives.

We need education of various types to equip us to succeed in life. Academic knowledge is important but not necessarily a must. Many people in the past have done well without it. Some of the essential qualities of those who are successful or great follow:

- Reliability
- Dependability
- Punctuality
- Faithfulness
- Sincerity
- Truthfulness
- Honesty
- Continuity of purpose
- Concentration of mind on one project at a time
- Ambition
- Passion for success
- Hard work
- Cheerfulness
- Decisiveness
- Imagination
- Strong will to succeed
- Loyalty to people and aims pursued
- Persistence
- Courage
- Generosity
- Faith in the future
- Readiness to make changes
- Kindness
- Careful planning

- Friendliness
- A positive mental attitude
- Optimism
- Compassion or sympathy for the less fortunate
- Inner joy
- Patience
- Self-discipline and focus

Take Initiative

Sir Edmund Hillary was the first man who successfully climbed Mount Everest. To do so required unceasing zeal, enthusiasm, and faith in his own strength. Without these qualities he would have failed to reach the top. Overcoming obstacles is like leaping over a big ditch. During a horse-riding competition, the one who spurs the horse and gives him a big kick when it comes time to jump over a wide ditch will overcome the hurdle with ease. Those who hesitate end up in the ditch.

Whenever there is a problem to be surmounted, give yourself a big kick (without hesitation!) to avoid falling in the ditches of life. Remember, fortune favors the brave. Train yourself to take calculated risks first, and you will be among those who mostly win. There is something very special about winning. The winner reaps two types of rewards: one in the form of money or a valuable object, the other an increased sense of self-worth, which goes up a few notches every time.

Those who take the initiative have a 50-50 chance of succeeding in a project. Those who do not have a zero percent chance. No one always wins. We have to battle against odds at all times, but the right kind of effort is absolutely necessary.

A lazy person will never go to heaven. The concept of success without effort violates a natural law. We can only succeed in the battle of life, provided we do our part. Those who are mentally and physically lazy generally blame God for not listening to their prayers, but God helps those who help themselves.
Initiative is the spark that incites us to action. The world owes a great deal to all those explorers who took initiative and risked their lives. Without their efforts, we might still believe that the earth is flat. Enthusiasm sets the fire ablaze; only enthusiasm releases enormous amounts of energy from the human body. Invest some time and take a journey within yourself to explore the capabilities you possess. Be totally honest, without any false modesty. The results will amaze

you. It is a serious mistake to believe that we are helpless beings at the mercy of some external force. Humans are the highest creation of God, and to be like a god, we must first be fully human.

Most people wrongly believe that higher goals are hard to achieve—harder than lesser ones, somehow—but this is not exactly true. The process involved in raising $1 million is almost the same as raising a $100,000. In order to make material progress, we must have a thorough knowledge of where we stand; we must review our specific achievements on material, intellectual, and spiritual levels in the past, plus the limitations of expectations we see as we look ahead to plan our goals for the future. A person who does not bother to take stock of life has little chance of success. Take stock today, and invest some energy in your own future. Every defeat should be taken as a challenge and every challenge as a test of our powers and mental prowess. It is only natural to become better—and then, finally, the best—if we keep trying.

About the Author

D. Ostaro is a nationally known Cabbalistic Hindu astrologer and has a practice in Manhattan. His specialty is transforming human lives. He has been featured in *The New York Times*, *The Wall Street Journal*, *The Daily News*, and *The New Yorker*. Listed in Marquis' *Who's Who*, D. Ostaro is a media veteran and has appeared as a guest on hundreds of radio and television shows. He is the host and producer of *The Ostaro Show*, a biweekly program featuring celebrity horoscopes on Time Warner Cable TV (NYC). He is the author of *The Art & Craft of Success: 10 Steps* (Svarg Syndicate, Inc.) and is a motivational speaker, a Toastmaster (ATM-B), and a member of the Screen Actors Guild. He has authored and produced *Cobra's Wish*, a digital movie. His next project is "Hell, No" (in preproduction). Visit his Web sites at http://www.ostaro.com and http://www.cobraswish.com. Article excerpted from *The Art & Craft of Success: 10 Steps*.

28

Turning Resistance into Competitive Advantage

Diane Turton

Resistance comes in many forms. It can be an unequivocal "no" or a polite "maybe another time." It might come in the form of crossed arms, a furrowed brow, or a silent stare. Resistance can also be disguised as feigned interest or displayed openly as outright rejection.

Regardless of the form it may take or the action that prompted it, rejection gives us an opportunity to have a conversation that will lead to the creation of a mutually beneficial relationship, if you follow a few simple steps.

You may be in a business situation, trying to persuade clients that your solution is superior. Or you may be at home, trying to convince your family that a new family exercise plan will really benefit everyone. Or you may be helping your friend see that the new partner in her life does not have her best interests at heart. Whatever the conversation, you can apply these concepts to any situation where you are trying to help another person appreciate the value of your contribution and—best case—agree with the points you have made.

1. **Convince yourself that your ideas, opinions, and thoughts really take the other person's interests to heart.** It is tough to sell an idea or concept when you are not convinced that your ideas will improve their lives or work in some meaningful way. It can become downright impossible when you are faced with legitimate objections that you cannot argue against. Be clear about how and why your suggestions provide clear benefits and keep them in your mind's eye at all times.

2. **Anticipate potential areas of resistance, and map out a plan for overcoming them.** Even if you are convinced that your idea or solution is perfect, anticipate every possible objection, and take the time to create

compelling counterpoints. For example, if your family responds that they are happy with a little extra weight, describe how exercise allows them to eat more without weight gain or that strong bones and muscle keep bodies healthier. If your customer claims that the product you are selling costs too much, discuss how the quality will save considerable money over the long haul. Never imagine that the other person will fall in love with your ideas, no questions asked. Far better to err on the side of assuming that several objections will crop up, and come prepared to have great responses at your fingertips.

3. **Discover the underlying reasons for resistance.** Very often, people give one reason for not saying yes, when in fact there is a different reason behind it. For example, if your friend insists that the latest person in her life is really "the one," her real concern might be that she is afraid she will not find anyone else that comes close to her ideal. In the case of your family they may be concerned that exercise might take too much time away from other pursuits.

4. **Paraphrase the objections, whether implicit or explicit, and test for understanding.** Let the other person know that you really understand and care about his concerns before you address them, for example, "You're concerned that I may be mistaken about the motives of this new man and that I am overreacting to the fact that he forgot your birthday and did not show up for your cousin's wedding. Is that right?" Before you address these objections, go on to surface other concerns, particularly those left unspoken. After all, objections that are kept quiet are virtually impossible to counter.

5. **Respond to the objections, and the underlying reasons, with facts or solutions that can reasonably address the other person's concerns.** If the price is higher than your customer planned to spend, explain how a slightly higher investment today will be repaid many times over. If your family objects to the time it takes to undertake a new exercise program, explain how the program you have in mind can be done right at home, without special equipment, in less than 30 minutes. Address each concern one at a time, pausing to observe the other person's response. For example you may tell your friend, "I know that you want to believe that this guy is really the one for you. But have you thought about how well he meets some of the needs you have told me are really important to you, like being respectful, considerate, and caring? I know of many great guys who would be interested in getting to know you if you're open to it."

6. **Know when "no" really means "no."** A promising business or personal relationship can quickly turn sour when the other person feels that he is not

110

being listened to. The other person will respect that you took the time to understand and respond to all concerns and that you put his needs and concerns above your need to convince him that you are right. As a result, you will be better positioned to offer him an alternative solution or to point him in a direction where he might find another way to meet his needs.

7. **Stay connected.** In the case of a friend or client, send a note, pick up the phone, or stop by to stay connected and build on your relationship. Find out how they are doing, and ask if you can help in any way. Not only will you cement your relationship in the case of the client, but you will position yourself to win referrals from neighbors, family members, friends, and associates of clients who are impressed with your caring and professionalism. For your family, consider other ways they can improve their health and present new ideas when you feel they may be more receptive.

8. **Learn from each experience.** Take the time to reflect on each interaction and assimilate what you have learned—especially when you have been unable to persuade the other person to accept your ideas and opinions. Were there concerns you were not able to ferret out and successfully address? Could you have listened more intently to their responses, which may have given you vital clues to determine another approach that might have worked better? Were you unable to offer alternative solutions that may have assuaged concerns? Should you have accepted the other person's "no" sooner and moved on to another option earlier? Reflect on your lessons learned in writing. Make sure to include tips and techniques that work well so you can leverage them in the future.

9. **Do not take rejection personally.** Remember that you are selling a product, a concept, or advice of some kind. Although it is true that in a way we are selling ourselves and our ability to hear and address the other person's needs, people make decisions based on any number of factors. As long as we present ourselves as caring people who respect our friends, clients, and family members and their choices, we have many more chances to win over these people another time. Rejection today gives us a great reason to have the kind of discussion that can lead to a stronger relationship in the future.

When people express some form of resistance, whether tacit or spoken, they are giving us the gift of the opportunity to have a meaningful conversation about their needs, concerns, hopes, and fears. Such a conversation has a way of opening doors that would never have been possible had the person not had a chance to surface hopes and concerns with someone who really cared enough to listen and respond thoughtfully.

So rather than trying to avoid issues that may lead to resistance, embrace those issues openly and proactively to give you both a chance to have an honest dialogue about what the other person needs, even if it means he or she goes elsewhere for a solution—this time.

ABOUT THE AUTHOR

Diane Turton is president and owner of Diane Turton, Realtors, a full-service real estate company, as well as Turton Financial Holdings, LLC, which assists clients with mortgage financing, title insurance, and insurance needs. In addition to contributing much of her time to a number of boards, Diane actively participates in a wide range of community activities and supports many deserving charities. Her efforts have helped thousands of people and have earned her numerous awards, including being named an Ernst & Young National Entrepreneur® of the Year Award nominee. Additionally, *Enterprising Women Magazine* named Diane one of its 2006 Enterprising Women of the Year, and she was recognized by *NJ BIZ Magazine* as one of New Jersey's Best 50 Women in Business in 2006. The company's Web site is http://www.dianeturton.com, and its toll-free number is (877) DTURTON.

29

Four Steps to Improve Communication with Your Family

~❦~

George Harris

Communication is one of the most important aspects of our lives that, ironically, many of us pay the least attention to. Regretfully, the main reason is that many of us have never been taught how to communicate in a way that benefits us and the person we are communicating with.

From the moment we wake up in the morning until we go to bed, we are communicating, first with family, then with coworkers, neighbors, friends, and so on.

We communicate either verbally, through our spoken words, or nonverbally, through eye contact, body language, and touch as well as through our thoughts, feelings, and passions. It has been estimated that only about 20 percent of our communication is verbal, and the rest is nonverbal. It is important, then, to pay attention to all the nonverbal clues we express to people as they speak more than the words we say.

For example, most people can remember when they were children and "the look" their parents gave them that expressed much more than words would.

Imagine if our communication with our spouses was clearer so that we knew how to express our feelings and ask for what we wanted—and we were heard. What if we, as parents, communicated from a place of personal power inside ourselves, expecting our children to listen and cooperate without having to yell?

Through verbal and nonverbal communication we let people know who we are, what we want, and how we feel. Therefore communication is one of the necessary building blocks for creating a solid and successful family environment.

Here are four steps that will enhance communication with your family.

1. Expressing Our Wants and Feelings

We all have wants and feelings. Once upon a time, in our youth, it was all right for us to want, and more so, it was even necessary for us to want. But many of us had parents who told us *no*, we could not join the big kids in the street, we could not ask for money or play with a certain thing, and that we asked too many questions. So "no, you don't want that" became the mantra of our lives.

How many times did we hear statements such as these: "don't argue with me"; "if you want to cry, I'll give you something to cry about"; and so many others that taught us to stuff our feelings and shut up. No wonder we have a hard time expressing ourselves.

This transfers into our adulthood to our spouses and children. When we do not get what we want, we tend to blame and attack others, causing upset and a belief that relationships are hard. In order to improve our ability to communicate and therefore improve our relationship with our family, we need to understand and release any emotions like anger and resentment and the belief that we are going to upset someone by stating our wants. It is when we release these that we can express our current wants and feelings, and we can then hear the wants and feelings of our spouses and children.

2. Making Others Right

Any time we make negative comments to people about something they are doing or about a feeling or thought they have, we are making them wrong for who they are. This is called *projection*: the tendency to *unconsciously* place onto others our own *undesirable* ideas and impulses.

How can you tell if you are projecting? The easiest way to know is if you are judging. How many times do you judge your spouse or your children for actions they take or feelings they have? No one wants to be ignored, accused, or made wrong. Think of someone right now that you have done this to. What was his or her reaction?

When we project, we think they are undeserving of our love or caring. Truly, the place to start letting go of judgments is within ourselves. The more we release our own judgments about ourselves, the less we project them onto our family members. We can then make them right and see them as important, having value, and being okay for who they are because we have seen that about ourselves.

3. Listening

What does listening have to do with communication? Why is listening so important? Listening allows us to get information, to learn about someone, and to understand another's feelings.

Research has shown that people are listening only 25 percent of the time and that they make up the rest of what they think they hear. Therefore the nonlistener does not learn what there is to know, and the relationship becomes a classic lose-lose situation.

There are many reasons why we do not hear what other people are saying. Some of them include talking too much, being too consumed with our own opinions, thinking we know a lot more about something than the person talking and planning our remarks and actions before the other person finishes.

A good listener gives his or her undivided attention, asks questions without interrupting, does not judge until comprehension is complete, sees things from all points of view, and, especially, exercises the mind.

4. Having Agreements Instead of Expectations

Since we have not learned positive ways to communicate due to holding back our feelings and not asking for what we want, we end up having expectations of others. We feel as if they can read our minds and know what we want without having to express it.

Expectation is defined as "a prospect of future benefit." Because of this desire for a future benefit, we habitually deprive or withhold something desirable from ourselves for some outward goal or the love of someone in our lives. This is referred to as *Sacrifice*. For example, you think, "I will do this certain thing for my spouse, and when I do, she or he will love me more for it." Another example is thinking "I will pick up my child's toys, and he or she will learn from that and then pick up his or her own toys."

We also have expectations of ourselves based on what we think others want of us, and they become *shoulds*; examples are "I *should* be a better parent" or "I *should* be happy around my spouse all the time."

Because of fears we carry within ourselves about relationships and asking for what we want, we hold these expectations as a desire or a hope, wanting them to come true. We then sacrifice ourselves with these expectations, depriving ourselves of our wants. We become angry and disappointed when they do not come true and then feel guilty for having expressed the anger. In reality, we are angry with ourselves for not speaking up and asking for we want and need.

To resolve this, we need to observe when we run our lives by shoulds or expectations and instead then communicate to others our desires and make agreements with each family member. Successful family relationships depend on how well we communicate. By using these tools, you will learn how to listen and communicate with each other. You will empower yourself and your family members. And you will create more joy, love, and peace in the family household.

ABOUT THE AUTHOR

George Harris is a relationship consultant and the owner and facilitator of the Family Living System, which is a system of proven effective tools and techniques to enhance the quality of experiences in all relationships. George teaches parenting and couples' courses as well as giving motivational talks, seminars, and other training programs for families of all kinds, including those at the workplace, offering tools for everyone to learn to *Be* whom they need to *be* in creating the relationships they want in their lives. He is committed to sharing his knowledge and vast experience with others who desire more effective and fulfilling relationships. To learn more, please visit his Web site at http://www.familylivingsystem.com or e-mail him at famlivsys@spinn.net.

30

How to Break the Feel-Good Addiction to Engage Big Things

Vickie L. Milazzo

How does a busy professional like you cope with the mounting demands and pressures of achieving your passionate vision while all around you, life intrudes? We are constantly sabotaged by nonproductive energy wasters that contribute nothing substantial to our success. Whether you aspire to start your own business while still working a full-time job or are juggling hot leads to be the number one salesperson, the key to achieving *big* is breaking the "feel-good" addiction.

The feel-good addiction is a craving for the small, easy, "feel-good" tasks that bombard us daily—sorting the mail, answering e-mail, checking voicemail, and organizing and reorganizing.

The feel-good addiction is insidious for those of us who get a charge out of checking things off our to-do lists. Sure you knock out some minor chores, but that check-mark high comes at a price. Before you know it, you are majoring in minor things. You accomplish lots of little tasks but achieve very little of significance. In the long term, it is guaranteed to frustrate you, overwhelm you, and stress you out. Breaking the "feel-good" addiction opens the door to achievement.

Start Your Day Big

The feel-good addiction begins with the way you start your day. Most of us like to ease into our workdays: "I'll just check my e-mail for any emergencies." After all, firing off an e-mail only takes two minutes. Since you are not yet feeling the day's time constraints, these tasks steal more attention than they deserve. Two minutes turn into 20 as one item leads to another. Soon the morning is gone faster than those first two cups of coffee. In a flash the day is over, and you have not accomplished one thing toward your passionate vision.

Start each day big with a clean desk, free of clutter, and a clear mind. Put small tasks out of sight and out of mind. Start strong, and you will finish strong.

Engage Big Things for Big Results

What you engage and focus on is where you will yield results. Doing little things gives you little results, drains your creativity, and saps your brain power. When you cease to accomplish big, you lose desire and motivation. The less important your accomplishments, the less important you feel. You start to believe you are not cut out to achieve the success you imagined.

Engaging big things guarantees worthwhile achievements, and you will become addicted to the momentum of accomplishment. That momentum is a far more lasting high than the transitory feel-good of checking off trivial tasks.

Once you are engaged in accomplishing big things, you will approach even routine matters with laser-sharp focus, quickly delegating or deleting. More important, with fewer distractions to sidetrack you, your creativity and productivity will catch fire, and the resulting momentum will keep you pumped.

Start Your Momentum Rolling with Eight Easy Steps

1. **Define three big things.** Your vision might be to start a new business within six months. To achieve your vision, a big thing might be to develop a strategic plan. Choose three important goals that support your vision, then zero in on one of these big things. Define your strategies for doing so and the specific time each day you will implement your strategies. Refer back to your big thing, and make sure each task is really important and necessary.

2. **Challenge your commitment.** Ask yourself if you are really going for it or if you will quit when it is too tough. Make sure you are fully committed to the big things you choose and that they are right for you. You will not do the hard work required to accomplish something big if it is ultimately not right for you.

118

3. **Set aside sacred "momentum time."** Schedule substantial chunks of uninterrupted time (aim for two-hour blocks) for projects that support at least one big thing. To carve out time, attach a time increment to your daily tasks, no matter how small. Examine every activity and decide how to eliminate it, delegate it, hire it out, or do it faster.

You will have to fight to keep your momentum time sacred. Learn to say things like "I'll be available in one hour. What time after that works best for you?" Claim your momentum time, and you will reclaim those lost hours you have been seeking.

4. **Let nothing stop you.** Set a start time, and stick to it. Do not lose momentum by "warming up your engine" with feel-good busywork. Banish all thoughts ("Will I be assigned the new account?") and interruptions ("Will my son make the varsity team?") that do not relate to your big thing. Put your phone on voicemail, and do not open your e-mail. You can do it all later.

Develop a ritual to cleanse your mind—music, a cup of tea, an affirmation. A cluttered or tense mind accomplishes little. If you get distracted, even briefly, acknowledge the distraction, and commit to stopping it. Keep a pen and some sticky notes handy for sudden bursts of distracting brilliance. Write down the thought, and put it away for later.

5. **Alternate momentum time with "weed pulling."** Miscellaneous routine tasks are like weeds—no matter how often you get rid of them (or how good it feels to pull them), they always come back. You will find that most of your feel-good tasks fall into this category. Eventually, they do have to be handled, and pulling a few weeds can provide a welcome break from more intensive work.

After each momentum session, devote 30 minutes to weed pulling—handling mail, e-mail, phone calls, or other minor chores. Clump small tasks together. If you devote a short session to opening mail, paying bills, and filing the receipts, you are being efficient at weed pulling. If possible, never handle any communication (paper or e-mail) more than once.

6. **Focus on one big thing at a time.** When you engage in too much at once, you risk finishing nothing. Finish your first big thing, or at least reach a significant milestone, before embarking on the next.

7. **Let go of bad ideas.** When my company decided to develop a product, we put extensive time into it, but we did not get the response we had anticipated. I realized that putting any more time or money into the project would be a bad idea, so I let it go. It still hurts to think about the hours and creativity we expended, but I am glad we moved on to something bigger and better.

When a "great" idea is not so great after all, you have to let it go. This frees you to work on the next genuine big thing. Be open to figuring out that some of your great ideas really are not—and be ready to let them go.

8. **Safeguard your momentum.** Accept that you will not please everyone. Someone is bound to be unhappy about the changes you make to focus on your big things. They will get over it. Stop feeling guilty, and stay true to your goals. Surround yourself with friends, family, and peers who support your vision. Discard all discouraging messages. This is your vision, not anyone else's.

Engage momentum today. There is more to feeling good than the feel-good addiction. You can have time in your life and still have the time of your life. Make that your big thing for today.

ABOUT THE AUTHOR

Vickie L. Milazzo, RN, MSN, JD, an *Inc.* Top 10 Entrepreneur, is founder and CEO of Vickie Milazzo Institute, a $14-million education company. She won the Stevie Award for Women Entrepreneurs–Mentor of the Year, and her company was named Most Innovative Small Business by Pitney Bowes. Vickie authored the business best seller *Inside Every Woman: Using the 10 Strengths You Didn't Know You Had to Get the Career and Life You Want Now.* She is a renowned keynote speaker and appears on national TV and radio as an expert on entrepreneurship and career issues. For information, visit http://www.InsideEveryWoman.com.

31

The Secret of Feeling Good

Jeannette Maw

What is the secret to making dreams come true? Do you know the one thing that matters most in getting what you want? Would you guess the key to success is hard work, perseverance, commitment, right connections, good timing, or lucky breaks?

You might be surprised to hear it has little to do with the above. Contrary to what we learn from parents, teachers, employers, friends, and whomever else shaped our lives, the secret to success may very well be the exact opposite of what we were taught all along.

The secret to a joyful life, to reaching one incredible dream after another, is highly underrated in our society and easily overlooked in the crunch of daily life.

That secret is feeling good.

Whatever your dream or desire is, chances are you were led to believe struggle, sacrifice, and continual effort were required to achieve it. If we want to lose weight, we think it takes dedicated diet and exercise. To earn a promotion at work, we believe extra hours and responsibilities are required. We equate improving our financial situation with cutting expenses or increasing income.

But those actions in and of themselves do not put us on the path to success. The only reason those actions might serve us is if they put us in alignment with our goal. If you have ever taken traditional action steps and not achieved results, it is because the crucial factor of "alignment" was missing.

Alignment means being a vibrational match to your desire. You can think of it as being in line with, in tune to, or on the same page as what you want. We cannot achieve something if we are not aligned to it. Boiled down, that simply means to get what we want, *we must feel good*. Taking action that *does not* feel good not only prevents progress but leads to frustration when doing the "right thing" does not produce results. And that frustration just creates more misalignment to our goal!

This phenomenon is explained by the Law of Attraction, which affirms that *like attracts like*. Everything in our world is made of energy, and energy vibrates, including you and me and all our thoughts and feelings. Everything we experience in life occurs because we are a vibrational match to it; that is, we attract what we vibrate.

So your thoughts and feelings create a vibration, which create your experiences. That is why feeling good is so powerful—it attracts more life experiences and circumstances that feel good!

Feeling good *now* is the best way to create alignment with what you want and to allow your dreams to materialize.

However, this is not the advice we typically get to reach our goals. Most will preach persistence and paying our dues for what it takes to succeed. You can relax and enjoy after you get there, they will tell us. The problem is that in "paying our dues," if we create thoughts and feelings that do not feel good, we hold success at bay.

For example, if I do not enjoy counting calories or working out at the gym, and yet that is the action I take to lose weight, it is unlikely I will drop the pounds. However, if I feel good eating smaller portions and adopting an in-home yoga practice, that could very well be my ticket to the body I want. Not because yoga and small portions are the secret, but because *doing what feels good* is.

There is not one given rule that fits for all of us about feeling good. What one person delights in, another is driven to depression with. Whereas following a strict budget may be empowering to one, it could drive another insane. Posting a personal profile online for romance might be exciting for one, demoralizing for another. It is not the technique, strategy, or action step that makes the difference—it is how we *feel* about it that dictates our success.

122

So instead of following the "rules" or "expert advice," if all we did was what *felt best* in moving toward our goals, we would naturally attract astounding success into our lives, however each of us defines that.

And yet our culture does not promote "feeling good" as a habit to strive toward. It is considered hedonistic and selfish to put ourselves and our happiness first. We are conditioned to put families, careers, and loved ones' desires before our own, which is an unwitting recipe for disaster!

The secret to achieving things that make us happy in life is to do what feels good. Get in touch with your internal guidance, and follow that because we will not get to "heaven" by following a path that feels like "hell."

Since most of us are not practiced at discerning and respecting our "feel goods," here are four tips to naturally attract your dream come true.

1. **Respect your emotional guidance.** Your emotions are irreplaceable for steering you in the direction of what feels best. We are often trained to leave emotions out of the decision-making equation, which can lead to disappointment and frustration. Learn to listen to and follow your internal guidance, no matter how much logical sense it may or may not make.

You are the best expert on you. All the answers you need are within, and your emotions will steer you to the quickest and surest steps to the life you want. Trust yourself!

2. **"Feel good" every day.** Joseph Campbell's advice to "follow your bliss" is as good as it gets. Make it a point to bring some sort of joy or smile to life each and every day. Whether it is a new habit of kissing your sweetie hello, indulging in a favorite treat once a week, or just enjoying an occasional hot bath, discover how little things can make all the difference in how you feel.

Following your "feel good" will create an alignment that allows more good things to come to you!

3. **Eliminate what does not feel good.** Unload the obstacles that keep you from feeling good. What is on your to-do list that you are dreading? Skip those! Delegate them, hire them out, decide to feel differently, or at the minimum, get

them over with once and for all. These "feel bads" put you in alignment with things that you do not really want to attract.

As you eliminate what does not feel good in life, you will recover a tremendous amount of energy you did not realize was missing.

4. **Stop worrying what others think.** Yes, it may rock the boat as you change the way you live. That is okay. Does it feel good to worry about others and what they think? Right, it never does. Do not handicap your "feel good" by worrying about others.

You cannot make anyone else happy. We each choose for ourselves how we feel, and we can only be in charge of our own happiness. The best thing you could do for someone else is set the example of pursuing personal joy. Ultimately, when you find your joy in life, you become a better spouse, parent, child, employee, neighbor, and friend anyway.

The secret of feeling good is that it does not just feel good—it is a success magnet! The better you begin to feel and the more frequently you do it, the more you will find life delivering pleasant surprises, fabulous opportunities, and an abundance of experiences and things to love. Although it takes conscious attention until it becomes habit, it is the single best strategy you could embrace for living the life you want!

ABOUT THE AUTHOR

Jeannette Maw is an attraction coach and founder of Good Vibe Coaching in Salt Lake City, Utah, helping clients get what they want, once and for all. More articles about how to use the Law of Attraction to solve life's challenges are posted on her Web site at http://www.goodvibecoach.com, along with a sign-up for free tips and strategies in her monthly "Get What You Want" e-zine.

32

Is Your Life on Track, or Have You Been Derailed?

Sharon Seivert, Steve Cavaleri, & Fred Reed

Improving your life means having some idea of which direction you want to go. Think about it: Do you feel that you are on track and moving closer toward your dreams? Are you clear about how to get there from here?

If you are like most people, the answer to these questions is probably no. Instead, you may feel that—somewhere along the line—you have gotten derailed from the life you want to lead. Feeling derailed may cause you to simply *push harder* to get what you want while still remaining on a wrong track—instead of looking for a better one. Pushing harder along the wrong track is simply not worth the effort and can lead you further away from your true destination. In short, recognizing the best way to improve your life can be challenging.

The one result you *are* guaranteed to get from well-intended but misdirected efforts is stress—as if you needed more problems! But what if stress is not all bad? What if stress is simply nature's way to help you find the right track to be on? Instead of being a problem, stress can be a signal to help you become more deeply aware of underlying conflicts in your life. In short, stress shines a spotlight on differences between *where you want to be* versus *where you are most likely heading right now*.

Timeless Tools for Getting Back on Track

Would it not be nice to have a *system* that you can use to move toward the life you really want—a way of finding the right track and staying on it? Throughout history, great people have pondered the question of how to create such a system.

Over time, a number of elements have emerged as being critical for achieving personal success. We call these the Five Elements of Success.

These five elements are like pieces of a jigsaw puzzle that symbolize different aspects of your life. Each piece must be understood individually and as part of the complete image of your life's puzzle. When combined together, these pieces create a "picture" for achieving success, where each element takes direction from *and* supports the other elements. Failing to give each element its share of attention prevents the system from working ideally.

These five elements must also be aligned together to provide you with a clear picture. Unlike a store-bought jigsaw puzzle, your personal puzzle does not come with the final picture printed on the box top. One of life's rewards is that you get to design it along the way, sort of like creating a masterpiece—bit by bit. Over time, you can add the important lessons learned from experience and insights drawn from personal reflection. This personal work of art brings together essential aspects of what makes you a unique person.

Persistent feelings of stress are a symptom of something being out of balance or misaligned among your five elements. When feeling stressed, life often seems as if it is not moving in an ideal direction. We may lose confidence in our ability to act to improve our situation. The philosopher Charles Peirce called this loss of confidence the "irritant of doubt" that spurs people to grow and adapt successfully to life's challenges. One way to grow and adapt is by allowing the Five Elements of Success to work for you.

The Five Elements of Success

In simple terms, they are
1. *being*—discovering and experiencing—your core self
2. *envisioning* a world where you can be your best possible self
3. *committing* to a mission that guides your actions toward your vision
4. *connecting* with others who support your mission
5. *crafting* the specific means to actualize all of the above.

The "secret" of success—we think—is found in keeping these elements balanced and aligned. The first step in doing so is becoming more familiar with the elements as they apply to you. Here is an exercise you can try whenever you feel a need to get your life back on track. Each step will help you to become more keenly aware of how the five elements can work in your life.

Step 1 (Being): How am I?

Sit quietly. Close your eyes. Make the world go away—just for a moment. Take a deep breath in, then a long breath out. Repeat. Then start a simple breath count.

Ask yourself, How am I? Acknowledge but do not dwell on any internal conflicts or ways you feel out of balance. Simply thank these "irritants of doubt" for serving as a friendly wake-up call.

Continue this process until you feel at ease. By focusing on your core self, you can resume being the powerful engine of your life, rather than a helpless victim passenger.

Step 2 (Envisioning): What is on my mind?

Now begin to focus on what is on your mind. Let those stress-induced thoughts pop up. Most of the time, we push right past these bothersome thoughts. Instead, deliberately put on the mental brakes, slow down this runaway train, and make a "what stresses me out" list.

Now think about possible changes in your world that would reduce these stresses. When you clearly envision your destination, your mind will experience it as if you have already arrived!

Step 3 (Committing): Move into action.

Now you can prioritize the stresses that popped into your mind. Ask yourself questions such as, What thoughts kept recurring? What gives me the most pain?

In this way you can turn agitation into action that is aligned with the life you choose to lead. Commit now to taking just one action within a specific time frame. Do not wait until you find some "perfect" task.

Step 4 (Connecting): Smile and the world smiles with you.

Now you can relax. You are committed to taking action and are on your way to success. Allow a big, warm smile to spread across your face. Feel the pleasant sensation of that smile flow through you like a healing potion.

Not only does it feel good, but that smile will help you connect to people who will want to help you make your life a masterpiece.

Step 5 (Crafting): Embody a new habit.

Now resolve to change one personal habit in your life to help you accomplish the action you committed to take. If you want to transform any part of your life, you will need to deliberately craft a new "infrastructure"—that is, embody new habits that support you in making this change.

Think of it as laying down tracks, one at a time, in front of a train that is moving to your desired destination—one where it will feel incredibly good to arrive.

This exercise provides an introduction to the Five Elements of Success that are the foundation of a broader system that can help you improve your life in many practical ways: personal planning, career transition, relationship improvement, and professional or leader development. Please use them to help you lay tracks to the life you truly deserve!

ABOUT THE AUTHORS

Sharon Seivert, Steven Cavaleri, and Fred Reed of The Coreporation, Inc. help people successfully put together the jigsaw puzzles of their personal lives, relationships, and work. Together and alone, they have authored a number of books and articles (including *The Balancing Act* and *Knowledge Leadership*); provided coaching and consulting to individuals and organizations; and developed specialized tools (such as the Personal Balance Profile and The Balance Beam personal manager) to help individuals use the Five Elements of Success to improve their lives. Visit http://www.thecoreporation.com/5Elements or call (617) 441–WORK (9675) for more information.

33

REFLECT on the Future

≈⸻≋

Halette M. King-Meyer

There will never be a more exciting time to retire than today. Retirement will pose opportunities and challenges that will make your journey an individual and very interesting one.

If you are like most preretirees and retirees, you hope to (1) spend time with loved ones and friends, (2) live a life that is meaningful and fulfilling, and (3) leave a legacy. The seven REFLECT elements—Resiliency, Equilibrium, Forgiveness, Life Meaning, Extending Gratitude and Enjoyment, Cultivating Gifts and Strengths, and Transition and Transformation—will help you recraft a meaningful and enriching retirement.

Begin to REFLECT by focusing on being rather than on having and doing. At first, this may feel radical to you, but still only do the things that are deeply meaningful to you. If you desire extra revenue, consider turning something you are passionate about into a supplementary income. If finances are not an issue, then find a volunteer or vocational activity to support your passion. Do not currently have a passion? You have the answers deep within. You just need a little time, and a bit of guidance, to find your truth.

One of the best ways to approach something unknown is to seek information from others who have gone before you. Some of the insights my clients have shared with me when asked what they have learned from retirement follow.

Resiliency

A number of changes comes with retirement, just as with any other life stage. A positive attitude about your ability to make a productive transition is key. If you do not feel hardy, there are techniques that can be used to strengthen your resiliency. Alice is a good example of someone who is recruiting her resiliency resources. Severe health issues facing her brother, husband, and mother impact Alice. She is managing the challenge using downward comparisons by recognizing others are experiencing worse crises: "My heart goes out to the children I see at the cancer center. I can only imagine how hard this must be for them and their families." She is reshaping the negative into a positive by being grateful she can be with her brother the last days of his life: "I'm grateful that I'm retired and that I don't have to try to balance work, and the chemo, and radiation treatment." She vigorously disputes any defeating thoughts that enter her mind: "I argue with myself as I would with my best friend when I get into a funk and I think I can't go on. I think of every possible reason why I am the perfect person for this challenge." She also is employing self-care measures to ensure she stays well balanced.

Equilibrium

Balance the time you spend in each area of your life. You most likely spent much of your time at work. Now is the time to focus on you and your self-care and development. Delve into spiritual renewal, leisure activities, and family and social activities. Replace work with meaningful service at home, in your community, or on an even broader scale. Anthony says, "Between work and daily living activities, I neglected myself to the point that I don't even know what I want the rest of my missing life to entail. It's time to explore me."

Forgiveness

Anger or animosity can torment you physically or emotionally. Release your hurt. Maureen says, "It helps to recognize we're all imperfect, to accept that I am also in some way a contributor to the situation." Do whatever it takes to release the bond your oppressor holds over you. Ask for assistance from a higher power; send love and good intentions to your adversary. To hold on to resentment only hurts you, not the tormenter. You cannot be a hostage and all that you can be simultaneously.

Life Meaning

To fully flourish in retirement, it is critical to have something you can sink your teeth into. Having fun is pleasurable; doing things you are good at, or becoming

130

good at things you always wanted to do is engaging. Yet real-life meaning comes from taking your gifts, talents, and strengths out into the world and making it a better place for others. The selfless act of mentoring, instructing, or perhaps healing others is what will bring deep meaning in retirement. Pete says, "I'm having a better time teaching in retirement than anything I ever did in my former day job."

Extending Gratitude and Enjoyment

Be thankful every day for being able to rise from your sleep. Be grateful for the ability to see the morning light and to hear the birds chirp. For the fresh water you drink. For the air you breathe. Perfect health is not required in order to be grateful. Be grateful for your beating heart, for your "good" leg, and take time to recount good things, perhaps in a journal. Express your gratitude to others. Your enjoyment of life will be multiplied if you recognize, savor, and record in detail the best things in life—which are often free! Sylvia has found great pleasure in her garden: "I'm in awe of the beauty that surrounds me outdoors that I didn't have time for before retirement."

Cultivating Gifts and Strengths

Each of us comes to this world with some innate talents. We later learn an incredible number of skills and lessons along our journey. Retirement affords you the opportunity to share your unique gifts and strengths. And it gives you the time required to pursue lifelong learning opportunities that can foster emotional, physical, spiritual, and mental capabilities. A wise sage named Mille reminded me that "age does not necessarily equate to wisdom. Age is a given. Wisdom must be earned." Be open-minded, curious, and willing to explore your memories and beliefs, your desires and your dreams, your secrets and your fears, and how you relate to others. If in retirement you experience a disabled body, seek ways to use your limitless mind in stimulating ways.

Transition and Transformation

Wanda says, "While life was good when you worked, it is even better when you retire." It is, once you identify pursuits that are fulfilling, endeavors that offer you ample socialization, and compensate you in a manner that is pleasing to you, that utilizes your time effectively, and that cause you to feel good about who you are and about what you are contributing. Once you have mastered this challenge, you will know that you have moved from simply doing to being. You will know you have transitioned when you feel content and satisfied.

Retirement is less about *doing* and more about *savoring* the process, enjoying the journey and fully experiencing life by identifying where you find meaning each and every day. A meaningful life to you will be different from that of your friends, neighbors, and yes, even than that of your family or spouse. You must find your hidden treasures by exploring the map that lies within yourself and no one else.

REFLECT, dig deep, and be willing to let go of old limiting beliefs and to test out new things. Explore, experiment, and give yourself permission to stop doing things simply out of obligation or habit, the things that do not truly bring you fulfillment.

Retirement is a journey you will enjoy. If you trust the process, if you have faith in the goodness that exists for you, and if you take the time to truly explore the truth that lies within you, the reward will be rich.

ABOUT THE AUTHOR

Halette M. King-Meyer, PhD, has worked with individuals in transition for 16 years at American Express, Catholic Charities, General Motors, and Goodwill Industries, among other companies. Dr. Meyer coaches pre- and post-retirees though the retirement phase of life. To increase an individual's baseline happiness, Halette offers Authentic Happiness Coaching workshops and one-on-one sessions. Halette also prepares women at a transitional housing facility for a life of independence. She has championed a welfare-to-work reform initiative designed to move welfare recipients to self-sufficiency. She has also guided associates and managers into the team environment and new hires into technical operations positions. To discuss retirement or craft a retirement options plan, visit Dr. Meyer at http://www.theheartofliving.com.

34

GOAL SABOTAGE

Are You Sabotaging Your Goals?

Jeanette Griffin

What lies behind us and what lies before us are tiny matters compared to what lies within us.
—Ralph Waldo Emerson

In today's society of successful people, there is a lot of talk about goals and the importance of goal setting. Yet for many, there is no real understanding of the most important part of taking the thought of a goal and carrying it to a successful end result. Statistics show that 95 percent of North Americans never write down their goals and that of the 5 percent who do, 95 percent never take it to completion.

Just as with so many things, there must be an unshakable foundation, a place that an idea can go from being just that to becoming a reality, a truth in your life. The foundation that supports the growth of any idea is founded in your desired goal by your attitude, desire, and belief. Life exposes us to many negative influences that create pessimistic, disbelieving attitudes. This forms a weak and unreliable foundation, the base supporting your life choices. When you free up your mind of all the negative self-talk that has been playing in the background, you begin rebuilding your foundation.

In other words, you sabotage your goals simply by allowing your mind to continually play a negative thought recording over and over. When you hear yourself saying things like "I could never do that" or "people like me are never successful," you lead the orchestra of a million and one excuses as to why you cannot succeed, and it is time to change the recording—it is time to build a new foundation. You create who you are and what you are to become simply with the thoughts that you think.

The strongest emotion leading your mind to create disbelieving, pessimistic thoughts is fear. Fear is tricky because it has so many faces; you are looking at fear when you see yourself failing, if you see yourself creating reasons as to why you cannot make changes in your life, and the list goes on and on. The greatest fear is fear itself. If you find that the fear of failing is an obstacle, a stumbling block in creating your desired life, it is time to get it out of the way. The first step in the process is removing the thought that there is such a thing as failure. The people known for their great works understand a truth: that what many of us see as a failure is life leaving us room for growth. Without mistakes, how could any of us ever learn to reach for better? We would never see the better and greater things inside of us waiting to be found. Thomas A. Edison once stated that he never failed at any of his attempts to create the incandescent light bulb but that he did find 10,000 ways not to.

The steps below, when put into practice, have very positive results in the area of eliminating the fear of failing.

1. **Persist.** Never give up; many people give up when they are right on the edge of succeeding. Try different approaches to reaching your desired outcome until you find the right one.

2. **Take action.** To overcome fear, you must take action; the bolder the action, the greater the proof you offer your mind that you will not allow your fear to hold you back.

3. **What could you do differently?** When you see that you are not getting the results that you want, review the steps that you took to see if there was anything you could have done differently.

4. **Always look at every event as an opportunity.** If you look for the value in every event in life, it will benefit you in a positive way. Learn from it, and use it for improvement.

5. **Never internalize a failure.** Failure is not a personality trait, it is a result. Recognize the mistakes that were made and move forward.

6. **Do not beat yourself up.** Every great and successful person throughout history has made mistakes. Some of the biggest mistakes have produced some of the greatest successes.

Remember that failure is only a state of mind; see it as a challenge from which greater opportunities are born.

The second greatest emotion that many struggle with when striving to reach a goal comes in the form of doubt. A person's self-doubt leads to the loss of many dreams. If you find that this is true for you, then you need to ask yourself, "How committed am I to doing whatever it takes to reach my desired goal?" Do you hear yourself arguing with yourself in conversations, such as "I am positive that this is something I would be good at, I'm sure I can do it," and then you reply with "I don't know what I was thinking, that is totally out of my range, I could never do something like that"? This is the self-banter of a self-doubting person, and this form of self-talk is one of the leading causes for "Lack-of-Goal-Reach-itis," a not so rare disease resulting in a lack of self-confidence.

The manner in which you mentally talk to yourself has tremendous impact on your performance. Feed your mind a diet enriched with strengthening beliefs, just as you feed your body a healthy diet to have it perform with strength. The diet of positive beliefs is filled with "I know I cans" and "I can do anythings." Reinforce your abilities with positive thoughts by focusing on the things that you see as your greatest attributes and skills, and spend time strengthening those skills. Simply by taking positive actions that are targeted at specific areas of your life, you will begin to see your confidence in your abilities rising with each new achievement.

I have listed some steps that, when put into practice, have very positive results in eliminating self-doubt.

1. **Rid your mind of all negative self-talk.** When you hear your mind filling up with doubt, review your reasons for wanting to reach your goal and how it can be possible.

2. **Never allow others' disbelief in you to affect your belief in yourself.**

3. **Always review your plan for reaching your goal and establish achievable strategies.** Be sure that you are spending time daily reviewing your goal plan and taking steps to ensure its achievability.

4. **Keep track of your achievements by recording everything you are doing that is bringing you closer to reaching your goal.** Review your strategy plan

and remind yourself how much closer you are rather than focusing on how far you still need to go.

5. Review the qualities you possess right now that support you in reaching your goal. Are there any areas that have room for improvement? A new skill will only add to your life of successes. We are meant to grow rather than stagnate.

All goals are reachable once you form a deep belief in yourself. Use the power of a strong positive attitude, a clearly defined desire, and an unshakable self-belief in your abilities to be all that you can be. Remember: All things are possible.

ABOUT THE AUTHOR

A dedicated wife and mother of four, Jeanette has spent the last 16 years home schooling her children and offering personal counseling. Her work as a motivational writer, life coach, and motivational speaker is founded on her desire to give back to the world the blessings that have been given to her. She bases her work on her own personal journey to living her life from a place of inspiration, peace, and happiness. Her greatest inspiration comes from leading others to living their desired lives. Jeanette is a cofounder of the inspiring Web site http://www.apositivelifestyle.com and all the blessings that her endeavors bring to others, to her family, and to her.

35

Boosting Your Success with Five Easy Happiness Tips

Christina Winsey-Rudd

What would it mean to you to achieve greater success? Studies on happiness and success reported by the *Psychological Bulletin* of the American Psychological Association state that "happiness contributes towards reinforcing positive emotions, which also motivates people to undertake new goals and succeed at them."

Dr. Sonja Lyubomirsky of the University of California and colleagues studied over 275,000 people. Their findings showed that "chronically happy people are in general more successful across many life domains than less happy people."

On the converse side, people who stay in jobs or relationships in which they are chronically unhappy miss out on the joy life has to offer and are at greater risk of chronic diseases.

It is important to be clear on exactly what happiness means to you. When happiness is some nebulous goal to be achieved "someday," then by definition, you do not have it *now*. Happiness is not some ultimate goal; it is a moment-to-moment choice. As Abraham Lincoln said, "Most people are about as happy as they make up their minds to be."

Abe was not too far off from the truth, but there is another important puzzle piece: brain chemistry. Brain cells communicate feeling states with each other through a complex biochemical process using neurotransmitters—little chemical messengers.

The brain makes a variety of neurotransmitters responsible for our emotions—Dr. Candace Pert, in her book *Molecules of Emotion*, states, "...not only the familiar feelings of anger, fear, sadness and joy; but also spiritual inspiration, awe, bliss, and other states of consciousness." More recent studies observe that neurotransmitters may actually be somewhat addictive. In other words, you may find yourself becoming angry regularly because you actually have an internal addiction to the neurotransmitter involved with the feeling of anger. The more you get angry, the more you get angry, and the more neurons get involved in that vicious cycle of anger to form what is called a "neural net."

The good news is that this process can be reversed. Through choosing happiness instead of anger, the neural net can be dismantled over time, and you can "train" yourself to be happy more of the time!

So how do we begin to experience more happiness? As simplistic as it seems, actually becoming conscious of and logging when we really and truly are happy is a basic beginning. You may be fooling yourself in thinking that you are not happy because you have not achieved some goal or that you do not live in some special home you want. But perhaps the truth is that you are actually pretty happy with your life overall. Your gut will tell you, but if you are really not sure, you may want to begin with this simple happiness gauge exercise.

(Note: While your schedule may not follow the below example, do your best to correlate these sections to your life/work schedule.) Give yourself a "Y" for yes or an "N" for no in each of the following parts of a typical day, during which you usually experience contentment or downright happiness:

Upon arising and getting ready for the day: ____
During breakfast: ____
Commuting to work: ____
The morning hours: ____
Lunchtime: ____
The afternoon hours: ____
Commuting home: ____
Dinner: ____
Early evening activities: ____
Later evening activities and getting ready for sleep: ____

How did you score? If you put a "Y" next to nine or more of the parts of your day above, congratulations! You may still benefit from the basic tips below. If you scored lower, remember that happiness is something that is really a choice, and it can be practiced. Here, below, are some key tips to help you amp up your share.

Live by *your* definition of happiness and success. Many people feel an ongoing sense of dissatisfaction with their lives or businesses because they are using someone else's "happiness measuring stick." Comparing your life and achievements to those of others and using *their* criteria rather than *yours* is a surefire way to lose the happiness game.

Strategy: You have heard of a rule book for games. How about putting together your own little book of rules for life—criteria for happiness and success? Having it written down makes it much easier to hold your own when others impose onto you their ideas about what you should or should not be doing.

Become a Pollyanna. Pollyanna, contrary to popular opinion, was not teaching denial or pie in the sky positive thinking. Rather, she perfected a mind-set of learned optimism and of seeing the glass "half full." Pollyanna's "Glad Game" turned around an entire town from being gloomy and pessimistic to being a happy, joyful place.

Strategy: No matter what life hands you, see how well you can make lemonade out of lemons. Not only will your sunny outlook help you be happier more of the time, but also, your "vibes" will positively affect those around you. If you are single, keeping a sunny disposition will make your "vibe" much more attractive. People like to be around upbeat people who make them feel good.

If you are in sales or are looking to climb a success ladder, you will be much more attractive to your ideal employer or ideal customer if your attitude is obviously an optimistic and happy one.

Have better relationships by living from both head *and* heart. Being too rigid and intellectual can really wreck the relationship "happiness quotient." The people in your life, just like you, want to hear expressed appreciation and be given more understanding. Sadly, it seems much easier in our society for people to express disappointment, criticism, and negative observations than it does the positive ones.

139

Strategy: Speak words of encouragement and appreciation freely. Also, ask for acknowledgment when you need it. When you give and take freely of appreciation, understanding, and praise, relationships are bound to flourish; after all, success in almost any endeavor is based on having good relationships.

Stay in the here and now. Most frequently, people think, "When I achieve this goal, I will finally be happy." Life is not "then." Life is right *now*! Future happiness is created by the cumulative now experiences of happiness.

Strategy: Make a habit of slowing things down. Savor those good people, experiences, and feelings in the very moment you are experiencing them. While you are experiencing and noticing them, inwardly say a thought of gratitude that you have this person, job, experience, feeling, or talent.

At the end of the day, review. If you have really practiced this "here and now happiness," the overall feeling about your day will be a good one. Eventually, you will find the percentage of happiness that consumes the majority of your days, weeks, months, and years increases measurably.

Quiet your negative self-talk. Many people are completely unaware of the numerous negative things they say to themselves throughout the day. Like criticism of others, negative self-talk never helped anyone perform better.

Strategy: Become your own detective. Carry a little notebook around with you, and whenever you are aware of some negative thoughts running through your mind, write them down. Then consciously and deliberately refute the negative thought with some positive observations.

Think of any and all good things you can to see things in a positive light. Here, again, because you are focusing on the positive, your "vibes" will be good ones, and people will like being around you. In fact, they will begin to think and feel about you the way you do. It is much easier to be successful when people like being around you!

These are just a few ways you can enhance the quality of your happiness experience and your life. Get creative, and begin thinking of your own solutions! They will pay big dividends.

<u>ABOUT THE AUTHOR</u>

Dr. Christina Winsey-Rudd ("Dr. Chris") is a human potential, stress management, and corporate coach, an expert weight loss coach, a retired chiropractic physician, writer, and speaker. She is co-owner of Dynamic GoldMind Strategies, Inc., a corporate coaching and professional development firm. Her rigorous postgraduate training includes applied kinesiology, Silva mind control, applied clinical nutrition, certification in neurolinguistic programming, the Coachville School of Coaching, and a certificate of completion in emotional freedom technique. Called the "I Can" Doctor, she empowers clients to tap into their own inner genius and to transcend blocks to personal success as they define it using cutting-edge whole-brain and mind-body-spirit techniques. Visit her Web sites at http://www.goldmindstrategies.com, http://drchris.interfaceias.com, or http://www.universityofmasters.com, e-mail her at TheICanDoctor@comcast.net, or call her at (941) 914–2433.

36

HEALING

The Three Steps to Healing: Awareness, Expression, Resolution

Robert S. Vibert

Have you not experienced success with the emotional healing techniques you have tried? Join the club. I recently realized what was missing in many emotional healing techniques: a systematic and comprehensive approach that would ensure that the three key aspects of the emotional healing process would be properly handled.

Since early 2001, I have engaged in a dedicated and intense research project on emotional healing approaches and modalities, which encompassed numerous workshops and conferences, books, articles, videos, self-study, and extensive discussions with experts in the field. I have also had the techniques applied to myself as well as to willing clients.

As I watched for patterns and underlying structures in these techniques, a clear picture emerged concerning the emotional healing process, the steps involved, and how well many methods achieve their stated goals.

My research reveals that there are three steps one needs to take for complete healing.

Step 1: Awareness

Before one can remedy something, he needs to know what it is that he is remedying. This involves an awareness of it at a deep level. For example, if one feels fear arise around speaking in a group, it is important to follow that fear and see if it is linked to another emotion or feeling.

I guided a woman through a healing session in which she started off feeling sad. As she healed the sadness, other emotions arose (hurt, unable to forgive herself, guilt) until we uncovered a feeling of shame. Once she healed that shame, a great feeling of release came over her—she had been holding on to that shame for close to 50 years. The other feelings still needed to be healed as they had only been identified and partially healed.

Fortunately, there are a number of good approaches to exploring our feelings, and as long as they are respectful of the timing, safety, and support that we need, most of them allow us to identify the primary feelings as well as those lurking underneath.

Step 2: Expression

Once we have identified a specific feeling to work with, it is often helpful to express that emotion, both as part of the awareness deepening and the acceptance of it. Being able to talk to ourselves about a feeling is a good first step. We can express it out loud, perhaps looking ourselves in the mirror and saying words such as "I feel fear."

Taking this process further, we could then describe the feeling to someone else. We need a good, patient listener who is not going to judge what we say, react to it, or try to fix it.

If we feel safe enough, after the words flow will come other expressions, which could include tears, shouting, sobbing, body sensations, and so on.

Step 3: Resolution

The third step in healing an unresourceful emotion or feeling is to achieve resolution around it. This resolution would include the following elements: a full exposure to the feeling; a diminishing of the intensity of the feeling to a level that is first comfortable and then truly absent; a feeling of peacefulness around the event or subject that triggered the feeling in the first place; and some insight into what was going on for us.

Most of the emotional healing methods I have explored do not achieve all of these markers of success and focus on only one or two of the elements. Some try to immediately get an insight as to what caused the feeling and then use that insight to "think away the feeling." Some try to put whipped cream on the cow patty by "reframing" a painful incident through rationalizing about it, verbally minimizing it, putting a positive spin on it, and so on. Some methods place a lot of value on the expression phase, having people scream, punch pillows, kick their feet, and so on. Some methods attempt to quickly reduce the intensity of the feeling by use of physiological actions: having clients do lots of slow, deep breathing, for example. Other techniques take advantage of the normal human desire to avoid pain and our built-in defense mechanism, disassociating, to simply further disassociate the client from the feeling.

Getting to Resolution

Having watched hundreds of people try various healing processes, with varying degrees of success, I boiled down the results to these four essential elements of a successful healing process. They are simple, practical, and easy to look for.

1. We experience full exposure to the feeling for as long as it takes for resolution to occur, and we remain fully associated. As this can be seen as counterintuitive, given the human nature to avoid pain, one must overcome the tendency to run away from the feeling. Having someone else guide you through a fully associated process a few times makes it easier. "Fully associated" means you feel the feeling and are looking out through your own eyes, not watching yourself as if watching a movie.
2. The feeling will diminish in intensity, first to a level that is comfortable and then dissolving completely. Stopping prematurely (once a comfortable intensity is reached) can lead to the feeling being possibly retriggered as it is not all gone from the system. The amount of time needed for a feeling to diminish can vary tremendously, so patience is important—it might take hours. There is no attempt to make the unresourceful feeling go away or change—it is accepted for what it is and allowed to run its course until it dissolves of its own accord.
3. Once the intensity of the feeling has reduced to null, a sense of peacefulness around the event or subject that triggered the feeling in the first place is reported. If that peacefulness is not present, it is likely that related feelings are present, and each in turn would be handled like the first, until the peacefulness arises.
4. Some insight into what was going on for us, what meaning we can give to the fact that we had strong feelings about an incident, can and often does arise after holding oneself in the peacefulness for a while.

There are a small number of techniques that I have found that incorporate processes to facilitate complete resolution of the unresourceful or excessive feeling, and in this article I shall mention one that if properly used, has a very high success rate: Emotional Freedom Technique (EFT). EFT makes use of a gentle interaction with the body's energy meridian system, usually involving tapping with the fingers on certain energetic intersection points. Some have described it as being like acupuncture without needles. EFT has been widely used by many thousands of people to resolve phobias, fears, pains, and emotional wounds.

If the healing process you are presently using does not give you long-lasting resolution (the problem keeps resurfacing, despite the temporary relief you experience), you may want to look for someone to guide you through a properly run, fully associated session of EFT or a similar process. You can find a link to EFT practitioners on the main EFT Web site (http://www.emofree.com). True resolution comes from honoring the feeling, and that means staying in it until it dissolves of its own accord.

I am not surprised by the resistance to this concept of resolution I have encountered from some practitioners of traditional cognitive-oriented therapies. Besides not answering the apparently common human tendency toward complicated methods, it is often difficult for a practitioner to watch someone else be in the depths of his pain without the practitioner's own pain being triggered. However, once we have healed our own pain, it becomes far easier to patiently support those doing their three-step healing work.

This article is excerpted from Robert's recent book *The Missing Link to Your Emotional Healing Success.*

ABOUT THE AUTHOR

Robert Vibert is a "big-picture" researcher of techniques, philosophies, and methods developed both in ancient and modern times to provide awareness, guidance, healing, and insight. He studies how our hearts and minds work and how we interact with each other and internally with ourselves. He then applies the results of this research in the real world, through his series of Missing Link books, CDs and DVDs, workshops, and private mentoring. Previously, he was a very successful businessman in his own right, having created several million-dollar companies from the ground up. You can find him on the Web at http://www.real-personal-growth.com.

37

On Purpose: Living Life from the Higher Octave

Caroline Sutherland

I am in the health business. My purpose is motivating people to leave aside their addictions and destructive habits and move toward healthier lifestyles. Given all the "feel-good" reasons for optimum health, there are none so compelling as the notion of destiny. This is the question that I am asked most frequently: "What is my purpose, and how can I find it?"

In order to anchor a deep respect for the physical body firmly into our minds and to give us the motivating factor for achieving optimum health, we must look to the ideas of purpose and calling as the driving force behind our intentions. It is time to live life from "the higher octave."

Sure, it is great to feel healthy and alive, and when we feel this way, we have the energy to do just about anything. But just feeling good is not all that is involved. When destiny gives us a project, however large or small, we need to have a healthy body to carry out our purpose and mission.

The passion of our calling does as much to excite the cells in our bodies as it does to keep our souls fulfilled.

All too often, I speak to large groups of highly evolved spiritual people whose physical bodies do not match the evolution of their souls. But the way is clear. As we take the steps to uncover our unique talents, the journey and the experiences along the way take us to our ultimate goal of completing our purpose in this lifetime. The discovery of our talents can be a powerful motivating factor for setting aside addictions, having a peaceful heart, letting go of blame, and seeing the bigger picture.

One never knows how someone can be motivated and inspired by another person's words.

I remember giving a talk in Los Angeles a few years ago. I mentioned the idea of optimum health being linked to spiritual purpose. Several weeks after my presentation, I received a letter from a man who said that he had given up chain-smoking the very next day after grasping this concept. He knew that he needed a strong physical body with which to complete his purpose as a spiritual songwriter.

Illness begins when the spiritual part of our lives is disregarded. We stay in jobs we do not like, we stay in relationships we have outgrown, we are content to feel old, lethargic, and in pain. When we realize that we have a finite number of years to live on this earth, living life consciously and purposefully takes on new meaning.

Andrea, a beautiful, capable young woman in her mid-forties, came to me for a consultation. She had spent eight years training for a job she did not like. She had low energy, lethargy, and pains in both of her ankles and heels. I had a sense that despite what her mind was telling her, she was way off purpose, and the flame of passion in right livelihood was missing from her life. I did my best to assist her from a nutritional and supplemental perspective, and her energy did improve, but her real Achilles' heel, where her pain was located, was in direct proportion to her lack of fulfillment in her job. Daily meditation and quiet contemplation assisted her in finding her inner voice, and she was led to calligraphy as a way to balance her daily work with a creative outlet while awaiting a new career direction.

What are the steps to finding and staying on purpose?

1. Align with a higher power that knows you better than you know yourself. This is a spiritual power or force that understands your deepest desires.
2. Write down all the things you enjoy doing. Make a long list, and leave nothing out. This can be anything from gardening to holding a baby to flying an airplane. What do you love?
3. Check in with your heart. All of your actions should "feel right." If it does not feel right, do not do it. Let this heart-compass guide you in your life. This is the higher, all-wise, all-knowing part of you that is leading you forward.

4. Let the universe deliver. Daily, you will see the magical unfolding of events in your life. Look for serendipitous happenings and chance meetings that can bring important pieces of the "purpose" puzzle to you.
5. Be patient. Destiny is a journey that unfolds one step at a time.

When it is time and the soul prompts us to move on or to move forward, we must be ready to take the ultimate leap of faith. We need to align with the universe, which has something bigger in mind for us. This takes courage.

The healing journey, like the life process, can be challenging, even unbearable at times. To stay in gratitude when life is falling apart and things are changing is a big test. To develop trust in the unknown, to be positive when in pain and to stay calm and present when there is nowhere to turn takes great discipline and mastery. The rewards for this discipline are great.

When we release great chunks of anger, resentment, and bitterness, the real gift is that our connections with the spiritual become deeper, sweeter, and more revealing. We also develop more compassion and understanding toward others—the cornerstone for living life on purpose.

As a result of this inner work, the facets of our own individual diamond personalities become finely polished and emit a radiance and energy that has far-reaching effects.

Many years ago, I had the unique opportunity of working in a beautiful heritage church. It was set in a little cove at the edge of the ocean, surrounded by trees and a lovely garden. Inside the church, there were dark wood beams, red carpets, and ornate stained-glass windows. It was a very popular location for weddings; but for as many brides that walked up the aisle, there were just as many coffins that were carried down. Working at a church gave me the opportunity to witness the very dramatic and transient nature of life. As I saw these important chapters unfolding before my eyes, I realized that life is too short to waste. This experience continually forced me to reset my inner compass and focus on what mattered.

To all of you who wish to see the fruition of your own dreams, keep yourselves healthy. Call upon your intuition, your inner guidance, and your body's wisdom to keep you on track. Let this instinctive part of you show the way to all the right choices that are part of manifesting your own destiny.

ABOUT THE AUTHOR

Caroline Sutherland is the author of *The Body Knows: How to Tune In to Your Body and Improve Your Health*, *The Body Knows Cookbook*, and the number one Amazon best seller *The Body Knows: Cracking the Weight Loss Code*. For the past 25 years she has lectured internationally as a medical intuitive and has positively affected the lives of over 100,000 people. Caroline is an internationally recognized medical intuitive, lecturer, and author of 27 products regarding health, personal development, and self-esteem. She is the founder of Sutherland Communications, Inc., offering medical intuitive training programs, weight loss programs, and consultation services for adults and children. Sign up for her newsletter, teleconferences, and online video programs at http://www.carolinesutherland.com.

38

The Top 10 Secrets You Should Know about Hypnosis

Nathalie Fiset

Hypnosis has been around ever since the dawn of man. This powerful tool is accessible to all human beings. Unfortunately, in the past, hypnosis has gained a bad reputation from all the misconceptions carried by the film and book industry.

Hence hypnosis is often perceived as scary or dangerous by people who do not fully understand its functioning. The truth of the matter is that hypnosis is a natural and normal state of the human mind, where a higher level of focus can be reached.

By simply pushing aside the conscious mind (the arguing part of ourselves), hypnosis opens access to the subconscious mind, where positive and powerful changes can take place easily. You will be amazed to discover the following top 10 secrets you should know about modern hypnosis.

1. **Learning self-hypnosis is within everyone's reach.** You do not need a skilled hypnotherapist by your side every time you want to go into hypnosis. Hypnosis is a learned skill and is attainable by everyone. I am a strong believer in the saying "give a man a fish, you will feed him for a day; teach a man how to fish, you will feed him for life." Most of my patients who have learned self-hypnosis in preparation for a natural childbirth told me they kept on using the techniques they learned even after their babies were born.
2. **What we think will happen, happens.** We program ourselves for our future. Therefore people who think like winners become winners. People who think like losers become losers. The good news is that *you* can control how you think and program yourself positively with the help of hypnosis.

3. **You can remember or hear everything while in hypnosis.** The depth of your hypnosis will vary from a light trance (like daydreaming) to "spacing out" and having the impression that you have been sleeping. Hypnosis is nothing more than a nice feeling of letting go. Many of my patients, after listening to one of my self-hypnosis recordings, are concerned that they might have fallen asleep because they do not remember anything that was said. I reassure them by telling them that if they were asleep, they would not have emerged on the count of three. It makes sense.

4. **Everyone can use hypnosis to gain better mental and physical health.** The average human uses only about 10 percent of his mental power. Hypnosis might be one way to find the keys that open the gateway to the hidden treasure our powerful minds contain. My personal experience as a hypnotherapist shows me that the old belief that a certain percent of the population cannot be hypnotized is a misconception. We drift in and out of hypnosis many times during any given day. Examples of this are when you miss your exit while driving on the highway or lose track of time while watching television.

5. **The hypnotherapist has no power and cannot control you in any way.** The hypnotherapist is merely your guide, like a sherpa who guides you up a mountain. You are the one doing the climbing. Many stage hypnotists want the public to believe that they hold great power. You do have to remember that stage shows are done with *volunteers*. Bottom line: No hypnotist, no matter how great, can have another person do anything that is immoral, illegal, or "fattening" in hypnosis.

6. **Hypnosis is not a truth serum.** A liar is a better liar in hypnosis. This is the reason why hypnosis is *never* accepted in court as verifiable proof. On the other hand, though, the human mind registers every piece of data presented to it and can recall it in hypnosis. For example, a person can be brought into hypnosis (voluntarily) and recall a license plate number—and then use this evidence as a starting point for a police investigation.

7. **The power of hypnosis is limitless.** It is as vast as the human imagination. Most very successful people have succeeded because they imagined and saw themselves being successful. Successful athletes call "being in the zone" that very focused and powerful state they go into when achieving top performances. This state is nothing else than hypnosis, of course!

8. **You can change your internal programming in hypnosis.** This is because it addresses your subconscious mind (your hard disk). Therefore if your childhood has been tinted with negative programming, such as that you were a burden or unloved and unwanted, you might have acted according to that

151

belief from the beginning. You now have the power to turn this around and become the successful, accomplished, loved, and loving person you deserve and want to be.

9. **A willing person can achieve a perfect, natural anesthesia of his body with the help of hypnosis.** There are numerous films of people going through major surgeries and natural childbirth with minimal or no discomfort at all—with only hypnosis as the sole anesthesia. The comfortable level of anesthesia learned and achieved by my patients in self-hypnosis programs happens too often to be considered pure luck.

10. **You cannot "lose" hypnosis.** It is a natural and easy way of life. With the help of hypnosis, you can achieve almost anything you want. I often compare hypnosis with love: a pleasant, natural state of mind that helps us become the people we aspire to be. Not unlike love, one cannot lose hypnosis. It is always present for us to grab and use.

In conclusion, I have opened a gateway for you today. It is normal that some fear and skepticism remain. For example, Franz Anton Mesmer was brought before a committee commissioned to determine if hypnosis was an existing phenomenon. Their conclusion would decide if Mesmer was really having an impact on all those people who claimed they were transformed by his hypnotic interventions.

The committee, which included Benjamin Franklin, concluded that hypnosis was not a recognizable phenomenon because it could neither be measured nor seen at the time. From that day on, Mesmer suffered a decline and gradually ceased helping people with hypnosis.

The irony of this story is that Benjamin Franklin later discovered electricity, which changed our lives greatly. Just like hypnosis, electricity was a phenomenon that could neither be seen nor measured, yet it undeniably existed and was very powerful…

Now imagine what can happen if hypnosis has the power to open your subconscious mind as fast as a light switch! Napoleon Hill said it best when he said, "Whatever your mind can conceive and believe, it can achieve."

ABOUT THE AUTHOR

Dr. Nathalie Fiset is a family doctor, a certified hypnotherapist, and a neurolinguistic practitioner. She is the author of the powerful hypnosis for childbirth program Hypno-Beginning© (http://www.hypno-beginning.com). She has also created the amazing Alpha-Power© program (http://www.myalpha-power.com) for best mental and physical health with hypnosis. You can consult her other complete and professional Web sites on hypnosis for well-being at http://www.aperfectharmony.com and http://www.a-1hypnosis.com.

39

Don't Die with a Million-Dollar Idea Still Inside You!

Vernon Myers

Did you know that you were brought to this earth for a specific reason? You are the only person who can fulfill the purpose and mission for which you were born. What is your purpose? What is your mission? You have within you the ability to create anything that you can imagine. The fact that you can think about a particular thing is evidence that you can create it.

A creative act is experienced from the inside out; first it is experienced in the mind, followed by outward expression as an idea, concept, product, or service. Napoleon Hill, author of the success classic *Think and Grow Rich*, said, "Whatever the mind of man can conceive and believe it can achieve." Can you believe that you have a million-dollar idea inside of you? You can and you will, if you believe you can.

We Live in an Idea Universe

We live in an idea universe, where Thomas Edison said, "Ideas are waiting to be discovered." Have you found your idea yet? Have you found the idea that will take you from where you are right now to the lifestyle of your dreams? Think about the idea that subtly entered your consciousness and left just as quickly. Think about the idea that caused your heart to race because there was no way you could accomplish it by yourself, yet the sheer size and scope of the idea caused your muscles to tense up and your palms to get sweaty with anticipation. Your million-dollar idea is created within the confines of your mind, and it is waiting for you to reach out and grab hold of it.

The problem with most people is that when the inkling of an idea enters their minds, they are not prepared for what comes next—the feelings and thoughts of doubt, disbelief, fear, and failure. Most people stop at this point—the idea is lost, and they go back to life as usual. Did you know that your brain is programmed to keep you where you are in your life and that the minute you try to do something different, you run up against the mental programming that has prevented you from being as successful as you should be? You must break through this mental wall of failure and pursue your ideas with focus, energy, and intensity. You must become so determined to see your idea become a reality that you either create your idea or you die trying to accomplish it. That is the high commitment level that you must bring to this life-changing endeavor.

Are You Creative?

Do you possess the creative ability to develop a world-changing idea? We are all creative, and we all possess the ability to produce fantastic ideas; in fact, you are an idea-generating machine that can create masterpieces where nothing existed before. How many times have you had a great idea, only to see it materialize somewhere else? We live in a time full of opportunity and possibility; in fact, businessman, author, and motivational speaker Brian Tracy says that "the average person has four ideas a year, which if any one of them is acted upon would make them a millionaire." Have you seen your million-dollar idea this year?

Everyone has a multimillion-dollar idea inside them, but statistically, very few will become millionaires because they will not bother to implement their million-dollar ideas. The real joy in creating novel ideas is in finding creative ways to put them into practice and then seeing the ideas grow. You have an unlimited opportunity to produce wealth and abundance in your life—today! There are over a million ways to become wealthy and prosperous, but there are only a few ways that are absolutely suited to your personality, skills, passions, and desires. You only need to find one idea in order to change your entire life. Art Fry of 3M created the Post-It Notes one time, and now 3M pays him one percent of total sales every year. Can you live with one percent of $100 million every year of your life?

Personally, I have always wanted to write a book—it is amazing how this desire came about by following through on an idea that I had for a totally unrelated project. I wanted to drive traffic to one of my Web sites, so I decided to create a template that I would give away as an incentive for people to join my mailing list. I created the template to help people outline and structure their ideas and concepts—this was only supposed to be a five-page template. Well, 115 pages later, I had written my first book, and I had a blast doing it. Recently, my vision for this book has expanded tremendously. Now I am building a brand around this book to include interactive software, a membership Web site, coaching, and many other products.

What if I had stopped at five pages? What if I had settled for "good enough" and decided to wait until the "right time" to write a book? What can you learn from my experience? What idea have you kept hidden away in your heart?

How to Get Ideas

How do you develop or create life-changing ideas? Ideas are all around us, yet they will not trip you up as you walk down the street. Ideas will not come knocking at your door, waiting for you to invite them into your home. Ideas are elusive and are only revealed to the discerning eyes of people who are ready for them.

You get ideas by actively searching for them. The quality of an idea is based upon the information you gather and the specialized or general knowledge you have to work with. You find ideas when you actively combine old elements or ideas into new combinations—that is the essence of ideation. Curiosity is another way to feed your ability to get new ideas because the more you search, the more you will find. The more you know, the more you will want to know. Continuous learning allows you to add new information, facts, and knowledge to your kit bag to help you create new and better ideas.

How to Implement Your Ideas

After you create the idea, you have to figure out a way to move the idea from concept to reality. You need a team to help you develop your ideas. Do not try to do everything by yourself—your team may be able to contribute time, money, resources, and support as you get your idea off the ground. You must develop a plan that outlines how you are approaching the development and deployment of your idea. The old adage goes, "if you fail to plan, you plan to fail." Get started building a foundation under the big dream that you are building.

Remember, teamwork makes the dream work. Creating a vision team is easy. Who do you know that is doing what you want to do? Who do you admire? Who wants to see you succeed and is willing to back this intention up with action? Create a list of these people, identify what you need them to help you with, decide what you can offer them in return for their service, and contact them immediately. You can contact them by e-mail or by phone. Ask each person to commit one hour every month to help you expand your vision of what is "possible" for your idea. Set up a monthly teleconference with your vision team, and allow them to help you take action on your great ideas.

Identify your skill and information deficits. What specific or general knowledge do you need to launch your idea? Can you learn it, or do you need to pay someone to provide the knowledge for you? Identify the specific skills and knowledge that you need to develop and create your idea, and go get it today.

What is it going to cost if you do not follow up on your idea? What opportunities will you miss? What mission will you not accomplish? When one person finds her mission in life, she helps 1,000 people find the missions for their lives. Find a strong reason to persist in creating your idea, no matter what the obstacles or circumstances. I have heard it said that there are 1,000 reasons why you cannot pursue your dreams; I challenge you to find one reason why you can pursue your dreams.

You are a walking miracle—there is no one on this earth that has the unique abilities and insights that you possess. You were placed here for a particular reason. Do not allow that reason to go to the grave with you. The idea, the plan, the purpose, and the dream are not meant just for you but for all of mankind.

Billionaire Ross Perot says that "it just takes one idea to live like a king for the rest of your life." I submit that one idea cannot only change your life, but one idea can change the lives of millions of people.

Imagine if Gandhi of India allowed his idea of nonviolent social change to die with him: Millions of people in India may have continued to be oppressed by the British Empire. In America, Martin Luther King, Jr. would have never studied Gandhi's principles of nonviolent social change, which means that black Americans might not have enjoyed the freedoms that they enjoy today.

Follow the example of these great men—express your idea, live your idea, create your idea, and share you idea with the world, but most importantly, **DON'T DIE WITH A MILLION-DOLLAR IDEA STILL INSIDE YOU!**

ABOUT THE AUTHOR

Speaker, author, and master idea creator Vernon Myers is an active duty army major currently serving as a program manager in the Army's Simulations Command in Orlando, Florida. This article is based upon his most recent book, *The Idea Journal (A Tool for Unleashing Your Urge to Create!)*. Get his free 5-week e-course to help you create and take action on your ideas at http://www.ideamerge.net/products. Reach him at info@ideamerge.net.

40

IN BETWEEN RELATIONSHIPS

Alone: Who are You?

Kim Olver

Relationships generally begin when both people are in the "alone stage." Although I am aware that affairs often begin when one or both partners are involved with someone else, it is my contention that relationships have a greater chance of success when both parties have spent some time alone and unconnected with a lover prior to their involvement with each other.

What do you do with this time alone? If you are interested in creating the relationship you deserve, then you must become the best person you can be. Each successive relationship we engage in provides us with lessons and information we need to reflect on. If you are attracting the "wrong" people into your life, then perhaps it is because you are not the person you need to be in order to create a relationship with the person of your dreams.

This also means that each "wrong" person you attract into your life is exactly the right person to teach you the lesson you need to move closer to the person you truly want. This is why I never look back on any relationships with regret. Maybe not in the moment, but over time, I have come to understand that I learned valuable lessons in each of my past relationships, and I grew, which then helped me to become a better person.

Whenever you find yourself in between relationships, it is not a time to longingly wish for the next partner to arrive. It is not the time to go out "prowling" for the next person to make you complete. The time between relationships is a very important healing time. It is a time to look back on the past relationship to discover what that person was there to teach you about life, love, and yourself. It is a time of introspection to determine who you want to be in a relationship. I am not talking about playing roles. I am talking about a genuine transformation of yourself into a person who deserves the relationship you seek.

No one dreams his entire life about meeting a mediocre partner—someone who thinks of him sometimes, who loves him a little, and who takes care of some of his needs. No one looks to get involved in relationships with people who lie, cheat, and disrespect her. No one asks for verbal or physical abuse in a relationship. So how can we break the pattern of choosing the same type of person over and over again? I believe the key is to look at each relationship as the perfect relationship you needed at that point in time and then go about attempting to figure out what it was about the person that made him or her perfect for you during that period in your life.

Once you figure this out, you will have learned a valuable lesson. If you take that lesson and put it to use in your life, then you have one half of the equation.

The other half is about preparing yourself to be the kind of person who will attract the relationship of your dreams. If you are seeking a person to be loyal and to stand by you no matter what, then ask yourself the difficult question of whether or not you have those same traits and characteristics. If there is something in your character that has caused you to be disloyal, then do some introspection to learn what you need to heal in order to become the person you truly want to be.

Relationships only act as a mirror, showing you those things about yourself you do not want to see. When you welcome the information and seek to learn from it, doing so will move you closer in the direction of becoming who you want to be.

It also helps during this alone time to take an inventory of the traits, qualities, and characteristics you want in your "perfect mate." It is far more likely that you will attract the person you want when you become crystal clear about exactly what you are looking for. My list included having someone to love me for who I am—not in spite of who I am. I wanted a partner with loyalty, integrity, honesty, good looks, intelligence, a sense of humor, romance, and availability (not involved with someone else). I wanted a man who was strong but gentle, decisive but sensitive, and confident without being conceited. I wanted someone with whom I shared common interests and someone who did not feel the need to control me or compete with me. Guess what? After I was clear about what I was looking for, the "perfect" person for me walked into my life.

Another thing that is extremely helpful during the alone stage is to remember that you are perfect just the way you are. You are totally complete without a significant person to share your life. So often, in the alone stage, you focus on what you lack, rather than on your abundances. You look at the one thing you do not have—a romance—and waste the time you have been given feeling sorry for yourself instead of putting the gift of time to use for the betterment of mankind in your own unique way.

In conclusion, allow yourself alone time. Do not be in such a hurry to jump into the next relationship before processing the last one. Take time to analyze the lessons in your past relationships. Use alone time to search introspectively to assess whether you are the person you need to be to allow the person you seek to come into your life. And finally, focus not on your lack of a relationship, but rather on what you can do to help others during this time.

Used wisely, your alone time can truly make an incredible difference in the way you experience your next relationship. Do not short-change yourself. Maximize and leverage the time you have been given between relationships. It is truly a gift.

ABOUT THE AUTHOR

Kim Olver helps men get more sex and women get more romance into their lives. By learning to focus only on those things over which you have control and learning to implement the Platinum Rule in your relationship, you will experience an empowering relationship with your partner, where each of you gets what you truly want. Visit http://www.therelationshipcenter.biz/couples.htm to learn more about Kim's products and services. While there, make sure to sign up for her free newsletter, packed full of awesome, practical, and little known tips and advice to help you create the relationship you deserve.

41

Innate Personalities

<hr>

Why "Secrets to Success" Fail

Jeff Allen

Many individuals claim they have found "the secret to success." But what does that really mean? How do you know which one to believe? And if there really is a secret, how come you have tried almost all of them but have yet to experience a significant, measurable change in your life?

As a life strategist, I have helped a wide range of clients with very diverse backgrounds, levels of education, and levels of income, from high-paid executives, entrepreneurs, and well-established business owners to divorcées and jobless individuals—not to mention teenagers and young adults who are taking life on for the first time. With all this diversity, is there really one master secret that fits all? Well, yes . . . and no. Sounds confusing enough, right?

Basically, it all boils down to this: To create significant, lasting change in anyone's life, there are three must-haves and one absolute. It does not matter what shape or size your background is or what your current circumstances are— the formula works every time. *But wait, you said there isn't necessarily a master secret, yet now you're saying there is a formula that works every time; what's the catch?* Okay, here is the catch—there is a variable in the formula.

First, let me discuss the three must-haves. I have watched my clients time and time again create absolute magic in their lives once they have understood and applied these three simple truths.

1. **Trust.** Trust the Universe, trust yourself, and trust others.
2. **Leadership.** Know how to lead yourself so that you can then lead others.
3. **Intention.** Know how to intentionally create your future.

Like I said, simple truths—have trust, be a leader, and be intentional. But let me ask you a couple questions. How do you establish trust? Is it through facts and figures, or is it through feelings and emotions? Also, how do you stay clear with your intention? Does your intention become clearer working as a group or as an individual? Is your intention best served leading the group or promoting ideas for others to implement?

As you can see, there are several possible answers to any of these questions. When clients first walk through my door, we go through a series of questions similar to the two questions I just asked you. Most of the answers I receive are very generalized or vague. However, after I have introduced them to the one absolute and opened their eyes to a whole new world, their answers become as unique and numerous as there are individuals. Everyone has a clear, specific answer. And often, it is not even related to the generalized response he originally had early in the process.

So what is this variable, this one absolute? The variable is that you must *absolutely know yourself.* Even ancient Greek philosophy tells us to "know thyself."

Well, what is so tricky about that, right? I mean, you have lived with yourself essentially your entire life, you should know yourself pretty well by now, should you not? The fact is that we are very dynamic creatures, and each of us is exceptionally unique in our own little way. Whether you know it or not, the fact is that we all have multiple personalities. I know that sounds a little discouraging, but it is not a disorder.

Each of us has three distinct personalities, and each personality has certain environments or situations where it becomes the dominant persona. Think of someone you know close to you and how different he may act when he is with close friends compared to when he is at work, and then differently again when he is in his home. You can begin to see that there are some subtle differences—as well as some drastic ones.

It is one thing to point out the different ways we act, but the true gem is in *why* we respond to varying circumstances the way we do. When you can harness the *why,* you can then have solid, meaningful understanding of how you specifically relate to the three must-haves—and when you have that, magic happens.

Your Innate Personality

Of the three personalities, the most important to understand is your innate personality, which is controlled by your unconscious mind. Your innate personality was given to you by nature; it is who you are at the very core of your being. It helps keep you physically safe and out of harm's way.

Your innate personality is the central source for motivation, a key component to achieving significant results. It also determines your primary learning style—particularly those hard "life lessons." The largest factor is that the innate personality is the most dominant of the three personalities. When it remains satisfied—*feeling safety and trust in its environment*—nothing can stop you from getting where you want to go. However, if your innate personality does not feel safe, then nothing seems to go as planned.

Your Intending Personality

The second most important personality is controlled by your conscious mind. I call it the intending personality. This personality was developed sometime in your high school years. Your conscious mind actively creates solutions and also plans for the future. You make decisions with this personality based on what you intend to do—thus the *intending* personality.

Ultimately, your conscious mind is where the seeds of your intentions are sprouted and then nurtured. When you use your conscious mind in its favored thinking style, you will experience higher levels of awareness in everything you do.

Your Imprinted Personality

The third personality is the imprinted personality, which is controlled by the subconscious mind. I call it the imprinted personality because it was taught to us by our parents (usually before the age of eight years old). This personality is how we look for acceptance from others, and it is constantly on the lookout, protecting us from emotional pain.

Another good way to describe the subconscious mind is *self-conscious*. When we are self-conscious, this personality kicks in and starts running our lives. It commonly has programs that served us as children but that are mostly stumbling blocks now that we have grown into adults.

Most people work so hard to be this *taught* personality that they miss their entire lives trying to be accepted and loved based on a learned behavior, rather than on who they really are.

Of the three personalities, I mentioned that the innate personality is the most important; I also posed the question in the opening of this article, Why are there so many different secrets that seem to work for others, but not for you? The reason some processes did not and do not work for you is because your innate personality does not relate with the particular method or process. It will work for certain personalities but, generally, only for a grouping of similar thinking styles. True, there are some fundamental processes that we each must learn, but we each relate to those processes differently. So until we truly understand who we are, we will not know which processes are important to us. Once you have a full understanding of what your overall personality is, you will then be able to use the right applications for success in your life.

To identify your innate personality and gain a better understanding of the types of processes that are most in alignment with you, visit WinningPersonality.com/free-profile (use the access code 101WAYS) and take the free personality test I have developed called the Identity Profile.

ABOUT THE AUTHOR

Jeff Allen is a business coach, life strategist, inventor, and entrepreneur. Jeff's lifelong passion for personal development and helping others achieve their potential found him studying under some of the top professional trainers in the United States. Ultimately, Jeff developed his Identity Profile, a unique, powerful, in-depth personality assessment that helps identify your optimum "life strategy" based on who you really are. To learn more about the Identity Profile process, visit http://www.winningpersonality.com.

42

The Secret to Freeing Your Inner Child

Marnina Reid

It is said that we all have what is known as an inner child. Our inner child is said to be the purest part of us that desires solely to love and be loved. It is the "spirit" or "feeling" part of us. It is also the playful part of us. It is said that in relationship to our inner child, we have three parts: the inner child, the adult, and the benevolent observer. The adult part of us pays the bills and sets the alarm clock to wake up in the morning. The adult grounds out the child's energy and redirects it. This means that the adult relates to the child, acknowledges the child, and nourishes the child. In a balanced relationship the adult becomes the parent the child most likely never had. (This is not about judging or condemning real parents; this is about taking full accountability for our feelings, our needs, and ourselves.) In contrast to the adult, the benevolent observer acts as a witness to life's happenings without attachment or judgment, as if it were observing someone else.

Many people have lived with a wounded inner child since childhood. We were taught by society and our parents that is it not okay to express our feelings or even to experience them. Can you relate to this? How many times have you felt sadness, anger, or any other negative emotion and then beat yourself up for even feeling it? How many times have you invalidated yourself for feeling somewhat emotional? This is really what your inner little girl or boy is feeling inside. It is your child that feels emotions.

Many people's emotions are to some degree stifled or repressed. We are simply taught by our parents or other significant adults to push them down, ignore them, and "put on a good front" when inside, there is deep turmoil. We learned to do that by being condemned and criticized—usually by someone else—for having feelings, and now many of us continue that same behavior to our own selves. This is often unconscious. It is a learned habit. Did you ever hear "stop crying, or

I'll give you something to cry about" as a child? Even if the threat was not in those exact words, can you feel the energy behind it? The energy of anger and frustration? The energy of dissatisfaction? In that very moment of being told to stop crying, you literally learned that it is not okay to express your emotions. This is often reinforced over and over throughout childhood. It takes only one initial demonstration by anyone to learn a belief or habit before the age of seven.

Emotional energy is actually very simple, and it is a natural part of being human. We are meant to be able to express our emotions. It is absolutely impossible to bottle up our feelings and expect that they will just disappear. It is extremely unrealistic; it is not the way the body works. Imagine a volcano or a wave. There is pressure building and building in both situations. At some point, the pressure peaks and goes through a process of release. The volcano erupts, and the wave crashes. Soon after, in both cases, there is a settling that happens.

Human emotions are the same way. Emotions are energy in motion. If you are not used to expressing your emotions, it is understandable that doing so would feel scary. Acknowledge that you feel scared. You are already doing it. That acknowledgment was an expression! In the past, I worried that if tapped into negative emotions, I would not be able to control myself, and the experience would be never ending. In other words, I felt that if I started to connect with my wounded inner child, I would be devastated all over again.

The key to healing your inner child and gaining a rich, emotional connection with yourself is to first start to connect with your child. You want to practice connecting just as you would with a "real" child that has been through trauma in its life and needs acceptance and nurturing. How would you talk to the child?

You could start by asking, "How do you feel?" Maybe you could also use an endearing nickname for your inner child to help with the connection. See if you can let go of any expectations and allow yourself to be real with your own self. You can elaborate more . . . your child may be ready and available, or withdrawn, sad, or angry. You may have to ask specific questions such as "are you feeling sad?" It is normal that at first, your child may not trust your adult enough to be vulnerable with his or her feelings. This is very understandable. Many "inner children" have a history of devastation and trauma and have learned to believe that their feelings are not important. It can be very challenging when they are asked to express those feelings.

You can ask yourself, "What does my child need from me to feel content and happy?" The healing really starts when the child has the experience of being heard. When you give your child total permission to be heard about anything and everything he or she did not get to express in childhood, major internal shifts will take place. Everyone wants to be heard and acknowledged for who he or she is. This is acceptance. This is healing. Once you can hear and acknowledge your own self for who you are, you will be capable of empathy, of acknowledging and accepting others for who they really are.

Let me give you an example. My client Yolanda never felt heard as a child, and she learned as a child that she was not good enough, that life is hard, and that her feelings were not important. She frequently felt angry that her mother would never be the mother she wanted her to be. As Yolanda started to connect with her little girl, she started feeling more powerful. Yolanda started to realize that *she* could be the mother she always wanted for herself by being heard by her own self and accepting that her needs are valid.

Start connecting with your little boy or girl energy! What are your favorite things to do? How do you enjoy playing in your life? Does your child like going to the beach, being outside, going to the spa, going to parties, playing sports, reading? What activities bring out passion and joy in you? That is your inner child, the "spirit" part of you that is timeless and is love! Use your favorite things to help you connect with your child. This is a process. It takes time to be vulnerable with yourself. But the more you do it, the more joyful your life will be! There is no replacement for you in the universe; there is no one quite like you. You are authentic. We all want to be deeply connected to.

ABOUT THE AUTHOR

Marnina Reid is a nationally certified holistic health practitioner. Marnina has a private practice in San Diego and facilitates trainings in emotional healing. She mainly works with women who have suffered from emotional trauma, helping them to remove the blockages from the past in their lives that are preventing them from moving forward. She is also the author of the e-book *Natural Cures for Chronic Headaches*. For more information on Marnina Reid, please visit http://www.findyourfreedominc.com. For free cutting-edge health tips that can enhance your life and prevent disease, visit http://www.naturalcuresforchronicheadaches.com.

43

INNER INVENTORY

===

What Does Your Heart Know?

Mara Purl

> The heart has its reasons that reason does not know.
> —Blaise Pascal (1623–1662)

> I'm beginning to wonder if the heart isn't just as much a thinking organ as the brain. It knows so much, yet its information isn't presented in verbiage. Have we lost its language? Is that why we can't hear what the heart is trying to tell us?
> —Mara Purl, *What the Heart Knows*

Your plane bounces through an air pocket, and your heart skips a beat. Your child brings you his brand-new drawing, and your heart opens. You fail to achieve a cherished goal and feel sick at heart. Your boss seeks you out to tell you how well you handled the meeting, and it does your heart good.

The heart: It is one of the central metaphors of life. And only by penetrating its deeper meaning can we get to the "heart of the matter."

Some important things in life seem to come from outside ourselves. We might count among these our sense of duty, the discipline that keeps us faithful to our jobs, and membership in families and organizations. Yet do we not also sometimes feel overwhelmed by the commitments we have taken on, swamped by the schedules we seem to have agreed to while not quite in our right minds?

Could this be because we have failed to consult our hearts about these important matters? Another word for *heart* in this instance would be *core*, as in core values. How do we know when something is truly of central importance to us? Certainly ıversations with those we respect will inspire deep thought. Still, ultimately, we will only know the true answers to this question when they resonate deep within. And this resonance can more accurately be described as a *feeling* than as a *thought*.

An Intake Inventory

Ask yourself, "How much of the vital information I process in my daily life comes to me through logic and from things I can tangibly see?" Then ask yourself, "How much comes to me through intuition and from things I may not be able to see?"

Here are some examples of tangibles you can see: the red light tells you to stop; the client gives a yes to your proposal; the tickets to the theatrical performance are available.

Now here are some examples of intangibles you cannot "see" in the usual sense: you get a very strong feeling you should call your friend Joe (later it turns out he was trying to reach you but had lost your number); while shopping for a gift for your girlfriend, one item seems to call to you, though as far as you know it is not on her list of desired objects (later it turns out to be the precise thing she was looking for).

Perhaps you have a critical decision to make. Protocol indicates the decision should be *x*. Yet your gut tells you to go with *y*. Our culture generally does not give high credibility to gut feelings. How are they treated? As anecdotal, "touchy-feely," and of secondary importance.

Yet all of us have heard stories to the contrary: the woman who "for some reason" walks home a different way and avoids the muggers lying in wait; the police officer who checks behind a building for no reason and saves someone's life.

Then there are the times we fail to listen to that inner warning. Have you ever said to yourself, "I knew I shouldn't have accepted a ride from a stranger, but I didn't want to be rude." These are cases of the head overruling the heart.

Three New Perspectives

Now I invite you to explore with me three new, what we might call "heart" perspectives:

- one that touches your sense of self
- one that touches your sense of relating to others
- one that touches your sense of service to mankind.

1. **What does your heart know that your head does not know?** Might it have something to do with self-esteem? Does your heart tell you that you are talented and capable? But does your head tell you that most of your true potential is untapped, that you never really did as much as you could have?

Would you agree nothing is more energizing, encouraging, and vitalizing than discovering what your true purpose is? Would it not be like discovering the most precious secret to know your true mission in life? So this is the first point to remember: *Give yourself room to listen to what your heart is telling you.*

2. **How can we use our "heart knowledge" more effectively in our relationships, be they personal or professional?** Can you think of a situation where your *heart* knows something that your *head* is overruling? If we use "head information" to form our first impressions, what information are we getting: how the person is dressed; how well they speak; how much homework they have done before meeting with you. These are all good things. Now what if we use "heart information"? The person may not be dressed well, but they give the overwhelming impression of being sincere.

What if you were visiting Thailand after the tsunami and did not realize there had been a disaster? What if you saw someone dirty and barely clothed? Would you help them? The external appearance may not tell us everything we really need to know to be sure, or even to be safe. So this is the second point: We are very accustomed to consulting our head for information, and it does a good job. *But nothing reports on the climate of feelings and the atmosphere of thought better than the* heart.

3. **How can we use our hearts to be of greater service?** Can you think of a situation where your *head* says the situation is hopeless, but your *heart* says something must be done?

171

The head is tremendously good at cataloging the past. It keeps track of what has happened and how it has happened and trains itself that this is how things should always happen. So our tendency is to "plan forward" from the past. When it comes to creating a vibrant community project, might we therefore usually respond with "I don't have time," "I did so much last year," "I shouldn't rob my family of my time," "I don't have the expertise," and myriad other excuses?

Now let us look at this from another perspective. The heart is tremendously good at what might be called wishing and hoping. But we could use clearer, more dynamic language to describe what the heart is really good at. We could say it is good at envisioning, imagining, and creating what has never existed before.

What if we were to live "into" that expanding sense of what we wish to create, rather than "out of" the past that tells us we cannot create anything more than what we have already created? Our heart is a built-in guidance system that can protect, inspire, and lead us into the extraordinary lives we wish to create.

Like any other muscle, the more you use your heart, the stronger and more reliable it will become. You have a wellspring of wisdom and inspiration within you. I encourage you embark on the great adventure to know what your heart knows.

ABOUT THE AUTHOR

Mara Purl is the award-winning author of *What the Heart Knows* (Silver Benjamin Franklin Award), *Closer Than You Think*, and *Christmas Angels* (CIPA Merit Book). Her radio drama "Milford-Haven, U.S.A." reached 4.5 million listeners on BBC Radio and earned the New York Festival Finalist Award. Mara Purl and Erin Gray co-wrote *Act Right* (Gold EVVY Award). Mara performed the role of Darla Cook on *Days of Our Lives* and was a journalist for *Rolling Stone*, *The Financial Times*, and the Associated Press. A speaker and mentor, Mara was named Woman of the Year by the Los Angeles County Commission for Women.

44

INTEND A MIRACULOUS LIFE

Stop Hoping, Start Knowing: Your Life Is What You Intend

Paula Onysko

Do you know the difference between hoping and knowing? Hoping has you wanting a new outcome—knowing has you living it. Hoping comes with skepticism—knowing stems from conscious intention. Whatever you call that Higher Being in your life, it is always delivering according to the strength and clarity of your loudest intention. Not your hopes or dreams. Your intentions. The loudest one.

If you want to know what you have intended, look around. Your life is the perfect reflection of your thoughts, words, and actions. In fact, every experience—good or bad—you have directed by the energy of your intentions. If you do not like what you see, the good news is that you can change it.

I know this firsthand. For years I had hoped for a child. But inside, I was torn. The truth was that I did not think I would be a good mother. I loved my freedom without children. I feared going through a painful delivery. Most days, the tug of war inside was enough to cripple any hopes for a child. My loudest intention was not to become pregnant—it was to avoid my fears.

So the Universe obliged, as it always does, without judgment.

Any time we live in fear and worry, we are doomed. That is because what we focus on, we become. *Worrying is like praying for the outcome we do not want.*

If your ego is saying that this sounds too simple to be true, I understand. It took me years to accept that no thought is idle. Every thought is charged with emotion, and that emotion sends a message into the world, which then reflects back to us an experience of similar vibration. We react to that experience, sending out more emotionally charged energy, which then attracts more experiences with similar qualities. And the cycle escalates.

Just as I was getting tired of my own merry-go-round, I got a sense for how powerful my word was. If I could use it to attract things I did not want, surely I could put it to better use.

So the experiment began. As I noticed low-energy thoughts, I would say "how interesting" and choose something more vibrant. If my ego would not allow this shift, I would lovingly set her aside, saying, "Don't worry. I won't abandon you, but we're bigger than this thought. How about something more inspiring?"

At first it was embarrassing to see many of my thoughts laced with guilt, resentment, or anger—all feelings that keep us small. But judging ourselves is never the answer. Loving is.

Changing my thoughts meant changing my life. Toxic relationships had to go. I stopped gossiping about others as seemingly "innocent" gossip was not about high-energy feelings. My work needed to speak to my soul's desire. My health needed my loving attention.

Each morning I would ask, "What magnificence can I partake in today?" Never mind all my tasks. First, I wanted to frame my day with brilliant intentions for health, love, and abundance.

Before bed, I would ask God to address a few things while I slept. Perhaps I was stuck in my writing or desired a new melody for my song. No sense worrying. It would be taken care of while my body and soul rejuvenated.

I began to notice a shift in my awareness. No longer could I relate to people who complained. I saw beauty in the simplest things. Nature became my art gallery. Money started flowing my way. Possibilities replaced problems. And the messages came.

The Universe is continuously sending us messages. Most times, we are not paying enough attention. I finally tuned in when an article in an old magazine of my mother's caught my eye. Entitled "Dust Off Your Dreams," it spoke of a man rekindling his passion for writing after 20 years of being lured away by positions touting financial security and prestige. That article was written for me. Next I stumbled across the perfect book, which guided me in examining my fears surrounding parenting. Then I met a dear friend whose journey paralleled mine, and we helped move mountains in each other's lives. The more I noticed and gave thanks for these messages, the more I received. I began trusting this brilliant process.

Honestly, I did not always like what came my way, but I would stop and say, "It is no mistake that I'm being given this experience. What am I putting out there to attract this?" Nobody does life to us. We direct our life stories, and then people show up for the scenes we want played out. There is great personal power in realizing why the plot unfolds as it does.

Soon it became obvious that my infertility was no accident. Rather, it reflected deeply rooted beliefs about my femininity. At a very early age I had rejected my beauty and my natural maternal instinct, and so my body protected me from my fears. Discovering this, I began showering myself with love. I revisited each childhood memory and comforted the little girl who still held on to painful experiences. Through journal writing I forgave people who had hurt me. They did not even need to know. Forgiveness was about *me* releasing *them* with love. And I began to set the scene for a new life that was not anchored to the past. What are my passions? Who do I dream of being? What do I want to leave as my legacy? These are delicious questions to contemplate.

Living our dreams is declaring what we are about before the evidence arrives. Often we let our circumstances determine who we are. I relied on my bank account to decide my wealth, medical test results to dictate my health, and broken relationships to determine my worthiness. Yet these results were all in the past. They speak nothing of what is possible going forward.

If I was to attract a child, I had to *be* a mother. I started buying parenting magazines. I read about hypno-birthing and midwives. I even envisioned telling my husband we were pregnant.

Imagine my surprise in the spring of 2005, when a pregnancy test came back positive. Even a miscarriage a few weeks later could not dampen my spirits. Through releasing beliefs that no longer served me, I had achieved what medical doctors for 10 years said was almost impossible given my medical condition.

Three months later, to my sheer delight, we received a call that we had been chosen as adoptive parents. I did not believe in miracles until Baby Hanna arrived. Now I know that anything is possible. What we seek is truly seeking us, if we allow it to. Often we think we know how life should turn out. Chances are that we cannot begin to imagine the amazing possibilities that await. Decide the qualities in life you desire. Take action and release what stands in your way. Stop hoping and start knowing—intend for miracles to unfold.

ABOUT THE AUTHOR

Paula Onysko is a voice with vision—a writer, singer, and speaker inspired to help extraordinary people break free from their ordinary lives. Visit http://www.paulaonysko.com and pick up a free copy of her latest e-book, *Heartwork is Artwork*. To contact Paula for speaking or singing engagements, e-mail writeme@paulaonysko.com.

45

You Look Like a Cow

Lynette M. Loomis

"You look like a cow." When Kristen heard this, she was delighted and clapped her hands. When Linda heard these words, she was mortified and fled the room in tears. Why? Because they interpreted the words in very different ways. Kristen was dressed in a costume she had made herself for a masquerade party and was proud "to have pulled it off." Linda had just topped the scales at 300 pounds and vowed never to wear a black and white print again.

While this may be an overstated example, the point is irrefutable. We always have a choice in how we interpret and react to the world.

Tirade Ted

Ted's supervisor calls Ted aside. "Ted, I'm not sure this project shows your best effort." Ted has a choice in how to feel and how to react to his supervisor. One approach is to flash back unconsciously to his father's frequent reprimands about his average performance on the football field in high school. With increasing anger he can recall humiliating moments when his father harangued him about a missed catch or a pass that fell short. He can feel the resentment that he never felt he measured up to his father's expectations.

Ted can become defensive, cut off the remainder of his boss's comments, turn beet red, increase his blood pressure, and start to yell, "I can't do it all! I do most of the work around here, while those idiots in the other department sit on their butts all day picking out screen savers and betting on teams. If it wasn't for me, this project would still be in planning."

If, however, Ted has put some thought into what motivates him, he might take another approach. His father's expectation of him was to be the "star." But that is not what motivates Ted. What motivates Ted is to be respected for his work and considered a good team player, who will always "come through." He also wants to earn enough money to put his two kids through college with a minimum of student loans (which he figures he will have to pay anyway).

So when his supervisor says, "Ted, I'm not sure this project shows your best effort," Ted can recognize the surge of some old feelings and take a couple of deep breaths to manage his mood. He can remind himself that this man is not his father, he is not in high school, and this is not football. Moving past that, he can ask for some clarification: "I'd like to hear more about how you see my performance on this project."

Ted can take his feelings of anxiety and use them to improve his performance. While his supervisor explains, Ted can evaluate each comment objectively. He may acknowledge that he had so many assignments that he passed over some critical details on the current project. Ted might disagree with some of his supervisor's feedback but recognize the need to put more structure in his workday in order to juggle all the projects without compromising his reputation and the final result. To listen and respond to his supervisor's feedback with an open mind, to be aware of "what sets him off" and what motivates him, enables Ted to be in control of his emotions and his life.

The Red Cottage

Old feelings can be favorable and evoke positive emotions. Every summer of my childhood was spent in a three-room cottage on the lake with my father, brother, aunt, uncle, and three cousins. We had bunks, a sofa bed, cots, a fireplace, and a huge kitchen table, all of which made it quite cozy. (Some people might have thought of it as cramped, but not us.) Everyone who showed up at breakfast time was welcomed by my father, who created each person's first pancake in the shape of his initial. We had the only phone on the dirt road for many years, so our cottage was frequently abuzz with friends and neighbors who lingered to visit with us after their phone calls.

To this day, I see a certain shade of red on a house, and I am favorably disposed toward that structure. Mind you, the foundation can be crumbling, the porch slanted, and the plumbing may predate World War I, but my initial reaction is typically "I love it!"

In this situation I need to be aware of my emotional triggers and manage my positive emotions. (Boomers-Trigger is no longer just a horse or part of a revolver—it is something that stimulates a thought or feeling.) I need to remind myself, "I am not 10, my father has passed away, my cousins live in another state, and the structure is crumbling. Buying this will not recreate my childhood. In fact, if I buy this red building, I could end up like the Wicked Witch of the West, with only my foot visible beneath the collapsed structure." Without this self-awareness and management of my reaction, I could be the owner of 14 red houses in jeopardy of being condemned as unsafe.

Being aware of what motivates me enables me to create the life I want without going into foreclosure on condemned properties. I can create the feeling the red cottage represents any place I put down roots. I can select friends who choose not to be "victims." I can gravitate toward men and women whose view of the world is compatible with my own. I can enjoy the company of people who possess skills and interests different than my own so that I can learn, laugh, and grow from our conversations. My time can be spent with people who support and challenge me but never tell me how I should feel and welcome my ideas and listen to my stories with pleasure. I can purchase (in fact, I have purchased) enough silverware to feed the neighborhood if I choose to do so. In other words, I can create the red cottage with any color I choose.

Being in control of our lives does not mean that we always get our way or that everything is picture perfect (how dull would that be?). Being in control is really about recognizing and managing our emotions and being aware of what motivates us. It means that rather than going off like a Roman candle, we think about the situation. True, if someone says to me, "You look like a cow," I may cast a surreptitious glance at my hips and peruse my outfit before thinking, "Perhaps they mean nurturing." When a client or colleague challenges me, I will stay in the present and not relive the angst of adolescence while listening. And perhaps, with great effort, I will not buy 10 red cottages.

ABOUT THE AUTHOR

Lynette M. Loomis, MA, MBA, is a certified coach, marketing consultant, and speaker and is president of Your Best Life Coaching, LLC. She focuses on appealing to different learning styles, with a touch of humor, to propel individuals and businesses to significant success. Lynette can be reached at yourbestlifecoaching@rochester.rr.com, or visit her Web site, http://yourbestlifecoaching.com.

46

Signs of Authentic Intuition

Lynn Scheurell

Intuition is the quiet inner voice or feeling that consistently guides us toward being and doing our best in every moment. So how do we know that voice or feeling is truly authentic? That it belongs to us? That we are getting the "right" information? Here are 10 indicators to help you know your authentic intuition.

1. **Intuition is a whisper—not a shout.** True intuition will not compete to be heard—it simply is. It is a feeling, a nuance, an inkling, a subtle knowingness that is always accessible but not always acknowledged. The speed of life has a lot to do with your ability to understand and work with your inner wisdom. Chances are that if your intuition is shouting at you, it is time to acknowledge that that light really is the oncoming train.

2. **There is a sense of calmness and certainty in the intuitive awareness.** While it is not always easy to trust intuition at first (mostly because that is not a generally accepted practice of socialization in our formative years), there is a feeling of confidence in the intuitive insight. Authentic intuition just feels right when it is.

3. **Your body experiences "breathing" in all ways.** When we are in a state of fear, stress, confusion, or indecision, our bodies are tight, our breathing is shallow, and we can be distracted. Experiencing our authentic intuition leads to a release of that heavy or constricted sensation. When our intuition gives us the information or answer that is needed, we feel a particular lightness, a freshness, a sense of breathing again—literally.

4. **It seems like your "life glass" just got cleaned.** The world is brighter and cleaner, shapes are sharper, even smells seem sweeter. Your intuitive insight has

gifted you with clarity; the distractions to appreciating your world are gone. Your vision and your senses are connected again to the world outside of you due to your intuitive direction. If you suddenly notice that your spring cleaning never did get sprung, you know you have had a solid intuitive connection. (So *that* is the upside of noticing housework. . . .)

5. **The solution feels easy and natural.** When your intuition gives you a genuine answer, there is a gentle and relaxed energy. This guidance can feel like permission or maybe even forgiveness. The insight is personal, and you know it to be true like you know being your own gender—completely natural and in sync with who you are at your essence. When it is authentic intuition, the message is effortlessly just for you.

6. **True intuition will not harm you (or anyone else, for that matter!).** Your inner wisdom is a compass guiding you toward what is in your best interest at all times. It is impossible for authentic intuition to share space with negativity or malicious intention. Intuition serves only your best and highest good. Your intuition may direct you to do something that you may not want to do but that is ultimately helping you. For example, it may be time to release a relationship, which may hurt either party, but overall, it is a disservice to prolong a relationship that has served its purpose. The healthy cycle of life (birth, living, dying) is inherent in every part of life and is inexorably linked with every phase of our lives—including intuition. The bottom line is that bad things do not come from good intuition!

7. **The intuitive insight conveys creativity in being.** Sometimes intuition is baffling in what it communicates, which could be a symptom of not knowing your internal intuitive language, or it could be that you are not quite ready to assimilate that information. Intuition is amazingly creative and yet perfectly simple. If something pops in seemingly from out of nowhere but addresses exactly what is needed in a kind, gracious, undiluted, and perhaps unfamiliar way, it is a message to be taken seriously.

8. **Authentic intuition speaks in repetition.** Intuition often shows up as consistent messages, such as hearing a word or phrase, seeing it in a magazine, then passing a picture of it on a billboard. There are no coincidences, only synchronicities. Many intuitive insights appear in dreams, where our conscious minds cannot censor the messages. Intuition will pass if you do not listen as it has no enforceable interest in being heard. Additionally, exercising free will in

making choices overrides even the best intuition. However, if something shows up often for you, it is time to take notice. If you ignore an important intuitive message, it will show up again bigger and louder until you cannot miss it. (Much like the movie *Groundhog Day*, it is a do-over until you get it right!)

9. **There is a sense of "flow" opening up in other ways.** The purpose of authentic intuition is to help pull you forward in being your best. It creates space for your life to move in a dynamic, positive way. Things will start lining up easily and effortlessly. There is a new sense of open energy, ready to receive what is being attracted to you. Authentic intuition is to your life what water is to an ocean—it is an integral, changing element that creates, reinvents, and connects all parts of itself by being and "flowing." When intuition is flowing, it is likely that your life is too.

10. **Manifestation blooms around you.** We are the creators of our life experiences. Intuition is a vital tool that illuminates all that is available to us in our relationships between our inner and outer worlds. Authentic intuition helps us to distill the bigger picture into something meaningful and accessible in our everyday lives. As a conscious creation instrument, intuition helps us manifest what we need and desire; upon connecting with authentic inner wisdom, you will know the power when you see (and acknowledge) the richness of what is manifesting around you.

What to Do When You "Get" Your Intuitive Signs

This is truly the greatest place for actively participating in the positive change choices that are possible and opening in your life—it is the awareness of the messages that are meant just for you. When your intuition is authentically speaking to you, and you hear it (or see it, feel it, know it, etc.), it is the time when you get to make a choice from your full knowingness. This choice will be demonstrated through your thoughts, words, actions, behavior, and therefore your results.

It is not generally a question of right or wrong choice because each individual choice point that you make from your intuition takes you down a different path. For example, when it is a choice between eating cake or a salad, your intuition will tell you what is better for you in the moment—and it could be either one, depending on what is happening in your life! If your best choice is cake, you will have one path, and if your best choice is salad, it is simply a different path, neither being likely to hurt you in the moment. However, you must exercise free will to follow the recommendation of your intuition. Additionally, over time, if you extend your journey on each of these paths, the result will be a very different experience (and one of them likely will result in love handles!).

The most important action you can take when you are in awareness of your intuition is to acknowledge and honor it. If you suppress, avoid, or reject it, you are setting up a process by which you are not only hiding from yourself, but you become unable to trust your own inner wisdom. When that happens, you may feel indecisive, disconnected, empty, or even lost, like you do not recognize yourself and do not know how to "come home."

So what happens if you miss, or do not "get," your intuitive signs? Worse, what if you think you do not have any? In this case, relax—your intuition is always with you. It is a part of the fabric of who you are, and when you want to access that part of yourself, it is waiting for you. If it has been a while since you honored your inner guidance, you will have to relearn its language. You may have to take a little extra time and create a quiet space to slow down to the speed of your inner self, but like all your other natural body parts, trust that your inner guide is always there for you.

Learning to appreciate and act from your intuition is a process. It takes practice, patience, and presence with your own inner guidance. Slow down to be aware of your inner voice as it is expressing itself right now—it is well worth the investment.

ABOUT THE AUTHOR

Lynn Scheurell facilitates positive transformation for her clients using both linear and intuitive thinking. Her company, Creative Catalyst, is a leader in initiating dramatic change for independent professionals and decision makers. Download your own free report right now to learn "Your 6 Power Points for Personal Success—and How What You Don't Know Can Cost You Years of Hard Work!" at http://www.mycreativecatalyst.com.

47

8 Points for Ranking Your Next Company: How to Avoid the "Lots of Eggs in the Basket" Syndrome and Help Yourself Decide Between Options at the End of the Process

Judi Perkins

You have assessed your strengths and weaknesses and made a list of your past accomplishments. You have committed them to memory so that they are readily on the tip of your tongue during interviews. You have examined your previous jobs to gain insight into what is important to you and motivates you.

Good! You are starting off on the right foot. All that homework is not only necessary, but commendable because the majority of people short-cut it and go into an interview cold.

But hold it! Before you jump at every seemingly viable option, have you prioritized what you *want* in a job? The temptation is to keep your options open and scoop up everything that sounds interesting—thus putting as many eggs in your basket as possible.

Most job seekers drop the ball early by sending out résumés and just waiting for responses. Finding your perfect job takes an immense amount of thought, soul searching, preparation, and attention to detail *before* you begin contacting companies!

Eight points are essential to your job search preparation because they force you to think about the attributes of your ideal job and to what degree—if any—you are willing to compromise. Why bother with this beforehand instead of just going job hunting, seeing what is out there, and figuring it out after the interview?

- It highlights opportunities worthy of a closer look. This saves time and gives you focus. Do not spread your time and attention too thin, or you will include options that sound good but do not really meet your requirements. The result is usually a job that "works" and is sufficient. It is neither quite what you wanted nor what you expected.
- Most people go on an interview and then decide if they like the job and want to pursue it. This is backward. If you do not know what you want first, you are not likely to go after it as hard. When you have assessed beforehand what is important and have prioritized those items, then when they are presented to you, you will know if and how they fit your bigger picture.
- If you are presented with two offers, each from a different company, you are assured of making an objective decision according to your goals and values. When you have not given careful consideration to what you want in a job before beginning your search, puzzling through which offer is best can be confusing and painful. There is too much attached to the outcome of the decision, too much fear of perhaps making the "wrong" choice, and almost every factor is looked at with a somewhat biased weight as a result.

The eight factors that apply to new job opportunities follow.

Location. The job's geographical location is important, whether you are relocating or commuting. The time to discover that you do not want to leave your house at 6:30 to be at work at 8:00 is not on the second day of your new job.

Growth. This applies to the company, your movement within the company, and your knowledge. The key is knowing which factors apply to you. Your progress up the ladder does not have to hinge on the company's growth, any more than the company's growth will ensure your progress up the ladder! But if you are looking for a promotion, you will want to know if the company posts jobs internally before looking outside itself.

Are they looking for someone to pick up new challenges? Will you need to adapt your skills? Will they be grooming you for a larger role? You need to know which scenario you prefer *and* which is applicable to the job for which you are interviewing. Make sure they match.

Philosophy. If a company's most important factor is bottom line contribution at all costs—even if it means perhaps compromising the customer—and you'd prefer to give up the sale rather than sell the wrong product to the wrong person, your performance in the eyes of your employer will suffer. What is more, you will be uncomfortable and unhappy working there.

The most productive way to find out the answers to philosophical questions is to ask the hiring authority directly. Be willing to ask tough questions, especially if there appear to be inconsistencies. This is your career, remember?

Chemistry. The money is great; the commute is easy; the company is an industry leader; the company philosophy sounds ethical and compatible with yours; and you love the idea of what you will be doing. But gee, the interviewer just rubs you the wrong way. What is more, you will be reporting to the person! You cannot quite put your finger on what you dislike. Do not discount that, but do not jettison the whole opportunity because of it either.

Set up another interview (or phone conversation). Can you meet with a prospective peer in the department? If so, include questions about your potential manager.

Stability. This applies to both the company and the position. Some ideas you will want to explore follow.

- What is the position's turnover rate? If it is high, chances are very good that it is more than a coincidence. You do not want to learn about it firsthand.
- Has upper-level management changed frequently?
- How long has your boss been in his or her position?
- Was the company recently downsized? Did a larger company absorb it?
- Is it a well-established company?
- Maybe you groove to the challenges that come with a small start-up. Is there a risk that comes with the position?

Money. If there is relocation involved, know the difference in costs of living. Are you willing to take a pay cut, and how much? Most importantly, know *why* you are making that trade-off.

Be aware that the willingness to take a pay cut is met with suspicion by most hiring authorities because they fear that eventually, you will become dissatisfied and leave. Frequently, people equate salary with personal worth. Even if you do not and money is low on your priority scale, you may have a tough time convincing someone else of that.

Can You Do the Work? If you are looking to change your responsibilities slightly or to shift in your industry a little, you need to make sure that you are realistic about your ability to perform the job or that training is provided.

Will You Like the Work? Do some research. The library, the Internet, job boards, and discussion forums are all excellent places to learn if what you *think* sounds like a great new career actually *will be* a great new career.

If your new job involves a promotion, make sure you know about new responsibilities, that you will like carrying them out, and that they are within the scope of your ability to learn. Be aware that sometimes what looks like dissatisfaction with your current title or job is actually dissatisfaction with your company or career choice and vice versa.

It is far easier to know if an opportunity meets these priorities when you have given thought to them in advance. During an interview you are less likely to be swayed by factors that sound attractive but do not really meet your goals.

Before you begin interviewing, list the eight points by priority. Later, when you find yourself debating a decision, come back to your list. For any opportunity you are struggling with, assign a value of 1–10 to each point, with 10 being the best. Total the scores.

Anything over 50 is fine, as long as your higher numbers are toward the top three priority items. A score below 50 means you need to ask yourself why you are considering the job in the first place!

If you are having difficulty making a decision between two offers, the eight points are ideal for helping you choose. Examine your priorities and their scores. You might find that some factors seem to be so attractive that they overwhelm what would otherwise be a clear signal to move away from the position.

Your perfect job might land in your lap by grace and good fortune. But more likely, you will need to look for it. It is there—but to recognize it, you will need to know what it *does not* look like as well as what it *does*.

188

ABOUT THE AUTHOR

Prior to starting her firm, VisionQuest, Judi Perkins was a search consultant for 25 years in both the contingency and retained market, including a short stint in the temporary and local permanent placement markets. She has owned her own recruiting firm and successfully assisted numerous repeat clients in hiring all levels of management. She is a career expert and forum moderator with http://www.CareerCube.net. To sign up for her newsletter and learn thousands of powerful concepts to find your perfect job, go to http://www.findtheperfectjob.com.

48

The 30-Day Point A Challenge

Grant Pasay

It is not about the destination *or* the journey.

Before I go any further, I will admit that I am among the thousands who have been helped by the saying "it is not about the destination, it is about the journey." The more I personally focused on and enjoyed the journey, the more I enjoyed life as a series of learning moments, a forum for character development, and a playground for exploration.

But somewhere along the way, I began to wonder about the life-as-a-journey model. More specifically, if a journey-focused life was more fulfilling than a destination-focused life, could there be another sort of life that was even more fulfilling than a journey-focused life?

The answer is yes. There is another sort of life that is even more fulfilling than a journey-focused life.

As I said, it is not about the destination or the journey.

What is it about then? Read on to find out.

What Is So Bad about the Journey?

Those of us who have gone from life-as-a-destination to life-as-a-journey know how much better everything becomes.

With the destination we experienced fleeting satisfaction upon reaching our goal, only to moments later feel the need to chase the next peak; with the journey we can enjoy every step we take, regardless of where it is along the way.

With the destination we vainly pursued our ultimate goal while it ever receded from us like the horizon; with the journey we walk, rest, gaze back to see how far we have come, smile, and walk some more.

So what is so bad about the journey then?

It is not a matter of good or bad, but of better and best. And though life-as-a-journey is better than life-as-a-destination, there is another life model that is best of all.

The Resemblance between Journey and Destination

In fact, the more you examine the life-as-a-journey model, the more you will notice its resemblance to life-as-a-destination.

For example, have you ever felt the exhilaration of the latest leg of the journey—the insight in a new book, the high of a convention experience, the discovery of a new friend—only to later find yourself looking forward to the next insight, high, or discovery? (Sounds an awful lot like feeling the need to chase the next peak.)

Or have you ever made a real breakthrough into new territory of the journey—abundance instead of scarcity, respecting yourself, speaking your mind—only to remember all your other messed up parts that still needed to be worked on? (Sounds like having an ultimate goal recede from you like the horizon.)

Here is one way to explain such similarities between life-as-a-journey and life-as-a-destination: If the above is your experience, you are still destination focused and are simply fooling yourself into thinking that you are journey focused. After all, chasing, need, and dissatisfaction are not supposed to be part of a journey.

The Journey as Destination

Here is another way to explain such similarities between life-as-a-journey and life-as-a-destination: Being genuinely journey focused can still mean experiencing chasing, need, and dissatisfaction. True, these negative effects might be less intense than in a destination-focused life, but they are still the same.

So why does life-as-a-journey not eliminate these negative effects? Because journey is a destination.

Think about it. You are currently at Point A. Your destination is Point B. The time and distance between Point A and Point B is the journey. If you are always focused on getting to Point B, you are destination focused. And we all agree that does not make for the most enjoyable life.

On the other hand, if you are focused on the time and distance between Point A and Point B, you are journey focused. Again, we all agree this makes for a far better life than being destination focused.

But did you notice what neither of the above scenarios is focused on?

The Despised Point A

That is right. Point A.

The life-as-a-destination model obviously does not focus on Point A because it is focused on Point B.

The life-as-a-journey model can appear to be focused on Point A because it promotes experiencing the here and now; it promotes being in the moment.

But if you recall, the journey is not really about Point A, but the time and distance between Point A and Point B. After all, the essence of a journey is to be going from one place to another—to be moving from where you are to where you will be next.

Which begs the question, "What is wrong with Point A?"

"Only an Idiot Is Happy with What He Is"

The only thing wrong with Point A is that we usually do not like it.

For the destination-focused person, Point B is infinitely better than Point A: better looking, better feeling, better living.

For the journey-focused person, moving forward is infinitely better than remaining at Point A: better understanding, better awareness, better evolved.

Besides, is accepting Point A really an option? Are we not naturally inclined to learn and grow and evolve? As an acquaintance of mine wrote in an e-mail, "Only an idiot is happy with what he is."

The Wisdom of an Idiot

Putting political correctness aside for a moment, maybe we can learn from the idiot.

Imagine for a moment what it would be like to be happy with what you are. Not a single criticism. Not a single longing for reform. Not even a single ambition— just Point A.

If that does not appeal to you, you are probably focused on Point B, or at least journeying beyond Point A. How could such a life model be responsible? Are we not supposed to better ourselves? Are we not supposed to make a difference in the world?

Absolutely—if you are destination or journey focused. It comes with the territory. Yet try as you might, it never gets done. Either Point B continually recedes like the horizon, or the journey never ends—in other words, chasing, need, and dissatisfaction.

The 30-Day Point A Challenge

Accepting Point A, or simply "being," must lead to stagnation, apathy, and a wasted life. At least that is what I used to think.

What about all the negative things in myself that demanded reform? If I simply accepted myself, would not those negative things go unchecked, possibly ruining me?

And what about all the negative things in the world? If I simply accepted things as they were, if I did not try to move beyond Point A, surely things would only get worse. How could it be any other way?

Amazingly, it can be another way. But you will never know it until you take the 30-Day Point A Challenge:

1. forget Point B
2. forget the journey
3. just accept Point A.

For 30 days, forget learning, growing, and evolving. Forget being "responsible" and making a difference. Forget reform, ambition, and even goals. For 30 days, just be. Do not even wonder what the result will be (there is no way you could possibly know, even if you are sure you do).

And if after 30 days you do not prefer how you see yourself and your world, feel free to return to your previous course.

My Hope for You

I hope you find what I found: that nothing is wrong with Point A, that nothing is wrong with you, that there is nowhere to go, and that that is a good thing. Be well.

ABOUT THE AUTHOR

Grant Pasay is a person just like you who reminds himself every day to accept Point A as perfect. Grant writes, teaches, and creates music and media while enjoying life with his partner and daughter in Vancouver, Canada. To learn more about the 30-Day Point A Challenge, how to accept yourself and the world as it is, and how to create a perfect life now, visit http://www.pointAchallenge.com. To learn more about Grant, visit http://www.grantpasay.com.

49

KARMA LESSONS

Sacred Visitations:
I Remember the Pink Poodle Tragedy

Ceci Miller

At age six I learned my first lessons in karma. My first-grade boyfriend gave me a first kiss on the cheek. I got my first pair of glasses and immediately lost my first little boyfriend, whose interest in me proved shallow. I read my first books, about Dick and Jane and Spot and the others whose names also boasted a single syllable. And I took my first cake walk.

I am not sure where the phrase "it's a cake walk" began, but it might just as well have begun at the Lily B. Clayton Elementary School carnival in 1964. For it was there and then that I learned that even though one's brown cat-eye glasses have suddenly made one homely enough to cause one's little boyfriend to turn and walk the other way at lunch period, in the realm of karma a certain balance yet exists.

My brother and I raced onto the scene of the carnival and left our parents trailing behind. Our school playground of asphalt had been transformed into a diminutive township of plywood booths draped in canvas and was peppered with signs promising exotic adventures at scandalous prices: *Catch a Fish! Win a Prize!—5 cents, The Great Fatima Will Tell Your Fortune—10 cents, Make the Principal Take the Plunge—A Dollar a Dunk,* and *CAKE WALK.*

"What is the Cake Walk?" I asked, watching as people of varying heights and widths arranged themselves on a circular path painted with numbers. My mother explained that it was like musical chairs and that when the music stopped, the person standing on the winning number won a prize. Then she pointed to a table stacked with the largest collection of birthday cakes I had ever witnessed in one place.

"I'm going to do the Cake Walk!" I declared. My mother ushered me toward the extremely tall teacher presiding over this human roulette, and somberly, she handed me a slip of paper bearing a number.

I looked at the slip of paper. "What do I do with it?"

"Go and stand on that number," she said, as though this made sense.

"*Stand* on this *number*?" I asked, gazing incredulously at the tiny ticket. I could not see how standing on it was going to win me a birthday cake.

"Well, not on *that*. Find your number on the wheel, and then go stand on it."

In no time at all music was blaring, and we began to walk in a circle. I shuffled along dutifully, glancing about at the grownups and older children. When the music stopped, everyone scrambled. The tall teacher called out a number, and I looked around for the lucky soul who would soon be whooping and hollering and receiving congratulations. No one piped up. All eyes searched around the circle.

"*She's* got it!" yelled one of the grownups, pointing at my feet.

I looked down, and there it was.

A small herd of grownups urged me toward the table to make my choice.
When I presented the frosted chocolate prize to my mother, she said, "Well, how 'bout that." Scanning the grounds, she added, "What are you going to do *now*?"

"I'm going to do the Cake Walk again."

They tried to discourage my gambling fever, but I persisted, going on to become the first six-year-old in the history of the Lily B. Clayton Elementary School carnival ever to win three Cake Walks in a row. After my second, the game's towering supervisor regarded me skeptically. "I think you have enough cake. How about a toy?" she said and led me to a table piled high with garish, nonfood items.

I spotted my love immediately. It stood 12 inches high: a plastic poodle on wheels, with a leash by which to rein in the surreal pet. It was hot pink, with

196

googly eyes that rolled enthusiastically as I pulled it along. Though my mother looked chagrined at this new appendage, I could not have been more pleased.

That day, I learned that sometimes life turns inexplicably good. Despite the recent setback with my eyeglasses and my little boyfriend, I had won two cakes and a hot pink poodle by walking around in a circle and standing on a number. I had not worked hard, had not even been especially polite. On that spring day in 1964 it had simply been my moment to take the cake.

Losing my first boyfriend and winning the Cake Walk were apt microcosms of every wrong and right that came thereafter. Years of good and bad experiences lined up one after the other in succession, until one day an entirely different sort of teacher appeared. Taller and wiser than any teacher I had met before, my meditation teacher said that the pairs of opposites were a trap. Back and forth, good and bad, up and down, yes and no, right and wrong, loss and gain, the mind and emotions buffeted in an endless game of ping-pong. True satisfaction, this great teacher said, allows you to rise above the back-and-forth of karma. True satisfaction comes only by knowing the Divine. And to know that, she said, you must come to know your deepest self.

How do you come to know your deepest self? Practice watching your life for clues. As you watch your life, remember that no matter what is happening right now, something else ("good" or "bad") will surely follow in time. The outer world is in a state of constant change, yet the true self never wavers. You come to know that self by watching your own awareness. As you watch your breath going in and out, as you watch thoughts of all kinds flowing through your mind, remember that pleasure and pain are two sides of the same coin: One always follows the other. This keeps you from getting too attached, from trying to hang on to (or push away) whatever is happening in your life. The idea is to remind yourself again and again, until your experience comes to rest in the self, that that awareness remains unconcerned with whether you win the cake or not!

Three weeks later, my mother, brother, and I drove to the doctor's for a checkup. In our rush to leave the pink plastic poodle was left behind in the waiting room, its white leash dangling. Halfway home, I discovered it was missing, but my mother refused to go back for it. For a long time I pined after my pet—much more pitifully, in fact, than I had pined for my first-grade boyfriend. If only things had turned out differently! If only I had noticed my poodle as we left the doctor's . . . if only my mother had driven back. . . . But such are the ways of karma. Easy come, easy go.

ABOUT THE AUTHOR

Ceci Miller is a longtime student of meditation and the author of *Sacred Visitations: Gifts of Grace that Transform the Heart and Awaken the Soul*. Ceci has edited and coauthored numerous books and is the author of two illustrated books on meditation for children. To attend Ceci's workshops exploring the 5 Steps of Sacred Awareness, to learn about the *Sacred Visitations* AudioCourse, and to hear interviews with people about their mystical experiences on the *Sacred Visitations* podcast in "Ceci's Journal," please visit http://www.SacredVisitations.com.

50

Learning through Life's Knowledge Diamonds

Steve Cavaleri

"Experience is the best teacher" may be a time-tested proverb, but in reality, learning from life's experiences is not always as simple as the conventional wisdom suggests. We each learn different lessons from life's experiences based on the knowledge we use for making sense of things that happen. While knowledge is important to us, it is not always reliable. All knowledge is limited and limits us. Yet we often ignore the flaws or narrowness of the knowledge that we have come to habitually rely upon. It is often only in retrospect that we discover that our knowledge is more limited or imperfect than we ever imagined it to be. How can we create better-quality knowledge that can really be counted on to guide us when we need it most? One answer is to view experience freshly through the lens of life's knowledge diamonds.

Nikki's Personal Journey

Let us consider how Nikki improved the knowledge in her life. After nearly 15 years of working for large insurance companies, she left that business behind to start a small business of her own. Her early success in the new business was driven by her work ethic, people skills, and buoyant optimism. Her "can do anything" attitude grew out of her childhood experience of growing up on the family's farm on the northern plains of America's heartland. By the time she reached age 40, Nikki found herself working ever harder to keep her business afloat. Feeling more stressed than ever, in a crumbling marriage, chronically tired, and nearly 25 percent overweight, Nikki knew that it was time to reevaluate her life. By the winter of 2002, Nikki faced a crisis. She developed a severe case of pneumonia and landed in the hospital. Her physician warned her that next time could be much worse. Her childhood spent on the family farm taught her the importance of relying on personal grit and determination to defeat hard times.

Did she reach the limits of her simple wisdom gained on the farm and growing up on the prairie? As she lay in bed recovering from pneumonia, Nikki discovered that *trusted knowledge* is not the same as perfect knowledge.

Paying Attention to Life's Knowledge Diamonds

What are the secrets to creating personal knowledge diamonds that will effectively guide us toward the lives we most truly desire? If we look at the diamonds of our lives' knowledge, we find that the many sides are shaped by the meaning we have given to the lessons of our lives' experiences. There is no form of knowledge that is as powerful as our own *life knowledge*. Knowledge supports our beliefs about which rules of action will potentially be most effective in guiding us in various life situations to achieve the results we most truly desire. It helps us know which actions have worked well at getting the sort of results we want in the same or similar situations. As opposed to external knowledge about how the world works, facts, or data, life knowledge focuses on understanding what has worked for you personally to get the results you seek. How can we create the high-quality life knowledge that will serve us well?

If we follow seven simple steps, each of which will help clarify one side of the diamond prism, we can move ever closer to seeing life's challenges and opportunities with the clarity that comes with being informed by the lessons captured in life knowledge. Let's look at the seven sides of the knowledge diamond.

Side 1: Continuously improve the quality of your beliefs about how things work in your life. Let life's experiences provide you with the raw material to create richer, more elegant stories and explanations for how things work in your life. Experiment with designing new theories about what might possibly work in the future, and create an explanation for why it might possibly work.

Side 2: Personal Life Knowledge is the most powerful type of knowledge. Focus your own knowledge-building efforts on being attentive to what actions tend to work reliably in producing the results you value most.

Side 3: When in doubt, look for evidence of success in the lives of others. If you have clearly lost confidence in the ability of your own knowledge to get the job done, then inquire into what has worked for others. Take a lesson from their success and discover how their actions differ from your planned actions.

Side 4: Capture the lessons of what has or has not worked by making a deposit into your own knowledge bank. Formalize your evaluation of what works best by asking the question "do I consider this little experiment with this aspect of my life a success?"

Side 5: When you discover something that works well, ask yourself why it works. More important, what does this recent success mean about how things work in general? Unless you allow surprises or unexpected results to inform your beliefs about what is possible, the experience is wasted.

Side 6: Use your best reasoning to apply your knowledge to new situations. The true value of knowledge is found in your ability to apply it to situations where you can leverage it to the greatest extent. Knowledge tells you how to act in certain situations, so if you can effectively recognize how certain knowledge applies in a given situation, you can reason how to use it to get the results you want.

Side 7: Create your best knowledge by actively learning from your experiences. Creating knowledge requires that you invest time into it. Time devoted to reflection, to imagining new explanations of what is or is not possible, and to experimenting with new approaches are all good investments in your own success.

Nikki's New Knowledge

What about Nikki? After a long period of self-reflection, she discovered that she wanted a simpler life that was based on more tangible, everyday experiences of being happy. Unfortunately, like most knowledge, the lessons Nikki had learned earlier in life were limited—her knowledge was narrower than she needed it to be. She needed to find a new and improved sort of knowledge that would help her to see her life in a new light.

Her illness and marital difficulties taught her that her old habitual knowledge led her to ignore many important aspects of her life, such as health and feeling good each day. Nikki decided to take control of her life's experiences. She sold her business and took a routine 9 to 5 job in government services—with fewer pressures. She also began a rigorous exercise routine, worked as a volunteer, and learned to savor the simple pleasures in her life. She lost the extra pounds, smiles more, has a healthy glow, and is now happily married again. Nikki discovered that she had been only paying attention to a small portion of the knowledge available to her. Once she began looking at life through more sides of her personal knowledge diamonds, she became capable of envisioning a much more exciting future that compelled her to transform her life. Can you find the knowledge diamonds in your life?

ABOUT THE AUTHOR

Steven Cavaleri is president and CEO of the Pragmatic Knowledge Institute. He has written five books, including *Inside Knowledge* and *Knowledge Leadership*. A former visiting scholar at MIT, Dr. Cavaleri has developed a simple yet effective way to help people learn to improve the quality of their lives. The Pragmatic Knowledge Institute offers training and franchising for executive coaches and corporate trainers. Steven has over 25 years of experience as a professor and consultant with such well-known companies as Dow-Jones, IBM, and Stanley Tools. For more details on putting knowledge to work in your life, go to http://myownknowledge.com.

51

Enrich Your Life

Doni Luckett

Every once in a while, we hear a sports hero, celebrity, or person of prominence decry: "I am not a role model." It is an interesting statement because role models, like heroes and mentors, often are not labels we give to ourselves—they are badges of honor given to us by people who find us deserving.

The awe, the inspiration, the hope, and even the joy we bestow just by being ourselves leads people to look up to us, emulate us, and ultimately assign us the status of a role model. A role model is a leader, perhaps a shy, reluctant, or clandestine leader, but a leader nonetheless.

I recently pondered these thoughts in addressing 500 attendees at the Women in Leadership breakfast. One dictionary definition of leader is "one who is in charge or in command of others." Whether that command comes from respect of a special talent, a unique skill, or physical or mental prowess, it evokes emotion from those who come into contact with that talent, skill, or prowess. And as long as you are the beholder of such command, you are a leader—on purpose, or by accident.

Being "at the top of your game," striving to "be the best," or "pursuing the ultimate" in a chosen field of endeavor will garner followers. It may be uncomfortable, unwanted, scary, or daunting, but often being a leader—or a role model—is not just your choice. When you inspire others, they will continue to look to you for inspiration. And when you are an inspiration, you are a role model.

Too often we think of role models as people in specific roles—as in a teacher, politician, or policeman. Positions such as these bear the torch of being "pillars of society," the actions of whom our children should watch and follow. But title alone is not enough to assume leadership; just one look at recent headlines— teacher misconduct with students, broken political promises or abuse of public trust—shatters our traditional picture of the role model.

The bottom line is that each of us is a role model, a leader to someone—whether it is our children, coworkers, subordinates, or even if we are the clerk whose smile changes someone's day. Each of us can model attitudes to emulate, carry out actions that inspire, or be a presence to admire. Every day can be the day you change someone's life. So whether it is a role you have intended or one you have stumbled into, make the most of it for yourself and those who look to you for direction.

Embrace it. Just as giving yourself the title of role model does not mean people choose you to be one, likewise purporting "not to be" one can be a futile course of action. When you strive to be the best—whether you have conquered challenges, overcome adversity, elevated yourself to the top of your field, or chosen to spread positivity in everyday life—people will take notice, and many will admire you for it. Instead of absolving responsibility for your actions, take pride in who you are and what you have become.

Be yourself. Often it seems those wanting to dismiss the title of role model feel it will limit what they can do, who they can be. Being a leader does not make you superhuman, devoid of faults and complex intricacies; rather the more human you are, the more people can relate to you and what you bring to the table. Part of the problem with the title "role model" just may be the expectation that accompanies it—expectations we ourselves see as part of the role or that others attach to the title. Remember, the very fact that you are *you* is much of why you are considered a role model. If everyone were the same, whom would we emulate? What would make us strive to be better?

Speak your truth. By nature, leaders defy expectations. Many of us allow ourselves to fall into the rut of expectation, modeling the path of what we *think* we should follow, rather than what we know to be true in our hearts. Dare to defy convention—even if that convention is a limit placed upon yourself in your own mind. Strive every day to speak your truth, choose to confront the fear that chains you to mediocrity, and truly forge a path to greatness.

When someone in your presence gives you that rare glimpse of recognition—the innate knowledge that your skill, your actions, or your prowess have gone beyond the ordinary to the impressive—rise to the occasion. Instead of backing down with a resolution of "I am not a role model," accept the challenge. Realize that you have a gift—a gift that can inspire others to greatness. . . .

ABOUT THE AUTHOR

Lifestyle expert Doni Luckett is chief executive of Divine Basics, a Colorado-based company that provides products, services, and information for women to connect with themselves and those most important in their lives. A frequent contributor to national media, including television, magazines, radio, and newspapers, Luckett's "Enriched Life" column can be read weekly in the *Denver Post* Sunday Style section. Each month, millions receive her advice on how to reduce stress, achieve goals, and enrich their lives. Divine Basics' award-winning products are distributed through thousands of stores in 15 countries and online. Connect with her at http://www.divine-basics.com, or e-mail enrichedlife@divine-basics.com.

52

Making the Connection: Mind, Body, Spirit

Dorothy M. Neddermeyer

Did you know that when you experience pain, either physically or mentally—any pain—it is your body's way of communicating with you? Have you ever considered that the origin of this pain may not be connected to the specific part of your body experiencing the pain? Have you ever wondered if the origin of the pain may be connected to another time or experience in your life that you have forgotten?

Through pain, your body is working to get your attention. The key is to begin to listen.

Your body is resilient and has an incredible capacity to handle stress and emotional issues—it can absorb a lot. But is it necessary to put your body through all this emotional effort on a regular basis? Is it worth it? When you deny your emotional issues or ignore the fact that your body is stressed out; sooner or later, your body breaks down, and you experience the pain—diagnosed as migraine headaches, MS, lupus, fibromyalgia, chronic fatigue, cancer, diabetes, TMJ, PMS, and the list goes on.

You do not need to play macho with your body, doing the "stiff upper lip" method—"I'm tough, I can take it," "I can handle anything," or "I'm responsible for everyone else" routine. Whether you pretend you are okay or not, over a period of time, your body just breaks down. You can give your body a break by beginning to resolve those emotional issues that are hurting you.

When you experience a pain in your neck, make the connection. Your neck is where your power to speak resides—the throat chakra. The question is, are you expressing your truth? Your throat chakra is connected to your feet. What is going on in your life that you cannot stand, thus causing you to give yourself a pain in the neck? Who is being a pain in the neck? If you are not addressing your truth, you will get stuck or blocked in life, and you will not move forward productively. You may think you are moving forward every day, but nonetheless, you may be stuck on a particular issue and not really moving forward. Do you have periods when everything you want to accomplish seems like you are walking up a steep hill or in molasses, even though what you want to accomplish is nothing new and you have done it a hundred times? Ask yourself, "Do I want to continue this project, or did I say yes because I don't want to say no?" What is your truth? What do you want? State this clearly and precisely.

Knee pain and other knee problems originate in the shoulders. Shoulders represent our ability to carry our experiences in life joyously. We make life a burden by our attitude—taking on responsibility that does not belong to us. If you feel responsible for everyone in your life, that is a lot of weight and molecules to shoulder. With that much weight, no wonder your knees are hurting in their effort to hold up all those people. Why have surgery to repair or replace your knees, when you can eliminate the burden from your knees—and shoulders—and free yourself of the excess weight? By having surgery, you will simply continue to create the same problem and be back to the same predicament in a year or two.

Sinusitis, colds, respiratory issues, earaches, and asthma are connected to your first chakra, which holds all your belief systems and your relationships, especially your family—irritation to one person, someone close.

Sinus medicine cannot clear your first chakra of emotional issues lodged in your sinus cavities. Only you have the power to resolve those for yourself. Herbal supplements can support your immune system so it can do its job, but you still need to clear the emotional issues to completely eliminate sinus issues. You need to uncover the reason for the irritation.

Your jaws are connected to your generative chakra—your hips. The consciousness of TMJ is directly related to the misalignment of this chakra and your creativity. So if you are experiencing TMJ or any jaw misalignment, listen to your truth: Who or what are you angry at? Who or what do you resent? Do you have a desire to have revenge? What are you creating? Are you clenching your jaws or grinding your teeth, thus blocking yourself from creating a more fulfilling life?

These are merely a few of the many ways our bodies communicate to us that we need to change something. From this point forward, when your body has pain, ask your body, "What is the pain about?" Pay attention to the response. For example, close your eyes, take a deep breath, and blow out the breath with a big whoosh. Ask yourself, "Why do I have a pain in my neck?" If the thought comes to you that you did something you are not comfortable doing, pay attention to that thought. Expand on that thought. Maybe you said yes to something you did not want to do. Maybe you talked yourself into doing something because someone else did it. Ask yourself many questions. If your response leads you to say that you want something, notice if the pain you were experiencing has subsided or is completely gone. If the pain has subsided or is completely gone, you can be certain you have the right answer. If not, continue to explore and ask the question, what is the pain about? Initially, this process may take several sessions over a few days, before you are certain of the answer. After you are accustomed to using this technique, you will be certain of the answer on the first or second exploration.

Many people want guidance in perfecting this technique and seek professional help. Mind, body, and spirit healing is the most effective modality in facilitating or teaching this process.

ABOUT THE AUTHOR

Dorothy M. Neddermeyer, PhD, author, international speaker, and inspirational leader, specializes in mind, body, and spirit healing and physical/sexual abuse prevention and recovery. Dr. Neddermeyer empowers people to view life's challenges as an opportunity for personal or professional growth and spiritual awakening. Visit her Web site at http://www.drdorothy.net.

53

Lessons from Legacy: Life by Design

Melissa Galt

Creating a Unique and Original Life

In order to lead an original and unique life, we do have to think outside the box and create our own rules and guidelines for accomplishment. The best among us always have done so. It is our privilege to observe and learn from the lessons these pioneers can teach us.

My great grandfather, the renowned American architect Frank Lloyd Wright, left just such a legacy. He never played by the rules but instead forged his own path and, despite many naysayers, created architecture well ahead of its time. His designs still serve as an inspiration today. Many said he could not do what he ultimately did. They said it would not work, would not stand the test of time, and would collapse. While many of his projects have undergone extensive renovation, the innovative concepts presented in such properties as Fallingwater and the S. C. Johnson Wax building are timeless and blazed a trail of originality.

Great grandfather was, at the same time, perpetually broke, often accepting bailouts from clients and indulging in his passion for collecting art rather than paying his debtors. His fondest saying was "Give me the luxuries of life, and I will gladly do without the necessities." Of course, he did not do without necessities, but what he found essential was far beyond what most people consider necessary. He lived a life apart and beyond his peers and even those closest to him. He lived a life of his own design.

What trail would you blaze if you made your own rules? What necessities would you give up to have the luxuries you most desire?

Making the Best Choices

We are each the sum total of the choices we have made. If we want a new reality, we have to make new choices. After all, the very definition of insanity is to do the same thing repeatedly and expect a different result. When we change our actions, we change our results.

A perfect case in point is my godmother, famed Hollywood costumer Edith Head. At age 30 she was teaching French at an all-girls' school in California, and because she had studied a semester abroad in Europe, the school assumed she could also teach art. She actually could not draw more than stick figures, but she took on the task nevertheless. While looking in the paper one day, she saw a contest for drawing costumes for one of the major movie studios.

She wanted a change in career and boldly borrowed some of her students' sketches and entered the contest. She won! When she showed up on the first day and was asked to draw, she was found out, but her courage and presumption so captivated the costume designer that he took her on. The rest is history, including eight Oscars for costume design over a 50-year career. She lived a life of her own design.

What have you not pursued because you did not have the skill set or the connections? Can you learn the necessary skills? Who can help you?

Living from the Heart

Life is in the living, not in the stuff. Stuff, more often than not, simply weighs us down and stands in our way. In order to move forward, to continue growing and changing, we must let things go. Those elements we keep with us must serve as inspiration and memories, not as baggage. What you bring forward is up to you.

My mother, Anne Baxter, was an Academy Award–winning actress. To me, she was a single, working parent, too often gone on location and on tour. But she taught my two sisters and me valuable lessons. She knew from age seven that she wanted to act and pursued it with a single-mindedness that few of us possess for anything in our lives. At the same time she managed to write an autobiography about her life with my father, and she was in the middle of a second one about her life growing up when she died. Mother lived each and every moment with passion, vigor, and commitment to give her best. She challenged us to do the same and instilled the values I describe here. She lived her life by her own design.

When Mother passed, over 20 years ago now, we each had only a file folder of mementos that she had kept. This was such a gift as opposed to the stockpiling that I see so often with clients. They keep hordes of baby clothes, tarnished bronzed baby shoes, faded elementary school artwork projects, broken trophies from days gone by, and too much more. Mother saved the best, the things that really counted to her, and hence they mattered to us. What better gift could there be? The most significant legacy she left was the memories of times spent together, not the *stuff* left behind. When you live from your heart and your mind, not by your hand and your purse, you will truly know that it is connections and relationships that define us, not our possessions. He who dies with the most toys still dies.

What stuff are you hoarding? How is it holding you back?

ABOUT THE AUTHOR

Melissa Galt is a renowned designer, national speaker, coach, and author. She entertains, energizes, and empowers audiences nationwide with keynotes and seminars on Designing Your Signature Life; Living the Life You Deserve; No Excuses Decorating; Change Your Interiors, Change Your Life; and 3 Steps to Guilt-Free Living. Sign up for your free subscription to "Design Destinations," her monthly e-zine loaded with how-to formulas for designing your best life now, and regular teleclasses to assist you in learning to make each day your signature life at http://www.melissagalt.com.

54

What's on Your To-Do List?

Paul Keetch

Do you have a to-do list?

I am not talking about a day-to-day list of tasks that need to be accomplished, although having one can certainly help you be more productive and give you the sense of satisfaction that comes when you can cross something *off* that list. No, I am referring to a bigger list—a dream list. A "can you imagine" or "what if" list.

Your big dream list, or Top 101 list, or whatever you want to call it, is the list of things you would like to accomplish in your lifetime. It can consist of small or big items; personal or professional; health based or success centered. It is an evolving, dynamic list of all those things that you will do "someday." I use mine for inspiration and to keep me grounded, especially when life gets a little crazier than I might ordinarily like.

So what does this list look like? And how do you go about creating one?

There is no right way to create your list. It is, after all, *your* list. But I do have some suggestions to get you started.

First, do not think too hard about it. Tell your inner critic to simply be quiet for a while. Tell it a little white lie, if you need to, and pretend it is all just for fun. After all, your dreams *are* all "just for fun."

Give yourself 20 or 30 minutes in a quiet place where you will not be disturbed, and get several blank sheets of paper to write on. If you have some music that always inspires you, put that on as well. Tell your family that you are not to be disturbed while you are working, and make sure you hold them to it. They will survive without you, for just a little while.

The next step is to actually start writing down ideas. If you want to create some headers under which to list your goals, go right ahead. In case you need help getting started, here are the six categories I use for personal goal setting:

1. physical health and wellness
2. education and learning
3. family and home
4. financial and career/business
5. spiritual/ethical
6. friends and community.

Or you might just make a big, long list full of all of the things you want to do in your life.

Remember: Do not edit yourself as you go, no matter how much your mind may want to. Anytime you start to hear your inner critic saying things like "that'll never happen" or "you're going to do that?" just smile, say "thanks for your input," then keep going.

Start with the biggest, most daring and seemingly impossible dreams you can think of. Think back to a time in your life when you did not feel the pressures of day-to-day responsibilities. What did you dream of doing "when you grew up"?

Do you dream of climbing Mount Everest? Put it on the list! What about learning to play the piano or speak another language? Write it down! Maybe you have always wanted to travel to Africa and work in a small village, helping the locals learn to farm. Make note of it! The point here is to write down anything you have ever wanted to do in your life—anything that you may have thought, hey, that would be cool to try.

There are no right or wrong answers here. It is *your* list. Taking the dog for a walk is *not* a dream, unless, of course, you do not have a dog and really want one.

Do you want to own your own successful business? Become a millionaire and retire in the Caribbean? Travel to distant lands and write a book about the cultures you encounter? Put them all on your list.

Spend 20 to 30 minutes doing this, and then post your list in a place where you will see it on a regular basis. The idea is to get into the energy of your dreams and remind yourself daily that there is a bigger world out there—even if you are already living a big life, you can always go bigger.

For some people, posting their dream list in a public place may not seem like a great idea, especially if family or friends are unsupportive. Don't let those "dream stealers" tell you that it is not possible or that you are just dreaming. Of course you are "just" dreaming—that is the whole point! Find someone with whom you can share your list, someone who will be supportive of your dreams and aspirations and who will encourage you to go after them.

If you can, post your dream list on the refrigerator door or somewhere else where you will see it regularly. Otherwise, find a more personal place—a file on your computer that you can open each day and spend five minutes looking at, immersing yourself in the essence of it.

You may not get to 101 items on your list in the first try—it is tough to start dreaming that big if you are not in the habit of it. But you can add to your list on a regular basis. And as you review your list each day, try to find ones that you can start to work toward. Do you want to fly in a glider? If so, find a picture of a glider on the Internet and make it the desktop background on your computer. Research local gliding or soaring outfits and find out what it would cost. Then create a savings account, and whenever you have 5, 10, or 100 extra dollars, put it in there. If you bank online, you may be able to name your account after your dream. How great would it feel to be able to put money into your "Glider Fund" each month, even if was only an extra five dollars?

Make it a priority to go after at least one goal each year, and although you are probably going to start small, do not be afraid to go after the bigger ones too. I personally have several accounts set up that I contribute to each month. There is the little one that I try to use each month or every other month. Then there is the big one—the one that says "Tibet/Nepal" on it. Am I going to get there this year? Maybe and maybe not. But every time I put money into that account and every time I get my interest report at the end of each month, I see that dream getting just a little closer.

I used to think Mount Everest looked big from where I live, but it is getting bigger every day. And one of these days, I will be standing at base camp staring up at the world's tallest mountain.

When I do, I will be thinking of all of you, moving closer—inch by inch—to your personal vision of a great life.

ABOUT THE AUTHOR

A writer, personal coach, and success cartographer, Paul Keetch has dedicated himself to assisting others to uncover their hidden genius and live a life of true happiness and success. He strives daily to exemplify his credo: "A man with nothing to hide hides nothing." Download a free bonus at http://www.PaulKeetch.com/101.

55

Breadcrumb Trails to
Create the Life of Your Dreams

Dolores Arste

To find your passion in life requires that you follow that path. The Universe will present the trail, you need only look for it and follow it. Wherever you are, you will find the forks in the road. One will take you toward your goal. The other will take you back to where you are.

In 1965, I found a bread crumb trail that took the form of matchbook cover with the words "become a keypunch operator." I had had no idea that those simple words would take me on an adventure that started at the beginning of the computer age.

The trail that leads you back to what you have always done seems like the safe way to go. It is familiar, comfortable. It does not force you to grow.

To live your passion, you must grow beyond what you thought was possible. The trail will be there. For each step you take, ask yourself if it will take you toward your goal or away. The trick of all this is to look for the smallest crumb: the slightest inkling that this might be toward what you are after.

At other times, perhaps we do not know where we are going. Nothing seems exciting anymore. We have done it all. We have been everywhere. And still, there is that offering of a trail that will stretch your imagination. We need only keep our eyes open and take that risk to take one baby step toward the unknown.

It is also important to remember that you can always turn back. You can always change your mind. As I was driving home from the last day at my last assignment, at just a half-mile from home, I received the call that offered the perfect job that would keep me where I was. It would keep me comfortable. But I had decided that it was time to move on. It was time to create anew. To share with others what I had learned about this bread crumb trail. We saw it in the *Wizard of OZ*. The road was full of adventure. Full of scary things, too. And still it always led home. All you have to do is think it, and the trail will open before you.

Before you can take that first step down a new road to change where you are headed and to follow the new trail that lies before you, it is important to take a look at where you have been and what is important in the *now*. You will need to have a dream or a twinkle of a thought in your mind about how it might be. It is this that will allow the bread crumbs to appear.

What strengths have you accumulated along the path of your life so far? What is yours to keep, no matter which road you follow? What have you learned that can allow you to see where the next step will be? Start by making a list of the things that you love and love doing. What do you love that you want to include in each and every day? For me, it is the horses. The horses are part of every decision I make. When I spend all day on the back of a horse or with people who love horses, I am in heaven. Nothing is missing. For you, it does not matter what you choose, as long as it is something you long to do and have enough passion to do it full time.

Once you have decided on the dream, it is time to spend time with those who are a match with what you envision. By surrounding yourself with people for whom the bread crumb trail has turned into a superhighway, the path will begin to open up. So take a good, hard look at those with whom you surround yourself. Determine if they vibrate in harmony with your desire. Those that are in harmony will become your best support network. Do you now know people who care about what you are passionate about? If not, now is the time to go looking for them. Find out where they hang out. Find out what they do in their spare time.

Only you can say no to anything. And only you can say yes. Start to say yes to every opportunity that comes along that may even drop one crumb on the new trail. Many times, we want to be fully prepared before we take a step, and so we never take a first step. Trust that if you do not know, someone does. Trust that you can find the way one bread crumb at a time.

The bread crumbs will show up based entirely on how we think. As long as we think "someday" or "when" or "if," the trail will always lead to where you are thinking: right back to where you are. You must begin to be the person that has reached her dream. Feel it every day. Ask yourself if each step you take will create the possibility of a step toward that which you want to see, even if it is as small a decision of whether to spend your last dollar on a candy bar or a lottery ticket. That candy bar may feel good in the moment, but it is impossible for it to take you down the trail. At least the lottery ticket holds the possibility! The world we choose to live in arranges itself in a most peculiar way. Many people do not see that they must dream and believe it is coming before the road will begin to open.

Many scientists are beginning to see that the physical world is one large sea of energy that flashes into and out of being in a fraction of a second, over and over again. Nothing is solid. And so it is with the bread crumb trail. The "now you see it, now you don't" is based entirely on how you are thinking and dreaming in each and every moment. Roads appear and disappear in the blink of a thought. This is the way the world works. It is all yours to create the bread crumb trail to where ever your dreams can take you. Stay focused on the trail of desire, and the road will open step by step in front of you. Be brave, take one step and then another, and pretty soon, you will be speeding down a trail that can only take you where you want to go.

Stop, Look, Listen

Stop. The first step to finding the bread crumb trail is to create the desire. To know, to feel what it is that you would like is critical for the trail to appear. Without a clear vision of where you want to go, you are just feeding the birds. Think about how many of us just feed the birds. We look to others to lead us to where we want to go, but others can only show you the way to where they have chosen to go. We never really believe that we have the power to create for ourselves. Do not be afraid to voice your wildest desire right now. Stop; just say it even if you think no one is listening.

Look. Now begin to look for the signposts that will lead you to the trail. They may be small at first. Really, smaller is better because if we were to see the huge highway to where we want to go, we may never get past the ramp. We might not believe that could possibly be our road. By keeping your desire in the forefront of your mind all the time, you will know at each step if this will take you toward where you want to go. Focus each moment on the crumbs that lead you. Imagine the possibilities, and more crumbs will appear.

Listen. Listen to the words of those around you. Begin to pay attention to their talk. Do their thoughts expressed to you play on your doubts? Do not listen to them. Find those that say you are wonderful. Find those who say wow when you tell them your dreams.

You do not have to be afraid. There is always a step you can take that is small enough to stay comfortable and still be on the path to where you want to go.

My successful career enabled me to follow my passion with animals. With horses always in my life, fate saw fit to send me a very special one in the person of Cadbury. Cadbury was the first son of my prized stallion and precious mare Cherry.

Cadbury was born on my farm and was different from most horses right from the start. He was independent and athletic and bold on the outside but frightened on the inside. Not all horses are born with the same, shall we say, ability to have a conversation with a human. This thought also applies to people in that not all people are equipped with the same skills to have a conversation with each other or with an equine. At the beginning of every new relationship we all bring what we bring—our perceptions, our prejudices, our stereotypes, our fears, and of course, our agendas and egos.

By tapping into my emotions and the fear that was generated by this horse and through the methods of releasing fear, I learned to put the experience of dealing with a difficult animal to work for me and my coaching clients with a unique method of turning off the fear. Baby steps. There is always a baby step. You have just to take one step. Otherwise, the birds will all get the bread crumbs, and you will be left standing where you are now.

ABOUT THE AUTHOR

Dolores, now CEO of Zen Guidance (http://www.zenguidance.com), has been following the bread crumb trails that the Universe has left for her. After a long career in data processing and the Web, she has embarked on a path of bringing what she has learned to as many people as she can touch. Dolores's coaching philosophy is that coaching provides powerful energetic support and extremely effective tools for the individual who is ready to make the life changes he wants. For these changes to happen, coaching must work at a holistic level that integrates thoughts, feelings, words, and actions.

56

LIVING SIMPLY

A Journey across the Cow Pasture? How Does That Relate to Life?

Dan Ohler

Life is an interesting game that we play.

Life is a chunk of time between when we are born and when we die. Everyone that I know goes through it. Most of us do not consciously know how long this whole process will last.

However, when we look at the smaller pieces of it, we know that each moment is gone almost the instant it is begun, and we cannot relive a moment. How, then, can we pack each moment full of wondrous experiences so that when we mount our white stallions and ride out into the sunset for that last time, we can look back on life and say, "Boy, Howdy, that was one hell of a ride!"

I am a farm boy. When I ponder deep stuff like this, I find myself looking to nature for metaphors and guidance. I do not mean an in-depth scholarly study of the harmonious pulse of our seasons and the interdependent interactions between the various flora and fauna in the microcosm. That is beyond me.

I see life as if it were much simpler, like a walk across the cow pasture from one point to another. I look for ways to make the journey challenging, satisfying, and fun.

Here are a couple approaches to life. Which one works for you?

Common Thinking: Goal Setting Leads to Success

A highly prescribed common practice is to set goals—personal and business goals. These goals are specific, measurable, and tangible achievements or acquisitions attained in a predetermined period of time. We are encouraged to set big goals, requiring us to stretch the envelope of our abilities. We set these whopper goals and convince ourselves that we are going to be really happy when we get there.

My experience with this process is that it is similar to putting on a set of blinders. We see only the goal of getting to the top of the high hill on the far side of the cow pasture. Our line of sight is focused and locked on to that lofty spot, but unfortunately, because of the blinders, we do not see the beautiful wildflowers and the spectacular view of the river to the left of us, our families and friends who are playing games to the right of us, the muck-filled holes, prickly brambles and briers, angry bulls, and fresh cow pies directly in front of us.

We spend our time struggling, fighting, and sacrificing to reach our goals in record time. We are scratched, bruised, and torn, covered with pungent, digested grass from nose to toes. We look back to see a much easier path, lined with people who were there to help us. And we think, "Why didn't someone tell me there was a better way?" or "Whose fault is this?" We feel a bit disheartened, disappointed, and maybe even angry. "This was a stupid goal. There must be more."

We look into the distance and see a higher, bigger hill farther off in the distance, with more trees, more sunshine, more view, and a pot of gold at the end of the rainbow. We say to ourselves, "Boy, am I going to be happy when I get there." We lock our sights onto that far distant hill, and off we go again, all by ourselves. We keep achieving our goals, being successful, but are we happy?

Uncommon Thinking: Meandering with Purpose

I'd rather look at this life trip as meandering through the pasture with purpose. The journey is about creating worthwhile and valuable experiences for ourselves and others. It is about creating happiness in every step on the way to the goal.

I agree that goals in the future are important. We need direction. I also know that the process along the way is what gives life zest and gitty-up-and-go.

When we consciously take the blinders off and look around us, life can become much broader, rewarding, and exhilarating. We invest time to smell the flowers, relax and savor the sunset, build healthy, loving relationships, and nurture a lost puppy.

We ask for help along the way and discover that when we choose to work together with others, far better outcomes are in store for all. We learn to build bridges over the muck holes and fences that will guide and aid others who follow in our footsteps. We develop trusting relationships with the bulls so they don't feel as if they are threatened by our presence. We walk briskly but carefully to avoid getting stuck in the B.S. We use the B.S. to make fertilizer, rather than to complain that our lives stink. We take ownership for our choices and our outcomes. We celebrate our successes and search for the lessons in our mistakes.

We eventually arrive at our destination, feeling satisfied, proud, and elated. Yahoo!

The Life Challenge (If You Choose to Accept)

- **Set goals that are congruent with the moment-to-moment experiences you want to create in your life.** The daily process is just as important as the goal in the future.
- **Be flexible and adaptable.** Things change. Be willing to adjust your course in order to keep the process challenging and enjoyable. Things may change to the point where your initial goal is not inspiring to you. Re-set the goal with another that fills your heart with passion.
- **Focus on relationships.** The relationships with self and others are the reason and the means to achieving the goal. Effective relationships tie together meaningful life and successful life—they are about creating balance.
- **Be accountable.** Take ownership for all of your outcomes—the ones you like and the ones you do not. Consciously or unconsciously, you have made choices that have put you exactly where you are. Accept that without blame. Avoid your own B.S.
- **Celebrate successes.** Recognize yourself for your abilities, passions, and accomplishments—big and small. Recognize others for their contributions, guidance, and support.

- **Learn from mistakes.** Failure is an event, not a person. Within every failure is the seed for a greater success. Even if it seems difficult or uncomfortable, search for the lessons.
- **Have fun!** Life is a game, and games are meant to be fun.

Life. The moments come and the moments go. Each moment is an opportunity to choose "new" lightness, love, and laughter or to drag forward "old" hurts, heartache, and dis-ease. When you look at it that way, it seems like a simple choice.

In my life I have tainted too many of my moments with stale memories of the past, struggling for material goals, neglecting my relationships, and blaming others. I do not choose to do that anymore.

What about you?

I double-dog dare you to accept my challenge. Stand tall, be proud, and venture forth on the journey across the cow pasture of life. Keep one eye on the prize and the other consciously mindful of your relationships and surroundings. Fill each fleeting moment with proceeding, exceeding, and succeeding.

Your boots are at the door. Gitty-up!

ABOUT THE AUTHOR

Dan Ohler is a speaker, coach, and author, and he is Thinkin' Outside the Barn! Dan is a country boy based near Edmonton, Alberta, Canada. His keynotes, workshops, and comedy presentations have a unique, grassroots flair. Through his insights and humor, Dan encourages you to learn to apply the basics of human psychology—timeless, natural laws that create life-long, flourishing relationships and abounding success. To book Dan for your next event, buy his books, or subscribe to his *free* e-zine, visit http://www.ThinkinOutsideTheBarn.com, e-mail Dan@DanOhler.com, or call (780) 785–9479.

57

A Primer for Creating Miracles

Susan Barbara Apollon

> There are only two ways to live your life.
> One is as though nothing is a miracle.
> The other is as though everything is a miracle.
> I believe in the latter.
> —Albert Einstein

Need a miracle?

You have the resources to create your own! Whether you need a miracle regarding your health, finances, or career, know that you are capable of manifesting well-being, abundance, or your heart's desire.

Blood work and a CAT scan confirmed a tumor in Anita's thyroid. Though she initially felt overwhelmed, Anita was determined to create a miracle—which she did. We quickly instituted improved and comfortable ways of thinking, feeling, and living that enabled her body's immune system to produce chemicals needed to fight her cancer. Anita's second CAT scan revealed no sign of the tumor. Interestingly, as she learned that the tumor had disappeared, the sacred thread she had been wearing (blessed by Tibetan monks) fell off, without her unknotting it!

In October 2000, our then 15-year-old golden retriever, Amber, was diagnosed with a form of mucocutaneous lymphosarcoma. In November 2001, I attended a workshop on Larry LeShan's Type I meditation techniques (LeShan has been honored by Harvard for his research on consciousness). For four days I engaged in intense healing meditation, focusing on filling with love and merging with universal energy and with Amber. When I arrived home, I was stunned to discover that beautiful, pink, healthy gum tissue had replaced Amber's ugly tumor. We had experienced a genuine miracle, and if I could help Amber heal, anyone could!

The following guidelines are based on two decades of research on the mind and consciousness.

1. **Remember: Vibration is everything.** You are an energetic, vibratory being. Every thought and image you focus on causes you to feel a particular emotion and vibrate at a particular frequency. Emotions such as despair, anger, shame, and greed reflect low vibrational frequencies. Experiences of love, joy, peace, and enlightenment are among the highest frequencies. Be mindful of what you choose to focus on!

2. **Remember the law of attraction: Like attracts like.** You attract that which you are vibrationally. Focus on negativity, and you vibrate at that level. Worse yet, you attract similar low-vibration experiences. Unfortunately, many tend to focus on their fears. However, focus on love and joy, and you vibrate at a higher frequency level, attracting to you equivalent vibrational experiences. It makes more sense to focus on feel-good thoughts.

3. **Miracles are born out of changing your perspective and opening your heart.** When you get out of your own way, when you move out of your head and out of the box in which you operate and come from your heart, miracles happen.

4. **Remember the power of intention.** Clearly visualize your dreams. Write down your intentions daily (such as being well or financially secure). While writing, feel enthusiasm and excitement as you anticipate the manifestation of your desires. This creates in you a high vibrational frequency, which attracts vibrational equivalents. Journal, draw, imagine, cut out pictures, and talk about your intentions. Intend to have joy!

5. **The power of choice: Choose joy and love over fear and "reality."** When dealing with a frightening diagnosis, do not focus on the diagnosis. Rather, do everything necessary for well-being—but do not think or worry about or discuss the problem. Notice your feeling, feel your emotion, and quickly release and replace it with feel-better thoughts and activities (anger feels better than sadness!).

- Journal your feel-good thoughts.
- For 15 minutes daily, sit, visualize, and feel the excitement of living your dreams.
- Focus on your passion, while making it happen.
- Focus on what will make you laugh out loud!

6. **Breathe!** Breathe consciously, and you will feel joy, peace, and experience a sense of connection with your own soul and those of others. For example, focus on breathing in up to the count of 8, 9, or 10; hold your breath to the count of 8 or more; then follow your breath out to 10 or more, while visualizing it traveling through your body, warming and relaxing your cells. A vibrational shift will occur internally, releasing neuropeptides in the brain for well-being. Focus on your breath (long breaths and normal, easy breathing) 15 minutes daily. Practice the breath anywhere (while waiting for your kids, doctor, or dentist). The more you breathe, the easier it is to shift to a higher vibration. And whenever you experience fear, breathe consciously. It works!

7. **Choose love and compassion.** While breathing, focus on a loving memory, such as when you first held a baby, kitten, or puppy. See and feel your heart filling with warm feelings of unconditional love. Give this a color, perhaps pink. Feel your heart overflowing and filling the cells of your body with love. Enjoy this as a warm embrace. You may wish to send this loving energy to someone special. You may also visualize universal or divine energy and then see and feel yourself merging with this energy. You may then merge with a loved one for whom you have concerns. Stay with this, enjoying the awareness of both the giving and the receiving of an embrace of love.

8. **Process unfinished business, forgive, and surrender.** Your inability to forgive draws more energy from you than it does from anyone else. Forgiveness serves you and not the other. It frees you energetically, permitting you to shift to a higher vibration and allow in your desires. Journal and process your unresolved painful feelings. Feel compassion for the other and for yourself, then surrender your feelings to the universe. Forgiveness gets easier with time.

9. **Learn the power of caring for others.** Find someone or something that needs you. Filling with love and compassion for others shifts you energetically to a higher frequency and enhances the functioning of your immune system. By volunteering, cooking dinners for the needy, or checking in on the elderly, you serve others as well as yourself.

10. **Give thanks.** Frequently give thanks for your blessings. Gratitude is calibrated as one of our higher frequencies. When you remember to be grateful, you naturally shift to a higher vibration. Your body enjoys the healing vibration of gratitude. For example, I automatically lift my face to the heavens when I leave the food market, giving thanks for the magnificence of the day and for the gift of abundant food. Giving thanks feeds your soul and your body.

11. **Know the magic of prayer.** I am not referring to anything religious here— know that prayer itself is powerful. Research on prayer in the laboratory demonstrates that prayer works. The simplest prayer is "help me, please." When in need, ask everyone you know and prayer circles to pray for you.

12. **Read about creating miracles.** Hirshberg and Barasch, Pearsall, and Raud are just a few who have written about creating miracles when diagnosed with life-threatening illnesses. Additionally, *A Course in Miracles* illustrates the power of love in the healing process. These materials broaden your perspective and open your heart to possibilities of miracles happening in your life.

May miracles always be with you!

ABOUT THE AUTHOR

Susan Apollon is a psychologist who has been practicing in Yardley, Pennsylvania, for 20 years. A researcher of mind, consciousness, intuition, healing, prayer, and life after life, she is also the author of *Touched by the Extraordinary: An Intuitive Psychologist Shares Insights, Lessons and True Stories of Spirit and Love to Transform and Heal the Soul*. Susan appears frequently on radio and television and lectures and conducts workshops on healing from grief, creating miracles in your life, developing your intuition, communicating with deceased loved ones, and living a joyful life. Her intention is to enable you to know your own power and ability to create your heart's desires. Visit her Web site at http://www.touchedbytheextraordinary.com, or e-mail her at susan@mattersofthesoul.com.

58

MEMORIAL GARDENS

Memorial Gardens Are Divine

Earl D. Erickson

It all started out as a birthday gift for my wife, Bobbie.

I bought her a beautiful, painted, concrete bear. It looked so real, and it was the size of a real bear. She loved it. I placed the bear in the center of a circular-shaped flower bed I had landscaped near our house. Then I added a miniature wooden windmill next to it. Then it looked so cool that we decided to plant roses around it. And last, but not least, I painted a big rock that was already there with the words "Bobbie's Mountain" in black. I painted the background of the rock sky blue and drew a picture of Mt. Rainier in white. Afterward, we named our property "Bobbie's Mountain."

After Bobbie passed away from cancer in 2001, I made the spot a memorial garden. The thing I like the most about a memorial garden at home is that it is always right there at your fingertips. A personal memorial garden should be a private place to pray and think about your loved ones daily. It is not practical to visit a cemetery daily, unless you live close by. Even so, having a memorial in your own yard is very special.

I think every person should have a memorial garden in his yard or a simple arrangement in his home. A loving tribute to a spouse, relative, friend, or pet can easily be set up in the home. It does not have to be a shrine. A simple plant surrounded by some photographs or mementos may be just fine. Every person or pet deserves to be honored one way or another. It is a celebration of life, and it is spiritually uplifting. It creates powerful messages to your heart and your mind. It reflects a feeling of love and honor. It represents a time and a place in your precious life you will always remember. It brings comfort and joy to your heart and gently reminds you that this person was special in your life and that you will never forget him or her as long as you live.

If you have a yard, what a perfect reason to set up a memorial garden. It does not have to be fancy. A few plants and flowers and a simple homemade memorial marker carved out of wood is perfect. It would be a great theme for the perfect country garden. Just imagine how it would make you feel.

Exchanging plants with another friend or member of the family who also has a memorial garden can be a lot of fun. Make a party out of it.

Remember what your mom or dad liked or what your parent reminded you of, and add it to your garden. If your dad reminded you of an outdoorsman, then fishing gear, hunting gear, hiking gear, or camping gear might be appropriate to add to your garden. If he was a sports lover, then items from golf, baseball, football, basketball, soccer, or any other sport may be what you are looking for. If your dad was handy with tools, then make a memorial of him on your workbench and create a theme for your workshop; for instance, "Harold's Workshop: In Memory of My Dad" would fit in nicely off to the side or on a pegboard. If your dad passed away and left you an old truck, hardly worth fixing, drill some big holes in the bottom of the truck bed for drainage, drop an inch of gravel to the base, and shovel on a heaping pile of topsoil, then have fun planting a memorial garden in his old pickup truck.

If your mom reminded you of gardening, put her favorite tools in your memorial garden and create a theme. When my mother passed away and we sold her house, I gathered up most of the plants and flowers she loved and hauled them over to my house. Then I carved a heart—shaped out of wood—painted it pink, and in red lettering I painted the words "Amanda's Garden." Suddenly, I had a memorial garden in memory of my mom. It was special because now I could tend the garden where she left off and keep the living plants alive.

If your mom was an outstanding cook, and you really are not the gardener she was or you do not have a yard, create the memorial inside your home—in the kitchen—by hanging a plate that says, for instance, "Dorothy's Kitchen: In Memory of My Mom." Any engraving shop can help.

When your brother or sister passes away, think of the things that remind you of him or her, then make a memorial out of those things. Your sister's busy cell phone or your brother's loud guitar or drums make great additions to a memorial.

The list goes on and on, but I am sure you get the idea. I got a little extravagant with my memorial garden, but I wanted to include my wife, my mom and dad, and my aunt and uncle. I bought a 30-foot flagpole and added the birthday gift I had given my wife when she was living: the painted, concrete bear. Then I bought a granite marker, almost the size of a headstone in a cemetery, and I had engraved the following words: "In loving memory of my wife, Bobbie Jean, my Yellow Rose of Texas, who affectionately named this land Bobbie's Mountain. And to my aunt and uncle, Edith and Vernon Thomson, who made my dream home come true. And to my parents, Amanda and Hank Erickson, who gave me life and love." Then I planted a couple Japanese maple trees, a couple hydrangeas and rhododendrons, some bear grass, and yellow roses with a crawling ground cover. It looks beautiful, and I am always right there to enjoy it. It gives me peace and comfort only I can explain.

Now it is your turn to get creative and make a memorial garden that will help you find peace and tranquility in your life, like mine has for me. After all, memorial gardens are divine.

ABOUT THE AUTHOR

Earl D. Erickson is a grateful recovering alcoholic. His love of writing inspirational stories brings him comfort and happiness, and he hopes his stories will help his readers to identify the struggles they have encountered in similar events in their lives. He is currently writing a book on his life and struggles with alcoholism, drug addiction, depression, suicide, grief, loss, and anger. His book is entitled *Abstinence Makes the Heart Grow Fonder*, and he hopes to be finished with that project early in 2007. He owns and manages five Web sites: http://SereneandSober.com; http://ComfortandLoss.com; http://BobbiesMountain.com; http://videosmusicandmore.com; and http://SqwearEnterprises.com.

59

MEMORIZATION SKILLS

How to Memorize Anything

Sten M. Andersen

How much do you think you can improve your memory? The answer may surprise you.

Did you know that your three-pound brain (approximately 1.4 kilograms) contains 100 billion brain cells that can form gazillions of connections? According to Karen DeBord, PhD, "there are enough brain cells to learn just about anything." There you go. If I were you, I would not worry about how much I could improve my memory. If I had to worry at all, it would be about *how* to improve my memory—how to do it quickly and naturally.

Use It or Lose It

You have heard before that your mind is like a muscle. And a muscle that is not used is lost by atrophy. You may rely on shopping lists for your groceries, a phone book for your phone numbers, a diary for your appointments, an alarm on your mobile phone to remind you when your appointments are, and a string tied around your finger to remember who you are married to. Need I say more?

A Gruesome Word

The answer, of course, is to practice. Now I have said it—the horrible word. I know, I know, a pill would be so much better. So easy. The problem is that easy solutions seldom work. Not in the long run. Steroids do work to build your muscles, but in the long run, do they do more good or harm?

The Good News and a Party Trick

The good news, of course, is that as you practice, the process of practicing itself becomes easier. Then it becomes like second nature.

Imagine this: You walk into a room and stay just long enough to take one glance around. You walk out. And then you make everyone's head turn when you recite each and every object that was in the room. Yes, every single object in sight. It is totally possible, but can it be done with memory tricks or super-brain-me pills?

The Secret Key

I do not have the room in this chapter to teach you the whole method, but what I can do is tell you the secret key. Just knowing this key, and applying it by practicing what I am about to share with you, should give your memory powers an enormous boost.

Are you ready? Okay, just before I share the secret key with you, I would like to say one thing: The method I am about to show you requires some earnest thinking on your part. Most people are just too lazy to indulge in such mental effort. The Norwegian philosopher Arne Næss used to say that "thinking hurts— and that's why so few people do it." Please, do not let that be you.

So here we go. The one big key to remembering anything is to *cultivate attention*.

So What Is the Big Deal?

Now, I am guessing you have one of the following two questions for me:

1. Isn't that really too obvious? That in order to remember something, you need to pay attention?
2. What does that mean, really, to *cultivate* attention? How do you do that?

Let us take the first question first. Yes, in one way it seems really obvious. Of course you cannot remember anything unless you really notice it first. However, strangely, most of us really do not pay attention that well. And when we try to, we are really not as good at it as we would want to be.

Still skeptical? Okay, I will prove to you that you do not really pay attention, even to the happenings in your own life. Let us perform a tiny experiment that truly shocked me the first time I tried it.

Try and see if you can recall the incidents of the same day as today, one week ago. Stop reading this book, look away from the page, and try recalling what you did exactly one week ago. Do it now.

How much could you remember?

Now try this: How about yesterday? How much can you remember from yesterday?

If you are like most people, you remember hardly anything from last week and only some occurrences from yesterday.

What would your situation be like if you were to testify in court regarding the happenings of the previous day or the day of the week before? Again, most people would be in a bad position if this were to happen.

But relax. It is not your fault. You have never been trained on how to use your memory properly. So why could you not easily remember what you did yesterday or last week? It is because you did not make an effort at the time to store those memories. You let them slip by you. You did not want to be bothered with the recollection of trifles, so you made the mistake of failing to store them away.

William Walker Atkinson teaches that there is an immense difference between dwelling on the past and storing away memories for future reference. To allow the records of each day to be destroyed is like shredding important business papers in an office just to avoid giving them a little space in the file cabinet.

Now why on earth would you want to do that?

How to Cultivate Attention

You would not! So let us stop that right now. And that is what question number two is all about. What does it mean, really, to *cultivate* attention? How do you do that?

234

Here is how I do it: First, I tell myself that this is a question of *will*. I need to *really* want it. I need to want to cultivate my attention. My mental powers and I as a person will grow through this process. So I want it. I want it bad.

Then I turn my attention onto something uninteresting, something I find absolutely boring, like the ceiling in my office. It is white and dull. I start studying its details. After having overcome the compulsion to tell myself that it is white and there is nothing to study, I start finding details. It is cracked in some places. The paint is not the same thickness everywhere. There is a yellowish spot right above the door. There seems to be a texture to it, like it is made out of concrete.

And I do this with many things throughout the day. I find that it develops my powers of voluntary attention and perception. *And that is the first requirement for memory development.*

So how would you go about practicing for the party trick where you remembered every single object in a room? Here is how. Let us say that every day, you walk past a shop window (most of us do on our way to work, but if you do not, the same strategy can be utilized in a number of different ways). Try, as you walk by, to just throw a quick glance into the window, and then see how many objects you can remember afterward. Write them down. In the beginning you will probably only be able to remember one or two objects. But after a while, you will remember more and more, and in the end you will quite probably be able to remember all the objects you laid your eyes on.

In conclusion, there is no reason for you to worry about how much you can improve your memory. The brain has enough brain cells to learn just about anything. If you are willing to practice the art of paying attention, doing so patiently and knowing that there is no royal road to a better, natural memory, you will see extraordinary results.

ABOUT THE AUTHOR

Sten M. Andersen helps you develop your memory in a natural way. For a free e-mail course, register at http://YouCantBeatMe.com/selfgrowth.

60

Mentoring: The Gift of Yourself

Maureen Staiano

As we move through our lives, we gather an abundance of knowledge and experience covering a myriad of areas. As we stop and reflect on all this knowledge, we may be struck with the desire to share with others our experiences and the knowledge we have gained. We know in our hearts that what we have gained in experience during our lives could be of benefit. So in possession of this knowledge and experience and with the desire to share it, where do we start?

How about Becoming a Mentor?

Mentoring has been around for a long time and has grown and evolved over the years. A mentoring relationship is one in which one person, often older, but always with more experience, guides another person's development. Mentoring can be utilized in almost any area of life, and both the mentor and the one being mentored both realize lasting benefits

Most everyone has heard of Big Brothers and Big Sisters of America, an incredible program matching adults with underprivileged children. The positive results experienced by the children participating in the program are truly impressive. This is only one area where mentoring has had proven results.

Where Are Mentors Needed?

Anyone having experience with a 12-step program will be familiar with the role of sponsorship and its importance to success in the program. A sponsor is a mentor, and a very important one at that, sharing his experience, strength, and hope for success in the given program of recovery. For anyone beginning in recovery, this special person can be just the lifeline the individual needs as he learns a new way to live. Where better to go for guidance in this completely new lifestyle than to someone who is already living it?

Teachers also have the opportunity to be mentors, encouraging students to reach for goals they may never have dreamed possible. Teachers, in particular, work so closely with children for so many hours of the day that they are given a wonderful chance to impact a child's life in a favorable way. Many of us can look back fondly in remembrance of at least one teacher who had a lasting positive effect on our lives.

Some school systems have implemented mentoring programs for children, enlisting the help of adult volunteers. The results have been well documented, including increased school attendance, improved educational performance, confidence, and self-esteem. The adults have been given a priceless opportunity to influence a child's life.

Business and the corporate environment have recognized the value of mentors and mentoring programs. In larger corporations a mentor will be assigned to incoming junior employees to give these newest members of the corporation the best possible start. Similar programs have been started in many schools to support new teachers coming into the educational system.

Any career path you are contemplating would be benefited by enlisting the guidance of a mentor, and many people already established in a certain career still work with a mentor to further themselves in their chosen fields. As a coach, I work with a mentor coach and find it an invaluable business and life resource.

With the increase of entrepreneurs forging ahead to start their own businesses, mentors will be in higher demand as their prior business experience and knowledge will be invaluable. The same holds true for any business owner targeting a niche market, where specific prior experience in a similar niche could influence success or failure.

As for the Person Contemplating Mentorship, What Can He Expect?

Mentoring is truly the gift of yourself that you share with another human being. It is a relationship you establish with the mentor in the place of more experience and the mentee the benefactor of your experience and guidance. Though at one time the mentor set the tone of the relationship, today, the mentee plays a more active role as to the direction the relationship will take, especially in the business world. In this relationship the mentee is aware of the areas in which he needs guidance in order to facilitate most effectively his career development.

Either way, both people truly benefit from this special relationship. The mentor will gain the pleasure of sharing her knowledge. She will also discover a new excitement surrounding the area in which she is serving as a mentor. When you observe someone else benefiting from your knowledge and experience, it is difficult not to feel a sense of pleasure and fulfillment. We all want to know we matter in this world, that we indeed have made a difference. Becoming a mentor is one of the great ways to have a positive impact on another human being.

Where Do You Get Started in Becoming a Mentor?

Take a look at what has excited you in your life. Where have you succeeded? Would this knowledge be useful to others? Do you prefer to work with adults or children? Would you like to work one-on-one, or would you like to work with larger audiences? Answering these questions will help you focus on where you would be of the greatest benefit.

Big Brothers and Big Sisters is always looking for volunteers to serve as mentors if working with children is your goal. In addition, there are many programs run on state or city levels. A phone call to your local school district will likely provide you with information as to any particular programs they may offer.

If you already work in a large corporation, check with the Human Resources department to see if they offer mentoring programs within the company. If you know of small businesses in a field that you have experience with, make yourself available. The Internet is a great place to start. There are many sites devoted to all types of mentoring. Business organizations are another good place to start. If you meet someone just starting in a field that you have experience in, step up and introduce yourself, and then offer your services as a mentor.

If you feel you would like to reach a greater number of people, consider your options. If you like to write, perhaps you can put your experience and knowledge on paper so it will reach a large segment of the population. Some of my most influential mentors are the ones I have found between the pages of a book. As I take in their experience, strength, and hope, I find myself applying it to my own life. Though our relationship has not been one-on-one, it has been of great benefit to me.

Once You Have Narrowed Your Options and Found a Place to Start, Jump In

As with many things in life, if you choose to change the venue in which you would like to serve as a mentor, you can always make the change. More importantly, get started somewhere; you have a gift that the world can benefit from. Do not keep it all to yourself—giving the gift of yourself as a mentor is one of the greatest gifts you can give, and what you will get back will exceed your expectations.

ABOUT THE AUTHOR

Maureen Staiano is a life coach specializing in working with women addressing all the wonderful challenges and transitions we face. Maureen lives with her husband Jim in western New Jersey, where they enjoy golf and travel as well spending time with the five children they share between them. Visit Maureen at http://www.achieveyourdreamcoaching.com.

61

MIND ATTACK

A Message from Your Monsters:
We're Here to Help!

Rod Louden

Dear Friend,

We here at Inferiority Control have been informed that you are concerned about the "monsters" and "tyrants" wreaking havoc in your life. I have personally spoken with several of these monsters, and here is what they had to say regarding this slander.

Fear assured me that it is working extra hard to keep you hypervigilent and worried about making any changes in your life. As you know, change is bad, especially personal change. Fear wants you to know that it will continue to make sure that you do not take any risks, especially to confront personal issues that may lead to change. Fear will continue to broadcast its "helpful messages" throughout the day. Some of your favorites it identified are "if you try, you might fail"; "if you try, you might succeed"; "if you confront an individual and share your true feelings, you will be rejected"; and your favorite, "it's better to be in a relationship (good or bad) rather than be alone." So do not worry, Fear has got your back.

Depression told me to tell you that it will continue to walk side by side with you. It wants you to know that finding little pleasure in most things in life is normal as humans are here to suffer. It hopes that you will continue to get all that sleep. It wants to reassure you that hope is a bad thing as hopes and dreams always get crushed out there in the cruel world. So stay isolated and keep to yourself. Depression is here for you. It is all you need. Whatever you do, do not start looking for a better life—it is not out there.

Anger got particularly irate when I informed it that it was being viewed as unhelpful and domineering. Anger told me to pass on the following truths. First of all, you have a right to be angry all the time. After all, it is the people in your life that are screwing up and making your life a living hell. And remember, you are perfect. Just keep pointing a finger at others, spread blame around, and never, ever, even for a minute, consider that maybe your life is the way it is because of your own choices. What a crock that is. I mean, look at you. You are doing just fine. It has been said that Anger is just a way to push people away from you. We both know that people need to be pushed away. If they get too close, they may hurt us—we do not want that to happen. Anger will fight for you.

Substance Use wants you to know that it is tired of the negative things people are saying about it. After all, it is doing a very important job—keeping you numb so that you do not have to deal with the harshness of the world. Substance Use understands that at this point, it is only a temporary solution and that it has to be used regularly in order to receive its wondrous effects. That is why it wants me to tell you that it is working on a whole new batch of drugs in order to keep you right where you are. One of the side effects continues to be death. But if you really think about it, death is not so bad. Actually, it is a good thing. Who really wants to grow old and be surrounded by loved ones anyway? So Substance Use says keep usin' and boozin' and remember that there is no such thing as substance abuse.

In conclusion, I hope that I have helped you to see that there are no "tyrants" who are trying to ruin your life. If anyone suggests that you need to rid yourself of these allies, do not listen to them. They are here to help you; they are not your enemies, but your friends. Make sure you stay right where you are.

Sincerely,

Therisa Nohopeforu
Vice President
Inferiority Control

Dear Ms. Nohopeforu,

I recently received your correspondence. I know that you are very busy creating pain and suffering, so I will make this short. You are fired! That is right—I am not falling for your tricks anymore. My so-called allies are really my enemies, and I am going to war! Fear, Depression, Anger, Substance Use, and the rest of the destruction mob can all take a hike. I am tired of being sick and tired, and I am going to fight to take my life back. I know that I have made some poor choices in the past. Instead of blaming the world, or myself, I am taking responsibility for the state of my life. After all, blame is a useless concept.

Instead, I am looking in the mirror. I am questioning my morals, my values, and my belief system. I have come to realize that the road map that I created to follow to success is full of flaws. It led me to the land of Failure, where you and your buddies were waiting to take over my world. I was vulnerable to your tricks and lies. I have wised up. I am starting a new quest—a search for knowledge that is useful and productive. I am going to question every belief that I have to determine if it is based in the real world, not on a fairy tale or some other rotten source of so-called knowledge that has led me to suffer. When I find lies, I am going to toss them out and replace them with useful information that I will use to forge a new road map. If that road map does not lead me to success, I will learn more about myself and forge another. I will not stop until I have created success, peace, and tranquility in my life.

One last thing that is very important: I am going to stop running from my emotional pain. It has been trying to teach me some important life lessons, but I have not been listening. You can bet that I am listening now!
In conclusion, I have no more time for you and your mob of losers. I have wasted enough time. I have a new chapter in my life to write. It is called "The Day I Started My Journey of Positive Personal Change."

Without regret,
Ima Takinmylifeback

ABOUT THE AUTHOR

Rod Louden is a licensed marriage and family therapist in Woodland Hills, California. Rod is a graduate of the University of Colorado, Boulder, with a BA in clinical psychology. Rod received his master's degree in clinical psychology from Antioch University in Los Angeles. In addition to running a private practice, Rod is a therapist at the Child Sexual Abuse Program in Van Nuys, California, and a Supervising Children's Social Worker for the Department of Children and Family Services for Los Angeles County. Rod released his first book, *Monster Relationships: Taming the Beasts That Are Killing Your Relationships*, in 2005. For more information, please visit http://www.monsterrelationships.com.

62

MOTIVATION

What Motivates You?

Russ Yeager

Motivation is the reason we get out of bed in the morning instead of sleeping all day. It is what drives us to get to work or the gym and work harder, smarter, and more efficiently than the day before. Motivation is the reason that great ideas are turned into great accomplishments. Motivation is what drives us to get things done!

Have you ever found it puzzling, and sometimes frustrating, that at certain times you are extremely motivated and feel like nothing can stop you as you work toward achieving your lifelong goals, while at other times your motivation seems to be almost nonexistent? Why is that? Are your goals really less important to you during those "unmotivated" times? Surely that is not the answer. There are normal cycles of emotions and levels of motivation that we go through. It is easy to do the right thing when times are easy. The key to success is getting yourself to do the things you know you need to do, even when you do not feel like doing them. That is what will set you apart from the masses and get you on your way to the magnificent life you desire and deserve.

Let us first examine why our motivation to stay on track sometimes waivers and then address how we can break this cycle and produce motivation at will. One of the main factors that causes us to lose our motivation and become less productive is being reactive to our environment. Did you notice how I wrote that last sentence saying that our environment "causes us to lose our motivation"? That is a very reactive statement. In order to live our lives on purpose, we need to accept responsibility for where we are in life and become proactive by controlling our thoughts, habits, and actions. Instead of waiting for outside influences to provide motivation, decide right *now* that you are a motivated individual who takes productive, positive action in order to get what you want.

For example, motivation to go to the gym every day and stay on a healthy eating program often decreases during the holidays, but this is normally due to outside influences and not the fact that we are not as committed to accomplishing our fitness goals. It is during these times that we need to remind ourselves what our long-term goals are and exactly *why* we do what we do every day to get closer to those goals. This will not necessarily increase your motivation instantaneously, but it will keep you on track until your level of motivation increases again—and trust me, it will.

Motivation can be found in many different forms and can come from external sources or can be self-generated. I believe it is most important to have self-generated motivation based on your personal principles and life mission. It takes this strong, centered, internal drive to keep us on track as we work toward our goals. But what about all of the external influences we encounter every day, such as other people, the weather, and other events and circumstances? Is it possible to utilize these external events to provide further motivation that can act synergistically with your internal motivation? Oh yeah it is!

One simple and effective strategy I have found is to look to others who are already successful at what you are doing. Seeing others succeed (via a DVD, video, book, or live in person) can be extremely motivating. This also helps you keep your end goal in mind instead of focusing on how you may feel at the moment. Associate yourself with positive people who have similar goals and interests as your own. Having a close network of people like this can be a huge source of motivation. Read motivational books and articles often. The more positive reinforcement you provide to your mind, the easier it becomes to take positive, productive steps toward getting what you want. The subject you read does not even have to be specifically related to what you are working toward. It is easy to become inspired by others who have passionately and persistently achieved greatness, no matter what form of greatness that may be.

Can we even use the "bad" situations and occurrences as sources of motivation? Sure! Life is full of surprises and we do not always know exactly what "good" and "bad" things it is going to throw at us. The good news is that we have complete power to decide at any moment what is "good" and "bad" and how we want to respond to a certain situation. Think about that for a minute. That is very powerful!

For example, when you experience any significant level of success in life or do things "differently," you are going to have people put you down or tell you that you cannot succeed. One way to respond is to get angry and defensive and either argue with the person until you are blue in the face or even let the other person's opinion stop you from following your dream. Why waste all that time and energy, though, when you will never change the person's mind, and even if you do, what have you gained? Instead, save your energy to keep working toward what you want. What if the person really gets under your skin or you just want to be angry at him? Okay, not my first choice, but if this is how you choose to respond, then utilize your anger! Use his negative attitude to fuel your motivation and work even harder with a "prove him wrong" attitude. While other people's opinions should never determine how you live your life, learning to utilize everything that happens around you, including criticism and negative comments, will allow you to rise to an even higher level of accomplishment and self-confidence.

Too often, I hear people blaming their lack of success on their circumstances. This is another complete waste of time and energy. So what if this person or that person started with more money, better health, or better "luck"? Focusing on what you do not have is not going to help you get what you want. Besides, I guarantee there is someone right now who has less to work with than you do who is extremely successful at what you want to do.

So what motivates *you*? No matter what it is, use the power of motivation to help you reach all of your goals and dreams!

<u>ABOUT THE AUTHOR</u>

Russ Yeager, CFT, CPA, is the owner and operator of Russ Yeager's Fitness Solutions. His mission and passion is helping others live life to the fullest by helping them transform their physical, mental, and emotional well-being. Russ is a lifetime natural bodybuilding champion, fitness and life coach, personal training studio owner, and writer. Russ has the unique ability of applying the mental skills and disciplines learned from bodybuilding and fitness to help others make dramatic improvements in any area of life. Many of Russ's clients describe him as "the most motivating person I have ever met." To learn more and read more articles written by Russ, visit http://www.russyeager.com. Also, to obtain a free copy of Russ's brand-new e-book *27 Must-Have Tips for a Complete Physique Transformation*, visit http://www.completephysiquetransformation.com.

63

Is It Positive or Negative?
You Decide

Katharine C. Giovanni

A few weeks ago, I took my boys to the neighborhood pool. When we got there, I quickly found some chairs near some acquaintances of ours and started to chat with them as the boys swam.

About 20 minutes went by when I began to notice that everything my friend talked about was negative. She said nothing positive, and all she did was complain. When she got to politics, I decided that it was enough and quickly excused myself and jumped into the pool.

As I swam around the pool, I could not help but hear other conversations. Imagine my surprise when I found that they were mostly negative as well. So now I was curious. Was everyone tired and grumpy? Why all the negativity?

I decided to test it, so for the next few days I paid attention to everything I saw and heard to see how much negativity there really was in the world. Let me tell you, I did not have to try very hard.

First, I went to the grocery store. As I waited, I started chatting with the clerk and soon was told about her trip to Japan. She was complaining that her trip was horrible because all they wanted to do was touch her blonde hair!

That evening, I switched on the news and was presented with 30 minutes of rape, murder, and other interesting pieces. In between these heartwarming stores, I listened to commercials about weight loss and adult ADD.

After the news, I flipped around and found *Law and Order* and *CSI Miami*, both great shows but hardly positive. It seems I was surrounded by murder and rape, all in prime time. I settled for a *Touched by an Angel* rerun and went to bed.

When I woke up the next morning, I continued to pay attention.

First, I went to the post office. As I drove, I flipped on the radio to my favorite radio station, and what did I hear? A woman singing "wounds won't seem to heal, the pain is just too real." I switched to another station.

At the post office, there was an identity theft poster by the door. At Target I noticed that they had TV monitors on, and the story running was about how to prevent your child from being abducted.

Are you seeing a pattern here?

I tried the computer. After logging on, I took a look at my home page and saw one story about Al-Qaida and another about a woman found strangled. I then checked my e-mail and received the usual number of spam e-mails, which generally included sales pitches and various offers about Viagra. Do not forget the e-mail from a man in Nigeria who wanted me to send my checking account number so that he could send me millions.

Later that day, I went to get my mail and saw my neighbor outside doing some yard work. When I stopped to say hello, he asked me how I was doing. I replied, "No worries, mate. I feel great today!" I really do not think he was expecting me to say that because he stopped what he was doing and looked at me like I had just escaped from an insane asylum. I just laughed and told him I would see him later.

When did it become politically incorrect to tell people something positive?

By the end of the second day, I was physically sick and incredibly tired: so tired I went to bed at 9:00 P.M. I just wanted to lie down and pull the covers way up over my head and forget about it all.

So what did I learn from this little test? I learned that you can seriously mess up your mind with this stuff! I felt like I had been dragged into a negative world filled with greed, fear, and hatred. A world where you always lack money and you never achieve your dreams because you are too fat, too thin, too sick, need a job, lost a job, and on and on it goes. In fact, my brain had been so saturated with negativity that I was in danger of becoming physically sick!

By the end of the second day, I was yelling at my kids, bickering with my husband, and grumpy to everyone. So I had a huge bowl of ice cream (which I am convinced cures everything), took a hot bath, and went to bed. The test was officially over. Two days was more than enough for me.

On the third day I decided to visit the same places I had gone during the last two days to see what positives I could find there. First, I went to the pool. As I watched, I saw people laughing and smiling while children played. The sound of happy children playing is really one of life's greatest sounds, and it put an immediate smile on my face.

I then went to the grocery store and saw isle after isle filled with food. Now here was abundance and prosperity! I saw people chatting and smiling and two children happily eating a chocolate doughnut.

I went back to the post office and started to chat with a very nice woman who was mailing a care package to her son in Iraq.

I logged onto the Internet and received a wonderful e-mail from a friend entitled "The Positive Side of Life."

Later on that day, I saw my neighbor again, so I asked him how he was doing. He turned and looked at me with a big smile on his face and replied, "No worries, mate!" As I drove away, I flipped on the radio and immediately heard a song called "I'm on Top of the World!"

That evening, I turned on the evening news and heard an extremely beautiful story about a woman moving into her first home, built by Habitat for Humanity. Then the weather came on, and I was told that sunshine would be in our area for the next few days. Later that evening, I watched a rerun on ABC called *Extreme Makeover—Home Edition*, an incredible show that helps needy families get a new home.

There is a spiritual principle out there that says what you put your attention to grows. Certainly the case here! I put my attention to all the negative "stuff" for a few days, and it slammed into me so hard that I wanted to cry from it all. It got so bad that I saw negativity and fear everywhere I went. It could make a person seriously paranoid! When I put my attention on the positive, it grew too. It was like it had suddenly stopped raining and the warm sun came out.

So how do you remain positive, healthy, and prosperous in a negative world?

- Surround yourself with positive people.
- Treat others like you want to be treated.
- *Turn off the news* and avoid newspapers as much as possible, although you should scan things so you know what is going on.
- Write down all the positive things that have happened to you in the last month, and post them where you can see them. "See" your life as a success! Do not see your life as a failure! Look at all the positive things that you have done.
- Put a positive/inspirational poster over your desk. You can also put a plus sign or the words *stay positive* over your desk to remind you to be positive.
- Read inspirational books.
- Turn someone else's negative day into a positive.

Now please know that I am *not* telling you to blindly ignore the reality of the world. I am telling you that you can see that reality and also see the *positives* as well. The world can indeed be a cruel place. Crime, poverty, and illness seem to be everywhere, but the world can be a beautiful place filled with love, warmth, compassion, and prosperity. Do you see the glass as half full or half empty?

Negative things will happen in the world. They happen to all of us! But look at it this way: Positive things will happen as well. Good things will happen to you. Joy will find you!

It goes back to the law of physics that we attract like energy. So if we put out negative thoughts and actions and constantly focus on the negative, then we will *attract* negative back to us. It will be all that we see! Conversely, if we put out positive thoughts and try our best to see the positive, then we will attract the positive back.

We live in a negative world. So be it. However, I refuse to be negative and will continue to remain positive as much as possible. I have had my share of bad times; trust me, I wrote the book on that one. The good news is that I do not have to stay that way if I do not choose to. I choose prosperity, love, and compassion.

ABOUT THE AUTHOR

Katharine has been a meeting/event planner and concierge for over 20 years and has set up five successful businesses: Meeting Planning Plus, Triangle International, NewRoad Publishing, XPACS, and Triangle Concierge. She is Triangle Concierge's senior trainer and speaker and is the author of their best-selling book *The Concierge Manual*. A dynamic public speaker, Katharine has been a speaker at seminars and conferences around the country and has appeared on both radio and television. She is also the author of the acclaimed inspirational book *God, Is That You?* She can be reached through her Web sites at http://www.triangleconcierge.com and http://www.katharinegiovanni.com.

64

NURTURING OTHERS

Angie

Haiyan Zhang

I met Angie in December 1993, on a cold, cloudy day, on the train destined for Beijing, after attending the funeral of my father in my hometown, the City of Lanzhou, some 1,200 miles west of the Chinese capital.

As the wind howled and darkness descended, the steam engine–powered train puffed and blew its way eastward, heaving, as it seemed to me, in inconsolable pain, much like my own sorrow. I started a trip to the city called "guilt" and loaded myself up with blame.

I dreaded and agonized over how I could pass the 34-hour journey as my mind was flooded with memories of my father. My father, the multitalented poet and artist who walked his way from an impoverished village to the provincial capital to become the first university graduate in his home county. My father, who was persecuted many times because he had received a university education prior to the Communists taking power and because he had married the daughter of a landowner. My father, who single-handedly raised me after my mother had perished during the Cultural Revolution. My father, the dedicated educator who poured his heart into nurturing the growth of his students whenever he could steal precious freedom from the political persecution imposed on him by the communist government. My father, who claimed to have had an elastic stomach that "shrank" so that his children could have bigger shares of meals when food was scarce. My father, who was proud to finally see his four children graduate from universities after the reforms made his background less of a liability in their careers. My father, who spent many sleepless nights following the situation in the Middle East, when I, his only daughter, covered the conflicts that stormed the Arabian deserts. My father, who, with much courage and understanding, accepted my decision to marry a white, English-speaking Canadian, even though he himself did not speak English and could not communicate with my future husband.

I wondered how life would go on without my father. I regretted not having written to him in response to his last letter reaffirming his blessings on my pending union with Mike, my future husband, whom I had met in Kuwait during the Gulf War. I was angry with myself for not having called him on the first-ever telephone installed in his own apartment. I chided myself for not having had the courage to hug him when I saw him last, as public expression of emotions between adults, including family members, was scorned upon at the time in China. Most of all, I felt guilty that I had not rushed home to his bedside when he became very ill and instead wasted precious time waiting for news from the Canadian Embassy on a visa that would eventually allow me to join Mike across the Pacific.

A nonbeliever in the supernatural, I found myself praying that somehow I could be given a chance to make up for my failure to give back to this extraordinary man who had nurtured me and hundreds, if not thousands, of other people. I would do anything for such a chance to return the love I had received!

Soon after the train started, the loudspeaker broadcasted a shocking piece of news: "A baby girl was found deserted on the train. The Captain appeals for help from doctors or nurses among passengers."

Although neither a doctor nor a nurse, I felt I had to see the baby and offer help.

There she was! A beautiful baby girl with a round face, a thick head of black hair, dimples on her rosy cheeks, and big, sparkly eyes. A bundle of smiling joy, surrounded by a circle of strangers curious about her predicament.

A young woman, presumably the mother, had left the girl in temporary care of a passenger for what was supposedly a short visit to the washroom. The woman never returned. The baby was wrapped in a small cotton quilt, with half a bag of milk powder, a bottle, a few cotton diapers, and RMB50 Yuan (US$6.00). No name. No address.

As most of the other passengers returned to their seats, I volunteered to care for the baby for the rest of the journey, with the help of another passenger, a gentleman named Qi.

We decided to call her "Yuan," or "sent by destiny." In English, "Angie."

The stewardess arranged for a cabin in the sleeping car, which Mr. Qi and I converted into a temporary haven for Angie and where I spent the 32 most rewarding hours of my life.

I fed Angie when she was hungry. I cried when she cried, and I smiled with her when she smiled. I told her stories that my father had soothed me with when I fell sick in my early years. I recited to her poems my father had intoned to inspire my interest in literature as a student.

Mr. Qi, a man who had never had a chance to take care of his own children when they were young, took on the duties of washing diapers, which never seemed to dry fast enough before the baby was wet again. Mr. Qi, whose name meant "complete," decided to adopt Angie on behalf of his niece, who had been trying unsuccessfully to have a baby of her own.

Angie seemed to be in a lot of pain, yet she responded to my stories and poems with the broad and carefree smiles of a true angel.

As minutes and hours passed, the burden of guilt with which I had boarded the train left me. In its place, a sense of joy, love, and promise enveloped me. The huff and puff of the steam engine became the symphony of comfort and an affirmation of life.

Neither Mr. Qi nor I realized that the baby was born with a fatal disease, and Angie died a few days after we reached Beijing.

Brief as it was, my encounter with baby Angie taught me an important lesson: The best way to honor my father was to live life as he did, as an authentic, dignified, hard-working, and caring human being. The meaning of life lies in nurturing others.

ABOUT THE AUTHOR

Haiyan Zhang is a certified management consultant (CMC) whose mission in life is to contribute to and facilitate the success of others through attitude, aptitude, and action. Combining Western business disciplines and Eastern philosophies, Haiyan's advice is grounded on insights gained working with senior leaders in a variety of organizations and on her personal journey living and working in China, the Middle East, and North America. Haiyan holds an executive MBA, MA (Shakespeare), and, as a professional speaker, makes frequent presentations in English, Chinese, and French. To find out more, please consult http://www.3alife.com.

65

Is Your Cup Half Full or Half Empty?

Leslie Gail

How do you typically embrace the world? Are you constantly waiting for the storm to arrive, or do you look forward to a day of uncertainty? Do you typically see the good in most situations, or are you constantly looking over your shoulder?

I am a firm believer that the lens through which you see the world can color all your experiences in life. I was lucky enough to have been brought up in a loving and enriching home, where we expected the best and survived the worst. My mother fought illness after illness with a grace that to this day I cannot comprehend, and still she stopped to smell the roses. She always saw life from the vantage point of the cup being half full, even at her worst.

We are all dealt situations in our lives that can alter and shift our foundations, diminishing our feelings of safety and security. We have the power to choose how to respond to these circumstances. Sometimes it is easier to have a pity party, which can be therapeutic. But then it is important to brush ourselves off, raise our heads, and move on with living.

Would it not feel better to walk into an unknown situation prepared and expecting the best than preparing for the worst possible outcome and then creating just that? Mentally preparing yourself ahead of time for a positive end raises your confidence and creates an atmosphere that supports your desired result. Even if the end result is unknown to you at the time, you have the power to think positively and expect the best. I guarantee you that the act itself of thinking more positively will create an environment that supports a positive outcome.

Let me share with you from personal experience exactly how this has worked in my own life. I have always assumed things would work out for me, both personally as well as professionally. This is my attitude in general—a bit of naïveté, if you will. When I embarked on my coaching career, I attained more in the first year than most coaches attain throughout their careers. I am not talking financially—I am referring to getting my name and brand out in the media. Within the first couple months the newspapers were printing my articles. Within the first six months I was a regular expert guest on a major morning radio show. Several months after that, a major television news station created a coaching segment with one of my clients and me. All this happened because I simply believed that it would. I had no reason not to believe that all these doors and opportunities would open for me. Again, I assumed the best and made it happen. The opportunities continued to present themselves to me, and again, I just kept going in the same direction. Assuming the best will give you an attitude of not giving up because you know it will happen at the right time. Your attitude and energy leave an imprint on those around you—how do you want to be remembered? Commit to looking at life from a different angle and see what doors open and how you feel. I guarantee that you will not be disappointed with the results.

Follow some simple tips to begin your progress in the right direction.

Action Tips

Track your thoughts. Just as you would log your finances to see where your money is going, track how many negative thoughts pop into your mind on a daily basis. Many of us are unaware how often our negative thoughts cloud our choices and decisions. Make a commitment to track your negative voice for a couple days. Make a mark every time the voice pops up, and at the end of the day, tally your marks. This will give you a visual of how you are influenced by the voice in your head.

Change your language. Now that you have tracked your negative thoughts, you need to replace them with more positive dialogue. What are you most critical of in your life? Do you put yourself down regarding your appearance? Do you criticize the job you do at work? Replace these thoughts with more constructive words that support you. Every time a negative thought pops into your head, stop it and reframe it more positively. A good tool to use is to buy yourself 10–20 index cards. On the front of the cards, write down the disempowering thoughts that cloud your mind on a typical day. For example, you might write "I am unattractive and fat." On the opposite side of the index card, write the exact opposite. You would then write "I am beautiful and healthy." I want you to read the positive index cards several times a day. Reading the positive cards will help you begin to see yourself in that light, thus creating an environment that supports those statements.

Start your day on a positive note. The way you begin your day, your outlook, lays the foundation for the rest of your day. No matter what the day has in store for you, take control by lifting yourself and your spirits right from the beginning. You can say a positive affirmation, focus on your strengths and natural gifts, or just create a positive tone before you embark on your day. Again, this only takes a couple minutes every day, but it will set a standard that you will ultimately reach for.

ABOUT THE AUTHOR

Leslie Gail is a certified life coach and owner of New Life Focus Coaching. Leslie conducts seminars, appears regularly on a morning radio show, KOSI 101.1 in Denver, and publishes articles in The Rocky Mountain News. Leslie sends out a newsletter via e-mail every Monday morning entitled "Monday Morning Tips" that will jump-start your life every week. Sign up for these tips directly at http://www.newlifefocus.com. Leslie supports her clients in achieving personal and professional success without compromising their values. Contact Leslie directly at http://www.newlifefocus.com or call (866) 779–0731.

66

An Amazing Interview:
How Jill Kinmont Boothe Turned
Tragedy into Triumph

Karen Wheeler Hall

Life presents each of us with a seemingly endless series of tests and challenges. It often seems that just when we catch our breath, the next challenge hits us. But regardless of our circumstances, we always have the power to choose how we will respond to life's difficult moments. Choosing to keep a positive attitude during tough times enables us to bounce back more quickly from adversity. This is the true story of a remarkable woman who refused to give up after a heartbreaking accident, choosing instead to fill her life with meaningful pursuits that brought joy to herself and others.

Excitement filled my mind as I called Jill Kinmont Boothe. This was two years ago, and Jill had graciously agreed to an interview for the book I was writing. I eagerly looked forward to hearing the inspiring story of how she rose above the tragic skiing accident that left her paralyzed and went on to become a teacher and painter. I clearly remember watching the 1975 movie about her life, *The Other Side of the Mountain*, and soon I would be talking directly to her!

I placed a stack of cassette tapes near the tape recorder, envisioning a long interview. After all, learning to cope mentally and physically with being paralyzed must have taken years of hard work.

Imagine my surprise when I discovered that Jill was not interested in reliving all the gory details of her tragic accident. Our conversation went something like this:

KAREN: Learning you were paralyzed for life must have been pretty devastating for you.

JILL: Well, it was, except that I had so much support from family and friends. There were moments when I was teary and said "why did it happen to me?" but generally I held myself up because everybody else had to be held up. Everybody had to be strong for everybody else . . . I was pretty positive from early on. I don't remember it being a horrible, horrible ordeal. . . .

And with that, Jill went on with her story and with the rest of her life. No whining or complaining, no regrets, uninterested in sympathy—I was not sure what to think at that point.

When Jill described her years as an elementary school teacher, I made a comment that I thought would lead to a candid description of the challenges involved. Once again, Jill's response surprised me.

KAREN: That must have been a challenge, being a teacher and dealing with little kids without having use of your hands and legs.

JILL: It was a challenge, but just like any other teacher faces! The kids were a great resource for me because they could do all the things I couldn't do. They could write on the board, they could organize the files, they always responded when I needed help. That was never really a problem.

Jill's matter-of-fact attitude about her paralysis stunned me. Our conversation lasted only about 20 minutes. When it was over, I sat there scratching my head and wondering if I had enough material to write a story.

I thought of Jill and her casual attitude about her life-altering injury many times over the next few days. I admit it—at first I was disappointed because she did not go into detail about her feelings and all the difficulties involved with being paralyzed. I thought those details were necessary to make a compelling story that would engage the reader.

But before long, the real meaning of her story hit me like a ton of bricks. Jill's brevity and laid-back attitude *were* the real story. Here was a woman who had been paralyzed for over 50 years—her Olympic dreams cut short, unable to do many basic life functions for herself—and yet she had no interest *whatsoever* in dwelling on those things.

If Jill had done what I expected and gone into great detail about how horrible it was to be paralyzed, I am quite sure I would have missed the incredible message her life brings us. Jill's legacy to us is simple, but powerful:

- do not dwell on unfair and painful things that happen to you in life
- always focus on what you *can* do rather than on "what might have been."

Although Jill is now retired from teaching, we can all continue to learn from her example. In life we tend to get more of what we focus on. We can choose to focus on our troubles, or we can focus on being the best we can be every moment of our lives. The choice is ours alone, and whichever option we choose will become an even stronger reality for us. If we focus on our problems and difficulties, they seem to grow in stature, and we have a harder time overcoming them. By focusing instead on our strengths and abilities, we open ourselves up to experience greater joy and fulfillment than we may have ever dreamed possible.

But we cannot accept the new if we are still clinging to the old. Had Jill stayed focused on what she had lost, she would have wasted precious energy that she instead used to make the world a little brighter through her love of teaching and painting. Owing to her accident, Jill let go of her expectation to have children of her own. Instead, she made her influence more widely felt by profoundly impacting the lives of hundreds of youngsters—teaching them not only how to read, but how to live life to the fullest.

Remember that in every situation we are free to choose our response. Jill's decision to focus on her abilities and how she could best serve others made all the difference in her life. With Jill's example in mind, let us all resolve to take a look within and see where we are selling ourselves short in life. Start by completely accepting yourself and your current situation, without judgment or regret. Refuse to dwell on your faults or shortcomings, and focus instead on your strengths and your passions. With joy and confidence, move forward day by day toward your goals and dreams. Learn your lessons as life presents them to you, progressing steadily year by year, and soon you will graduate to new levels of success and happiness.

Keep these principles in mind, and you will find there is no limit to what you can accomplish in life, despite any challenges you may encounter in the school of hard knocks.

ABOUT THE AUTHOR

Karen Wheeler Hall is the author of *Illumination—Inspiring Stories about Finding the Silver Lining*, a collection of powerful true stories about people who discovered that painful events in their lives actually turned out to be blessings in disguise. Visit http://www.KarenWheelerHall.com to learn more about *Illumination* and to download your free copy of Karen's e-book, *Positively Incredible!* Karen received a B.S. in dietetics from the University of Texas and an M.A. in human services from St. Edward's University. She lives in Austin, Texas, with her husband, Greg.

67

PARENTING

Use Encouragement Instead of Criticism to Help Children Improve

Judy H. Wright

Our words are very powerful tools, especially with impressionable children. We need to pause and think before we give corrections and feedback on what our children are doing.

Criticism Is Punitive

Our children judge themselves on the opinions we have of them. When we use harsh words, demeaning adjectives, or a sarcastic tone of voice, we literally strip a child's core of self-confidence and make him less likely to try to please us.

Studies have shown that verbal abuse is more likely than physical abuse to damage children's self-esteem. Not only does it damage their souls, it is counterproductive to cooperation and lasting change.

Encouragement Is Uplifting

Encouragement is the process of focusing on your children's assets and strengths in order to build their self-confidence and feelings of worth.

Parents need to convey, though words and gestures, that we appreciate their efforts and improvement, not just their accomplishments. We need to make sure they understand that our love and acceptance is not dependent on their behavior or winning the prize in soccer.

Positive Correction That Changes Behavior

A very effective way of communicating is to create a verbal encouragement sandwich:

1. **Start off with a slice of the bread of life,** for example, "I really admire the way you are learning to take better care of your things."
2. **Next, add a little mayo spread lightly:** "I felt happy when I saw you hang up your new jacket last night."
3. **Then, the slice of sharp cheese:** "However, I noticed you left your bike outside in the rain again."
4. **On top of the cheese, a little spicy mustard to catch the child's attention:** "Please put it away every night, or we will have to lock it up for a week each time it is left out."
5. **Finally, another slice of bread:** "All in all, you are a responsible kid, and I have confidence you will choose to take better care of your bike."

Does the child get the message of the mistake of leaving the bike out? Yes, but it is not by attacking him personally, and this method of correction gives him an incentive to do better.

Nurturing Better Behavior

Some parents and caregivers, particularly those who did not receive much love or encouragement in their childhoods, often fail to see the importance of nurturing the inner core of a child. The sad part of this is that encouragement and kind feedback will bring about positive change, whereas criticism brings about rebellion, anger, and loss of self-worth.

Encouragement Works

Zig Ziglar, an internationally known motivational speaker, has said, "When we have positive input, we have positive output, and when we have negative input, we have negative output." As a parent educator, mother, and grandmother, may I suggest that you need to be very careful of the words you choose to motivate your children?

It helps if you break up the word to read "en" courage, which means giving a gift of courage: the courage to keep trying, to keep up the good work, to focus on next time and not give up. This courage helps the child realize that he can make mistakes and yet will still be loved and valued, whereas "dis" couragement or criticism takes away the courage to try new things or work harder for fear of getting in trouble and displeasing the adults.

What Choices Could You Make Next Time?

Help the child and yourself recognize that mistakes are never final and that frequently, we get a do-over or a second chance. The past is done; we can learn from it and then focus on the future. You will find a free listing at ArtichokePress.com of encouraging words and phrases.

Thank You for Doing a Great Job

Those of you working with children on a daily basis do the most important work in the world. I applaud your efforts and "en" courage you to choose your words carefully when you want the children you care for to improve their behavior. Words have the power to build up or destroy. As caring adults, the goal is to strengthen the character of the child as well as get the jackets, bikes, and toys picked up on a consistent basis.

ABOUT THE AUTHOR

This article was written by Judy H. Wright, parent educator, family coach, and author of over 20 books on family relations. Feel free to use it in your newsletter or publication, but please give full credit to the author and mention the contact information of JudyWright@ArtichokePress.com, (406) 549–9813. Her Web site http://www.ArtichokePress.com has a full listing of books, tapes, newsletters, tele-classes, workshops, and additional free articles which will assist you in finding the heart of the story in the journey of life.

68

PERSPECTIVE

Eyes Open?

Shane Belceto

As I sit here now, I feel the warm sun on my face and hear the children afar. I notice the walkers, bikers, skaters, and strollers all scoot by me. I hear the humming of the highway adding to the noise behind me and birds of many kinds in the trees above. I see the sand as it runs into the water. I smell the hot dogs being sold down the way and the freshly cut grass off in the distance. Chomping down on my cone, the mint of the ice cream tingles my nose and freezes my forehead. The crunch of the chocolate chips, and well, one can get lost in such a beautiful place and never return. I begin to wonder. . . .

I know a person who sees nothing. Nothing in his life, nothing in his past, nothing in his future, and nothing in his hands. He sees nothing for him, nothing for his family, and nothing for happiness. In fact, his view of himself has led him astray and on the path of drugs and alcoholism—his nothingness in life has pointed him on this path. Now, just turned 50 years old, he finds himself alone and on the street. The nothing he sees is now his reality, and what he sees still, at this point, is nothing. One could see him and think he is blind. He was born of perfect mind and body, born with all the needed qualities in life, born to a loving and caring family, born to live in this land of opportunity, and yet he is blind to who and what he is. Sitting here now, I wonder how one arrives at such a place and can see life this way. I am this man's only son.

I find myself now sharing with you what I see, but the ironic thing is that I am what some would call a blind person. I see with my eyes some, but only to a point. Being legally blind, or a person with a vision impairment, I am often asked, what do you see? From this question I now bring you these thoughts.

Many of the great have told us many things. For example, Jim Rohn says, "For things to change, you need to change." Isn't that the truth? I have challenged that statement once or twice myself, and it always seems to come out true for me. The lasting changes come from my changing each time.

Now, do not get me wrong: I love my dad dearly and always will. He and I both know I am there for him, and he makes choices each new day. The future is his to see, and he will decide how he sees it.

The question, then, is what do I see? I do not see things from a distance. I do not read unless I have to, and then it is with a highly powerful magnifier. I do not have extra special senses such as touching, hearing, tasting, and smelling. However, I do feel I have learned to utilize my other senses more than the average person. I especially rely on my hearing a lot more than most people do. Not that I hear better—I just have learned to use it for seeing things.

From this I have discovered that anyone can further take advantage of each and every sense more. Really, it is as simple as being aware of the sense and then deciding to strengthen its use like you would a muscle. Listening is a skill you can develop to learn to hear more. Listen to tones in people's voices, listen to the pauses or lack of pauses in their words, listen to the volume of what they say. Look to listen, too, at how they move while talking to you. Being aware first is the starting point. From there you will play and work with your senses to see how you can learn to "open your eyes" to all that happens around you and to you.

So I sit here now . . . what do I see? Great question, really. Do I see that hot dog stand? Yes, I do. I walked by it on the way here and can picture it now as the smell reaches my nose. Do I see all the people passing? Sort of: I hear the little wheels of the skate board and the weaving of the kid on top. I see the four wheels with two feet attached by a handle in the rear. Now, do I see faces? No, I do not, but I do see people: I hear a voice and know the one pushing the four wheels is a woman excited about the trip coming up this weekend. I hear the flash of metal of a man announcing, "On your left!" So really, I do see.

What do you see? Are your eyes open? Sit down here with me and let me know what you see.

See the sand? See the sun? How about those people passing by? Where would you say we are sitting? Some beach in California, Mexico, or on some tropical island?

I ask you now, while you are sitting here with me, are you going through your life with your eyes open? Or are you going through life blind, so to speak, like my dad? Sadly enough, many people do walk through life blind, not even knowing they are in control. I, too, could have decided to follow in his footsteps like so many of my other family members. I feel really that it all comes down to choices—choices made, both big and small, each day.

From a distance I do see. I see people can choose to see things differently, even from the same vantage point. I see that people can see what they want to see, be it true or not true. I notice that people need to be more aware of what is going on around them and pay more attention to choices they make in relation to their results in life.

Since you are sitting here with me now, let me share something with you: Open your eyes just a bit more. . . .

See that warm sun that hits our faces? Some would not see that sun—some would see the dark clouds off in the distance and the fact that it is March 3 in the Pacific Northwest and only 48 degrees.

See the children playing? Some would see the one arguing with his mom trying to get his way.

See the walkers? Some would see the gang of kids and fear for their safety.

How about the sand and water? Well, some feel that this is a filthy, dirty duck pond that needs to be removed and replaced with metal and concrete. Some would hear that the birds are several crows yelling at each other and the highway behind us full of noisy horns and sirens.

I think you see where we are now. We are sitting here together on a bench by a tiny park that needs upkeep. Here, on a bench where my dad would choose to sleep while it was cold and dark until the police woke him and told him to move along or some other people stopped to harass him.

From this bench, from the same vantage point, we each see something different. We choose what to see each and every day from each and every bench we sit on.

Next time you sit on another bench, I encourage you to pay closer attention to what it is you are truly seeing. Better yet, pay close attention to the choices you make based on what you see. Continue to ask yourself each time you sit down, are my eyes open?

ABOUT THE AUTHOR

Shane Belceto is an energetic, smart-aleck, stay-at-home dad who discovered the world of personal development and success once he was introduced to Jim Rohn. Believing that all of us should use all the senses we are given to their fullest potentials, and not letting his visual disability get in the way, Shane is now developing PersonalDevelopmentSuccess.net to take his passion for personal development online and to the world, providing a safe place for tools, support, and *fun*, while proving that anyone can succeed, no matter what.

69

Do Not Let Physical Pain
Keep You from Your Full Potential!

Joanna Wasmuth

One day, as I listened to a life coach teach on the power of transformation, somebody asked him, "How can a person do all you're talking about if they're in constant physical pain?"

His response shocked me. He condescendingly said, "Just do it." I was incensed by his insensitivity and lack of understanding—talk about adding insult to injury.

When you live in energy-sapping pain every day, you often do not have reserves to push through things and "just do it." So how do you grow if "just doing it" is not an option?

I would love to give you three easy steps to make everything better so you can live the life of your dreams, but we both know that just is not possible. What I can offer you, though, is a few insider tips from someone who has lived with chronic pain for 17 years and has navigated the sometimes overwhelming and unsympathetic waters of the self-improvement industry.

Personal growth is about becoming our best selves so that we can contribute significantly to the lives of those in our spheres of influence. It is the intentional process of minimizing our weaknesses while developing our strengths and funneling them into use for a higher purpose.

Here are a few ideas on how to sustain personal growth when your body hurts a lot of the time.

Let Your Purpose Guide You

One of our greatest desires as humans is to know that we make a difference. When we are sidelined by pain, it is easy to start believing that we do not contribute anymore and do not have meaning.

But I want you to know that you are uniquely created to contribute to the world, in spite of—and because of—your special circumstances! *You have a purpose.* You can make a difference, no matter where you are in life and no matter what stands in your way.

When you grab hold of purpose in life and contribute to others, you naturally have more energy and are less focused on your pain. Developing a personal mission statement is a great way to clarify your purpose! It will help you make better decisions about how to spend your time and resources. My mission statement is "to inspire wholesome thinking." I am able to do this in all areas of life, from conversations with friends, to my attitude toward physical therapy, and even my interactions with checkout clerks at the grocery store. A mission statement will empower you to infuse meaning into even mundane tasks, making your life much more fulfilling and rewarding.

If you are unsure of what makes you feel meaningful, try launching a PassionQuest. Spend two weeks watching for things in your life that you get excited and passionate about. What do you love to talk about? What stories do you tell? How do you contribute to others? What do you read? Your answers are good indicators of passion points. As you write all this down, looking for themes, you will soon have a strong idea of what to spend more of your time focusing on! This is not about squeezing more things into your already full schedule. It is a process of saying no more to some things and yes to others.

Set Yourself Up for Success

Growth and change rarely happen overnight. But that is often what we expect, is it not? Both with our health and our personal improvement. And then we get frustrated because we do not see it, so we short-circuit the process and quit. But resilience and personal growth are like muscles. They take training to build strength!

272

There are a few ways to end this cycle.

1. **Set achievable expectations.** It is important to set your expectations, taking into account your current health reality. Start out small, and work up! Success breeds success.
2. **Adapt and alter methods.** You are the best expert in what you need. When you embark on a path of growth, experiment with adapting and altering the methods to support your development. Self-improvement methods are not meant to be rigid. They provide structure and context but are flexible to move where you need them.
3. **Track your progress.** Chronic pain can make us foggy and forgetful. It can be hard to remember what we did yesterday, let alone the progress we have made over the last six months. Using an evidence journal to record your shifts in perspective and your personal triumphs will spur you on and keep you moving forward! I have a small journal that I record bullet point reflections in. This keeps it quick and easy to track my progress. In the mornings I write down five intentions I have for how I want to be or what I want to do that day. In the evening I write down at least five successes I had in attitude, mind-set, or action.

Reinvent Your Dreams

Your pain does not have to stop you! You can reinvent your dreams! I invite you to make a list of dreams and goals you have had in life.

Choose a few that leap out at you. As you do this, you might hear yourself saying things like "yeah right. Not anymore! I hurt too much to do that." If that is true, I think you will get tremendous value from this exercise. Brainstorm creative ways that you could reinvent the dream so that you could still make it a reality. Ask for input from friends if you get stuck. For example, I used to love hiking, until my health problems turned any attempt at a hike into a painful nightmare. So I reinvented that dream—maintaining the essence, but adjusting the method. Now I enjoy the beauty of nature in a way that is conducive to my current health by going for short walks on flat paths in the woods, or sitting on the beach, or riding my bike leisurely through the park. Be committed to your dreams.

Be Gracious with Yourself

We are often our own worst critics! Try not to compare yourself to others. Just look at yourself. What do you want? Where did you start? How far have you come? What is your next step?

You do not need to force yourself to keep up or go to rigorous conferences if you are not up to it! Get the CDs or DVDs to listen to from the comfort of your own home. Teleclasses and online resources are another great way to learn!

Develop a Growth Team

Who in your life would support you and want to join you as you embark on a journey to become your best self? With a Growth Team, you can help each other learn new skills and research different methods and help each other master them. You can brainstorm when you face challenges and attend workshops together. The synergy of a great team has unstoppable potential! Make a list of potential team members, contact them this week, and see what transformations happen in your life with a supportive Growth Team!

Always keep in mind that you can be *your* best and make a difference in the world, even if your life is marked by pain. I invite you to embark on a journey to make the comeback of your life.

Do not let pain keep you from developing your full potential!

ABOUT THE AUTHOR

Joanna Wasmuth is an expert in the day-to-day impact of chronic pain, having lived with fibromyalgia for 17 years. But she is a thriver and now specializes in empowering achievers with chronic pain to make the comeback of their lives. She is a certified dream coach®, speaker, and author, and she created the LifeThr!ve Personal Coaching Series for People with Chronic Pain. Prior to founding Harmony Coaching Group, she was an award-winning marketing and design consultant for more than 10 years. She is sought after for her innovative and creative solutions that get results. You can contact Joanna at grow@harmonycoaching.com or at http://www.harmonycoaching.com.

70

The Keys to Thinking Positively

John Ellis

Recent studies into how our minds work have revealed that you can be shown how to think positively. You will discover, to your delight, that you have a powerful friend just waiting and willing to help you through your life. This friend, when asked in the right way, will be happy to make thinking positively a truly effective part of your life. Your friend is your unconscious (or subconscious) mind.

Your unconscious mind likes to support you by carrying out what it thinks you want to achieve. It obtains this information by listening in to your thoughts and internal conversations. Unfortunately, however, it often hears internal statements like the following: "I'm going to fail"; "I'm going to panic"; "I feel sick"; "I feel trapped"; "I'm worried about flying"; "It could go wrong"; and so on.

Your unconscious mind hears "I'm going to panic," so it says to itself, *Oh . . . John wants to panic. Fine, I know how to make John panic—I've been successfully doing this for ages.* Before you know it, you are panicking because your unconscious mind is carrying out what it thinks you want it to do.

Have you ever heard of a self-fulfilling prophesy? That is precisely what you experience because your unconscious mind reacts according to your internal thoughts and conversations, by creating the subsequent actions and feelings to fulfill your prophesy.

So how do you change things? Actually, it is very simple, and you have probably already deduced the answer, but you need to incorporate it into your daily life to make it effective. The solution is to always think about and say what it is you *do* want to do or how you *do* want to feel. For example, instead of the thoughts shown above, you need to have thoughts such as "I will be successful"; "I am calm and relaxed"; "I feel fine"; and so on.

However, we now come to a quirk when we look at how your unconscious mind processes instructions that many people consider to be positive, such as "I'm not going to worry"; "Don't be tense"; or "I'm not going to get it wrong"; and so on. You will notice that all these "positive" instructions actually contain a negative word—either *not* or *don't*. You will also observe that each of these instructions also contains words that may cause you a problem, that is, *going to worry, be tense,* and *going to get it wrong*, so you are actually drawing your problems to the attention of your unconscious mind, which is the last thing you want to do.

In addition, and rather interestingly, our unconscious minds do not process negative words at the first attempt. In fact, when it hears "don't be tense," the process is as follows: It hears *don't*, but at that moment it does not know what it is it should not do—it could be anything, and it tends to disregard this word. Then your mind hears the words *be tense*, which it takes as a command, and you are left thinking about and becoming tense, which is the total opposite of what you actually want.

Many people say to me that the harder they try not to think about a particular thing or try not to feel a particular way, the more they seem to be drawn to doing that very thing or feeling that way. You have probably noticed this yourself, and you can now understand the reason for this phenomenon.

So again, the solution is to rephrase your thoughts into what you do want, for example, "I will keep myself active"; "I am calm and relaxed"; "It will go really well."

It will certainly pay you rich dividends to always think about precisely what you *do* want because you will then harness the wonderful power of your friend and make thinking positively a really effective part of your life.

Also, watch out for words like *no, never, can't,* or *won't* as they also signal that you are formulating negative suggestions, which you will need to rephrase into the positive. If negative instructions slip out, as they will now and then, tag onto the end the instruction "instead do . . ." (whatever it is you do want to do or have happen).

276

A word of warning about *why* and *what if* questions, for example, "Why does this always happen to me?"; "Why do I always behave this way?"; "What if it doesn't go as I planned?" Have you ever noticed that when you ask yourself any *why* or *what if* question, you always receive a whole host of negative answers and thoughts? Again, this appears to be another quirk of our unconscious minds—to always answer this type of question with negative reasons and answers you really do not want to hear. Consequently, totally avoid *why* and *what if* questions because they are counterproductive to thinking positively.

Similarly, with children, we should always say to them what it is we *do* want them to do and not what we *do not* want them to do; for example, instead of "don't drop it" (*crash!*), say "hold it firmly." How many times in a day do you hear children being told not to do this or that? Instead, always ask children to do what it is you *do* want them to do. Parents and teachers can benefit enormously by practically applying this information because it helps children to improve their behavior.

If you still experience difficulty in thinking positively, this is probably because you regularly experience negative emotions in your life, such as anger, sadness, hurt, rejection, fear, anxiety, stress, worry, or guilt. If this is the case, have you ever considered just letting go of these disabling emotions? Or have you thought that this is just the way you are and that consequently, it is not possible for you to change and let go?

The good news is that there are a number of therapies that are able to help you remove these unpleasant feelings. The ensuing calm, resourceful, and happy states of mind will then allow you to become totally positive by using the above suggestions.

So always remember: Don't *don't!* Start training your friend to always think about precisely what it is you *do* want and how you *do* want to feel. It is definitely worth the effort because this will help you to produce positive self-fulfilling prophesies . . . and how good will this make you feel?

ABOUT THE AUTHOR

John Ellis was drawn to study and qualify as a master practitioner of Time Line Therapy™ because it is natural, elegant, and very effective. It also produces results that are fast and lasting. John additionally is a master practitioner of Neuro Linguistic Programming (NLP), and he successfully combines both disciplines to help people, mainly from the United Kingdom, to overcome their emotional problems and phobias. After clients have let go of all their negative feelings, John shows them how to think positively so that they can move on and enjoy their lives to the full. Visit him online at http://www.myproblemsgone.com.

71

Academic Probation, a Summer Alone, and a Bowl Full of Blueberries: A Tiny Life Lesson

Joan Pasay

Before we get to know each other any further, I think it best to get one of the best-kept secrets about me out in the open right away: I failed grade 10 math class. It was not really due to my inability to learn. It had more to do with my ability to dream away my time, thinking about my future. I had so many questions. How would I work my life out? How would I reach all of my goals? Would I really have to master geometry to be fulfilled?

My life really sucked. Not only did I not understand how I would get from classroom 202B to everything I wanted in life, I was teetering on the brink of not being able to graduate. Apparently, passing math was required, and since I was failing the class, I was put on academic probation.

My parents informed me via a "family meeting" that academic probation was something that colleges did not appreciate, so I was enrolled in grade 10 math to be completed during the summer break—via correspondence.

While all my friends were whooping it up at summer camp, I was at home, alone, in my bedroom, staring at my correspondence lessons. If I could pass this course, I could move on to the next math level in the fall semester, get off academic probation, and be on track to graduate.

For the first part of the summer I spent most of my days in my bedroom with my correspondence lessons still enclosed in their airtight plastic wrap, my brand-new coiled notebook cracked open to page one, and me staring out my half-opened bedroom window trying to devise a way I could pass this course without doing any work. Day after day, I failed to come up with a viable plan of action that would get me the results I wanted.

When I would get frustrated with trying to figure out how on earth I would ever graduate, I went back to what I was doing in my first math class: thinking about my future. This proved to be quite a downer too. How would my life work out? How would I get past this summer and what seemed to be an insurmountable barrier? How would I get off academic probation, get my diploma, see and do the things I wanted to experience, and all the other stuff that I was thinking about when I failed grade 10 math the first time?

It was during one of these days in late July, after a few hours of lots-of-thinking-and-no-doing, that I decided I deserved a break and went to the kitchen to forage for a snack. When I returned to my summer math haven with sandwich in hand, my mother was standing in my bedroom holding my plastic-wrapped correspondence lessons. I swallowed my unchewed mouthful of sandwich and realized I was in trouble. *This would have been a great day to actually have opened that package*, I thought. Too late.

My mother flung herself on the bed, burst into tears, and assumed a fetal position, all while still clutching my stack of correspondence lessons. Maybe it was a good thing they were still in their protective wrapping—my mother was crying buckets.

Long story short, my mother agreed to stop with the tears and wailing and leave my bedroom if I agreed to at least unwrap and try to decipher the first assignment.

My mother left my bedroom whimpering and silently closed the door behind her. Off came the plastic wrap. The correspondence lessons breathed their first breath out of their airtight jail and puffed up in size about two inches. I sat up straight, positioned my coiled ring scribbler into writing mode, grabbed my freshly hand-sharpened HB pencil, and started reading the first section. It was all about comparing distances using geometry.

Question one seemed pretty easy. Actually, it was so simple that I closed my lesson book and checked to make sure I had received grade 10 math correspondence and not a lower level by mistake. The question only required a yes or no, and I proudly put the obviously correct answer of yes and moved on to question two.

I felt a nudging to stop and look at question one again. Had I missed something? I read the question aloud just to make sure my eagerness to satiate my weeping mother had not clouded my judgment:

Mary and Frank are standing side by side both facing east. Frank turns north one degree away from Mary to face northeast. If Mary and Frank each walk in a straight direction for five miles, will they both end up in the same place?

I pondered Mary and Frank's details. I sketched out their journey on my white notepaper. What was the big deal? All Frank had done was turn one single degree to the north. Would that tiny action really have resulted in him not ending up where Mary did? I drew a Mary and a Frank on my notepad. I made sure they were equal in stature just so neither would have an advantage. I got out my pencil and extended an arrow away from Mary due east. I did the same for Frank, with his arrow heading straight northeast. I charted out each step that Mary and Frank made. My eyes moved away from my notepaper and looked out my bedroom window toward the field behind our house. I imagined Mary and Frank walking and walking under the hot summer sun. At the beginning, the two stayed pretty much close together. However, to my surprise, the farther they walked, the farther they moved away from each other.

Who knew! Frank and Mary did not end up in the same place! At that very moment my bedroom door creaked open, and my mother, all freshened up and with a smile from ear to ear, walked in with a big bowl full of fresh blueberries. She placed the bowl on my notebook, leaving a blue circle stain right over top my artist's rendition of Frank's one-degree-of-difference journey. The sudden interruption jolted me away from my vision of Frank and Mary walking under the hot summer sun. I sat there for the rest of the afternoon eating the blueberries one by one until the bowl was completely empty. I thought about all the life pondering I had done during grade 10 math class (round one) and realized that my life did not suck, that I would be more than capable of seeing everything I wanted to see, that I would experience everything I wanted to experience, and accomplish everything I wanted to accomplish. I simply had to turn myself one degree toward the direction I wanted and walk in a straight line. Oh sure, I realized that at the beginning I would not be very far away from everyone else or from where I started. But over time, my one-degree shift would take me miles away from my starting point. Little by little, over time, my one-degree shift would take me where I wanted to go.

ABOUT THE AUTHOR

Joan Pasay passed her grade 10 summer math class, aced grades 11 and 12, and was able to graduate with her friends. She is now a 30-something business and marketing consultant, college instructor, entrepreneur, author, musician, and parent. She lives in beautiful Vancouver, British Columbia, Canada, with her family. You can learn more about Joan, find out how to contact her, and read more of her articles at http://www.joanpasay.com.

72

Talkitout:
How to Become a Powerful Speaker Fast!

Halina St. James

When Jane came to see me, she was terrified. She was a living example of that old saying "I'd rather die than speak in public." For a minute I wondered if she really would die before she gave her speech. She could not look me in the eyes. She turned bright red. There was sweat on her brow. She stammered, and that was all before she gave her one-minute presentation. I loved her! I just knew she would be my greatest success.

Jane was a receptionist for a large company with a strong public profile. She was sent to me along with four company account managers to spruce up their presentation skills. That was a smart move on the part of her boss. He knew the importance of public speaking. The company wanted everyone to represent it with confidence. And Jane was important because she was usually the first person people met.

Presentation skills are critical for everyone, whether you are a receptionist, account manager, sales person, CEO, president, teacher, preacher, broadcaster, or homemaker. Poor presentations are costing corporations tens of thousands of dollars—in lost orders, wasted time, and mistakes. They eat away at your reputation and confidence.

Every time you open your mouth to speak, you have two choices. You can inspire, make the sale, get your message across, influence others, and make a powerful impact; or you can bore, lose the sale, embarrass yourself, or, worst of all, make no impression whatsoever. The choice is yours.

Of course, there are a lucky few who do not have to make any choice. They were born with the "gift of the gab." They can stand up fearlessly and delight and inspire us. Most of us, though, were not born that lucky. For whatever reason we are simply terrified to speak in public, or we do it badly. It is not our fault. Nobody ever showed us how to do it properly.

There are two key ingredients to being a great speaker, whether you are speaking to 1 person or 1,000. First, be passionate. Believe and care about what you say. People may disagree with you, but they will respect you. You will never convince everyone anyway, so figure out what is important to you, and speak from the heart.

The second key ingredient is to be yourself. Do not try to sound like someone else by imitating him. Your audience will know immediately. You will lose their trust. You are a wonderful gifted speaker if you just trust yourself to speak in your own, true voice.

Being passionate and being yourself is that foundation that you build on as a speaker. Now you need the right technique. Almost everyone uses the wrong technique when he prepares for his speech or presentation. Do you do this? You sit at your computer or grab pen and paper and stare at the blank screen or paper. You think.

Then the thoughts pour out of your brain and get tap-tap-tapped into the keyboard as sentences to be evaluated by the eyes. Your eyes move the words around, and your fingers follow through. You carry on like this until finally—hours, days, or weeks later—you finish. What a waste of your precious time.
The trouble is that this process bypasses two vital organs. The words are never tested on the lips. And the content is judged purely on how it looks to the eye, rather than on how it will sound to the listener. Now there is nothing wrong with this method if people are going to read what you wrote or, heaven forbid, you are going to read it to them. It does not work when you are preparing a speech or presentation. You cannot write something that is going to be heard the same way you write something that is going to be read.

Have you ever tried to bake a chocolate cake using a lemon pie recipe? No matter how fresh your eggs and juicy your lemons, you are not going to make a chocolate cake. You have the wrong recipe. If you want people to really listen, to be inspired and to learn when you speak, you need to prepare your material using the right recipe.

Here is the right technique. Imagine your audience in the room in front of you. Now say your first idea out loud to them. Do not write it. Whether it is one word, one sentence, or a story, talk it out loud. Speak the way you always do. Listen to yourself as you do. Do not whisper. Talk it out loud in your normal speaking voice. Get used to talking out loud and listening to yourself. If you cannot bear to listen to yourself, how can you ask an audience to listen to you?

Be creative. Try saying your thought out loud a few different ways. Keep doing it until you hear the best way. Now write it down. Look at the sentence you just wrote. Now say it out loud again, and continue speaking the next sentence in different ways until you hear the best way. Now write that down. Keep talking it out, then writing it out like this until you finish your speech or presentation. What you are doing is preparing it the way the audience will hear it. You are writing for the ear, not the eye.

Before the computer, before the typewriter, before the pen, we talked. We told great epic stories without writing them out first. Today, with all our technology, we make lousy presentations, tell uninspiring stories, and bore our audiences to tears. We have to go back and do what the Romans and Greeks did. Talk it out loud before we write it. That is the right recipe.

The beauty of this technique is that every time you go back a few sentences and talk them out loud, you are rehearsing. By the time you finish writing your speech, you will know it. And because you are talking out loud all the time, the words are your own true voice. You are not imitating anyone. This technique works regardless if you are a seasoned pro or a nervous novice like Jane. It makes great speakers, not just great speeches.

At the end of our session Jane delivered a passionate, inspiring speech. We all had tears in our eyes as we applauded her success. Jane was stunned she was so good. I was not. I knew right from the start she would be a success because all of us, given the right tools, are brilliant speakers.

ABOUT THE AUTHOR

Halina St. James is the internationally renowned communications coach and professional speaker who developed *Talkitout*. Her technique guarantees that you will become a powerful, persuasive speaker in minutes. Through her company Podium: Media and Communications Coaching, Halina delivers workshops and speeches in communication skills and media management to corporations, governments, and broadcasters. She is the author of *TalkItOut: Discover the Secrets of Powerful Presentations* and *Dealing with the Media*. Halina has been a globe-trotting television news producer, an actor, and a teacher. Visit her Web site, http://www.podiumcoaching.com, to book your personal or group workshops.

73

The Divorce and Dysfunctional Relationship Solution

Ken Donaldson

Know someone who has been through a divorce? Maybe you or a loved one? Have you seen or felt the pain? Would you like to prevent it from happening again? Yes, I am sure you would. In this chapter you will learn three Passion, Power, and Purpose Principles that will enable you to have the healthiest relationships, *if* you apply them

First, a few short questions: Why are you here? Where are you going with this life of yours? What is most important to you? If you do not know who you are, where you are going, what is important, or your relationship requirements, how can you ever expect have a full and passionate life, much less a lasting relationship?

It may seem easier to just go along with what you have been doing or do what you think others want you to do. *Easier*, however, results in disaster when it comes to **not** planning your life or relationships.

Do this instead: Know and walk your True Life Path, which means knowing your values, your purpose, and your life vision.

Vision gives your life a target that represents everything you want to do, be, and have in your life. With your vision you know exactly what you are aiming for. Here are two exercises that will help you create your vision.

Exercise 1: *A miracle occurs tonight while you are sleeping, and tomorrow, when you awake, your life has everything you have wanted. What would it be like, look like, sound like, and feel like, and who would you be sharing it with?* Start writing, and do not stop. Go through all the primary areas of your life: social, emotional, spiritual, financial, relational, familial, vocational, and recreational.

Exercise 2: Create a vision map. Gather magazines and photographs, and cut out pictures, images, words, phrases, and symbols to which you feel drawn. Glue what you have cut out onto a piece of poster or mat board. Add glitter and sequins, a frame, bits of fabric, and, with markers or paint, draw, color, and write other words and symbols that you want in your life.

Hang your vision map prominently in your personal living space, where you will be exposed to it daily. Meditate about it, visualize it, or do other attraction and manifestation exercises with it, but the main thing is just to have it in your living space.

Next, read the first exercise out loud, every day for a month and at least once a week thereafter. Read it in the first person (using *I* and *me*) and in the present tense (*now*), as if it is all actually happening for you in this moment.

For example, if you have a vision of wealth, health, and relationship fulfillment, you might visualize and say the following: "My bank account has $100,000 in it, and my portfolio shows a net worth of over $1 million; I exercise every day, eat healthy food, and meditate twice a day; my relationship with my life partner is perfect as we work through every issue that we have; we are harmonious with each other and cheerfully share in all the tasks and responsibilities of running a household."

This vision work can bring an onslaught of prosperous and abundant opportunities your way as you begin to allow your vision to pull you into your Ultimate Greatness—for you and all humankind!

- **Passion, Power, and Purpose Principle #1:** Create your vision, and you will have the magnet that will pull you into your ultimate and utmost future.

What are your core values? Not sure? If you find yourself having difficulty making decisions (especially in relationships), completing tasks and projects, or often feeling overwhelmed with too much to do in too little time, then it is time for you to create a value-driven life to guide you. This is a process of establishing your values and prioritizing all decisions and actions based on those values. Why struggle when you can live your life with greater ease?

Essentially, your values are the elements of your life that you regard as most important. Below is a small sampling of some value terms:

> **Accomplishment**
> **Communication**
> **Decisiveness**
> **Discipline**
> **Empowerment**
> **Faith**
> **Gratitude**
> **Health**
> **Imagination**
> **Joy**
> **Love/romance**
> **Money**
> **Prosperity**
> **Quality of work**
> **Openness**
> **Peace**
> **Spirituality**
> **Teamwork**
> **Truth**
> **Trust**
> **Unity**
> **Variety**
> **Wealth**
> **Well-being**
> **Wisdom**
> **Zest**

Spend some time reflecting on what is really most important to you and identify your top 10 values—the 10 that you most stand for.

- What would you risk embarrassing yourself for?
- What would you not be afraid that everyone knew about you?
- What would you risk being rejected for?
- What would you risk dying for?

People do not live a value-driven life because they want to avoid conflict with others. They are simply afraid of what others think. By avoiding this perceived conflict, these same people then create a debilitating inner conflict for themselves because they are not living according to their values.

Who do you want to live your life according to? You or others?

Commit yourself to a value-driven life, and you will attract people of similar values and people who will support and encourage you to continue to live accordingly. Ignore your values, and you will attract other people who ignore their own core values as well as yours.

- **Passion, Power, and Purpose Principle #2:** Allow your values to be the guides and markers on your path that keep you going in the proper direction toward your vision to fulfill your purpose.

We each have a unique purpose. When *you* know what your purpose is and live according to it, you will experience an amazing sense of empowerment and passion.

Answer the following questions to get started:

- What is it that really turns me on?
- What is my unique gift or talent?
- What do I do, or have wanted to do, that would make a huge difference in the world today?
- What is it that I do that gives my life the most meaning?
- Where and with whom am I the happiest?
- If I had one billion dollars to spend on one cause, what would I spend it on?
- If I were to describe my ideal or perfect day, what would it look like, sound like, and be like?

Look closely at what you have written here and what you also defined in your vision work and your values clarification. What are the common threads that keep showing up? What is the *fire in your belly* that wakes you up in the middle of the night?

Work with this process until you come up with the completed statement, "The purpose of my life is_____." When that statement resonates as a 10 on a scale from 1 to 10, then you know you have found your purpose.

- **Passion, Power, and Purpose Principle #3:** Allow your life purpose to be the flashlight to keep you on your True Life Path.

When you are on your True Life Path, you will find the highest degree of passion and empowerment. This is the place where you will be in your integrity, which means to be in your wholeness and in alignment with your values. In other words, it is the place where your *walk* will match your *talk*.

And this is *the* place in which you will make your best relationship decisions. Understand the importance of marrying yourself first! Know who you really are, what your purpose is, what your values are, and what your vision is. Get whole with yourself *first* so you will not look to someone else to complete this for you. As Shakespeare once wrote, "This above all else, to thine own self be true."

ABOUT THE AUTHOR

Ken Donaldson is the author of the life and relationship success book *Marry YourSelf First! Saying "I Do" to a Life of Passion, Power and Purpose* (http://www.marryUfirst.com). Ken founded the REALationship Coaching programs to empower people to have more successful lives, businesses, and relationships by building a powerful relationship with themselves first. He is a licensed mental health counselor, is board certified as an addictions professional and clinical hypnotherapist, and is certified as a master relationship coach. He has been called "a blend of Dr. Phil mixed in with Buddha and Salvador Dali." Visit him online at http://www.REALationshipCoach.com.

74

RELATIONSHIP SATISFACTION

Satisfying Couple Relationships: Some Common Sense Approaches

Sheryl R. Brown

What gets in the way of a satisfying couple relationship? There are many things that prevent a couple from really enjoying each other. Differences of opinion, misunderstandings, power struggles, unmet needs, and lack of time together are just a few. In order to be successful in our approach, we first need to understand what is going on. Let's identify and consider some major stumbling blocks and where they originate and then find ways to navigate, if not remove them.

What are these obstacles? Generally, I see them falling into the following basic categories of challenges.

Personality Differences

Here I am referring to the regular differences that we all have. As people, we are all individuals—no two are exactly alike. In addition, we are often drawn to people whose traits are opposite to ours, thus complementing us. These differences can result in communication fall-outs and conflicts, ranging from major to minor—and everything in between—or they can be a means of creating balance. One partner communicates more with words, the other more with actions. One likes to include others in most outings, the other wants more one-on-one time. One makes plans, the other enjoys spontaneity. One has ideas, the other gets things done. One is sharp-thinking with analysis, the other majors in diplomacy. One spends generously, the other saves wisely. One keeps everything in its place, the other creates new places for things on a daily basis. All in all, these are not either right or wrong ways of being and doing; they are preferences or differences of style. Personality inventories such as the Myers Briggs can help assess and describe each person's profile.

Values, Faith, and Beliefs

Differences in this category may result in insurmountable obstacles. Each couple has to make their own determination as to how important it is to go to the same church or synagogue together, how to identify or discover their individual beliefs, and whether or not to have their children baptized or to wait until their children declare their own faiths. Some have successfully created ways to live with mutual respect and acceptance of differences. Some try and then decide the partnership is unworkable. On the other hand, agreement in this area does not guarantee relationship success.

Mistreatment and Control

On some level, we all experience and mete out something we might label as "mistreatment" of each other from time to time. The question is whether this behavior is relatively minimal or infrequent, such as your partner leaving a mess in your working space or eating the last piece of cake, or whether it is serious abuse that threatens your safety and well-being. It is essential to get outside help in such cases. Whether it is verbal or physical or both, it does have an emotional impact, and the damage can be great. Feeling threatened or controlled in a relationship does not make for mutuality and equality. Happiness and satisfaction are thwarted. For best results, control is shared, and each has self-control.

Maturity and Personal Development

If one or both partners are lacking in personal growth, or if one forges ahead in working on personal issues and the other does not, this can become a hindrance to enjoying the relationship. One scenario is the couple who has been used to a particular way of arguing. One partner decides that it is not productive and no longer participates in the same way. The other then feels some form of disengagement and may either continue trying to provoke the other into the usual fight or may withdraw, feeling abandoned or cut off. It is not impossible to find some satisfaction with your partner in this setting (consider the "kiss and make up" theme common in stories), but it can bring up chronic frustration in the one who wants to move beyond this pattern.

In all these differences, I see a continuum, just like there is a continuum or range in the pitch of musical notes, the volume of sound, colors on a spectrum, and the intensity of light and dark. Your problems will range from differences you expect in a relationship and do not worry about to issues that are aggravating and intolerable. You may not decide to part ways with your partner if he or she squeezes the toothpaste a different way (or refuses to use it!), but you may decide not to join up with someone who wants children when you do not.

How can these obstacles be navigated successfully?

- **Reading books or articles.** Many couples are able to arrive at workable solutions by helping themselves to information in print form or online.
- **Discussion with others.** Talking to others who have faced similar issues and figured out what worked for them may be enough to help you with yours. This may come in the context of friends, family, acquaintances, church and community forums, or support groups. Grassroots support is a valuable resource that can stand alone.
- **Consultation with a professional.** This may take place in an individual or couples counseling setting with a professional marriage counselor. One benefit of this mode is that the focus is on you and your unique combination of challenges. As a therapist, I tailor make strategies in the moment, using your input, with you and your partner and your current circumstances in mind. Personally, my common sense approach has been derived from years of reading, education, and experience, resulting in a distilled wisdom uniquely my own.

Your success in crafting a satisfying relationship with your partner is your own to achieve. Many resources are out there for you to employ. Knowing where to give in and let things go—to transcend the problem—and where to look further into getting your needs met is the critical balance to find.

May your partnership be all you have imagined and more!

ABOUT THE AUTHOR

Sheryl Brown, MS, is a Licensed Marriage and Family Therapist with a private practice in Issaquah, Washington, and is the owner of Sunray Counseling, a place for hope and healing. She provides individual and couples counseling for those who want more satisfaction in their relationships. Her training as a systems therapist uniquely equips her to understand the issues an individual presents in the context of his or her family background and cultural and community influences. Visit her Web site at http://www.sunraycounseling.com.

75

REMEDY FOR COMPLAINTS

Cures for the Common Complaint

Betty Mahalik

"If you complain, it will remain." My 84-year-old mother shared these words of wisdom with me recently. That message, close kin to the statement "what you resist persists," set my mental wheels in motion, wondering what my world would be like if I gave up complaining. So here, in this public forum, I am making a declaration: I am giving up complaining (at least for today), and I challenge you to join me in the quest for a complaint-free world!

Most of us complain to relieve tension, avoid taking action or responsibility, or just as a mindless time filler. Hang out around corporate water coolers any day of the week, any hour of the day or night, and you will find people complaining about everything from the dismal state of management to the food in the vending machines. Think about the last social event you attended. The conversations were likely filled with complaints about the traffic, how lousy the weather person is where you live, the state of the schools or other social institutions, or the state of the world in general.

And while it can feel good, worthy, or even justified to complain, complaining is like mental/emotional superglue: It keeps us stuck in an unpleasant state of mind and not doing one thing to improve our world. Here are some recommendations for how to begin eliminating the complaint virus from your life.

1. *Ask yourself if there is something you can or need to do about a situation.* Most of the time, when I complain about traffic, I admit it is because *I* have underestimated the amount of time it takes to get anywhere in Las Vegas and am mad that the other hundred thousand or so drivers on the road, plus road maintenance crews and traffic control engineers, have failed to consider my busy schedule! In short, I can take responsibility for my timing or where I choose to

live, but I can do nothing about the condition of the roads, timing of traffic lights, or other drivers.

2. *If there is really nothing you can do about a situation, then get over it!* Why pollute your mind, waste time, and stick yourself in a negative place if there is nothing you can do about a situation? It may require you to finally accept that sometimes life and what it hands you are unfair. It will require you to stop holding on to what you never had control of anyway. Get over it.

3. *Act, if you can do so without blaming, judging, making wrong, criticizing, or otherwise adding insult to injury.* I recently read a letter to an advice columnist from a woman asking how to handle the following situation: It seemed the office manager where she worked was always sending others to professional training seminars, while the writer of the letter was "left in the office to do everyone else's work." She said she was "tired of being treated like a second-class citizen."

The columnist wisely suggested that instead of complaining, she find a class she wanted to attend and then ask the manager if the company would pay for her to go. In short, she had to stop being a "volunteer victim," take responsibility for her happiness, and make her needs known in a professional, mature manner. Asking is no guarantee that the other person will automatically grant the request, but it sure beats complaining!

Complaining does not improve situations. It certainly does not improve our minds, and it contributes to a toxic environment around us. Because complaining is so deeply entrenched in behavior, you may have to do as they advise in 12-step programs: Take it one day at a time . . . maybe just one hour at a time. *Just for today, I will not complain. Just for today, I will take responsibility for my actions, change what I can, and get over what I cannot.*

I may be dreaming the impossible to think I can actually cure myself of the complaint virus. But I imagine a world without complaints: a world where people accept what is, accept responsibility for their decisions and actions, and a world where we make requests rather than waste our most precious resources—time and energy—hoping others will finally figure out what we need and give it to us, instead of us having to ask for it. The vision is so compelling, the possibilities so appealing that I, for one, am willing to try . . . one day, one hour, one minute, one complaint at a time. Will you join me?

ABOUT THE AUTHOR

Betty Mahalik is a life and business coach, corporate trainer, and facilitator who has been teaching people to communicate effectively, set goals, manage stress, and deal with change for nearly two decades. She founded her firm, Dynamic Solutions, in 1987. A former television news reporter and anchorwoman, Betty worked for eight years in the field of public relations prior to starting her own business. "My mission is to help people transform their potential into performance." Contact Betty at (702) 658–4425 or bettym@dynamic-coaching.com, or visit her online at http://www.dynamic-coaching.com.

76

Shooting for the Summit:
A Metaphor for Life and Business

Paula Gregorowicz

Recently, I took a much-needed vacation to Zion National Park in Utah. At the time we planned the trip, we had no intention of tackling one of the park's crown jewels, the Angels Landing trail. We had read about it (strenuous, not for the faint of heart), heard about it ("I was never so scared" and "unlike anything else I have ever done"), and decided to embrace being chicken, play it safe, and stick to more moderate hiking. However, about two weeks prior to the trip, I got the bright idea that we should do the hike and use it as a metaphor for life. Needless to say, this brought sideways glances and "you've got to be kidding" looks from my partner.

Let me start by saying that Angels Landing is not Mt. Everest, and plenty of people hike it each year. That being said, however, it is one of the most challenging and unique pure hiking experiences in America's national parks. Angels Landing is a 6000-plus-foot peak. In order to get to the top, you must hike 2.5 miles one way to the top and climb 1,500 vertical feet. What makes it special is the last half mile, which rises 500 feet on what seems to be a razor's edge on the back side of the peak. It involves a lot of rock scrambling, the use of chains driven into the rock, and navigating a path that is as narrow as three feet wide (go ahead, measure that out now), with a 2,000-foot sheer drop on each side. That is a lot of air and a long way down. Even the hiking guides and signs state that this trail is not for the faint of heart, anyone with vertigo, or a fear of heights. Considering that I cling to the walls of 100-foot lighthouses, sob on Ferris wheels, and death grip the lap bar on the calm sky rides in amusement parks, you would wonder what makes me want to do this.

To cut to the happy ending, we made it. It was tiring and heart stopping at times, but we got to the top and actually had a fun time doing it. It was a wonderful exercise in staying present in the moment and letting everything else just melt away. Coming back down gave me a new perspective on what it means to stay balanced, keep your center of gravity low, and focus on where you want to go (and not the vast amount of air space and hang time just waiting for a wrong move).

What I learned on this little journey is that sometimes you just have to get very clear on what success means to you, set your sights on the top, and move up and onward in spite of the fear. While my whole "metaphor for life" crusade was originally more a motivating mantra than anything else, I discovered 10 key success factors for life and business amid my journey up and down the mountain.

Preparation

While we decided last minute to hike this trail, we would not have had a prayer of hope had we not already spent many months maintaining excellent physical conditioning. A little due diligence, foresight, and planning gives any endeavor a higher probability of success.

Direction

If you do not know where you are going, how will you know when you get there? In this case we had a clearly defined path and summit, which made this piece of the puzzle very easy. Do you have a clear vision of what you want your life or business to be about? If you do not, how will you know if you are heading in the right direction?

Judgment and Common Sense

The world is an unpredictable place. The weather is even more unpredictable, especially in the canyons. En route to the summit, we had to pass through Refrigerator Canyon, a small slot canyon. Part way through, we heard a large crack of thunder reverberate all around us. We stopped and wondered if it would end our summit because in the desert the flooding happens in a flash, and exposed cliffs pose extreme lightning danger. At that moment, and every step along the narrow path, we had to use our judgment to assess the situation and risk. How do you periodically assess the steps along the path within your life and business?

Perspective and Focus

There is nothing like standing in a canyon between massive cliffs or being atop one of them to gain a little perspective. Grasping the bigger picture is crucial. Just as critical is the perspective you bring to any situation. Both can make or break your efforts. Focused vision is required to tap into a laser-like focus, removing all distractions from your attention and staying in alignment with your goal. Do you have an idea of your big picture, and are you focused on the goal? Or are you doing today the same thing you did yesterday just because it is what you did yesterday?

Balance

On the edge of 2,000-foot drop-offs is no place for two left feet or a klutz; the margin for error is tiny. Balance is important, physically and emotionally. The ability to maintain an inner calm and a faith in a higher power, despite ups and downs, is critical to personal mastery.

Flexibility

On the mountain it meant being able to stretch and contort our bodies to fit the allotted spaces. At times I simply shouted to my partner, who has shorter legs than me, "Just grow, will you!?" In life and business, flexibility is needed to go with the flow and respond to the constant changes and challenges in today's environment.

Strength

It takes a lot of inner strength to achieve a goal. In this case it took physical strength as well. Keeping yourself strong through attention and self-care on all levels—body, mind, and spirit—will provide you a strong foundation to build the life and business of your wildest dreams.

Stamina

A deep well of energy and resources to tap into is important for the long haul. Treat your life and business like you would a distance run. Pace yourself, take breaks along the way, and remember to stop and refuel.

Persistence

Keep at it, putting one foot in front of the other. At times on the hike, fatigue would set it, muscles would burn, or fear would take over. Our lives are not defined by any given moment. Being able to make consistent, empowering choices over time is what separates success from failure.

Support System

The people, places, and things in our lives form the environment and support system so vital to keeping us alive and well. On our hike it meant food, water, layers of clothing, and connecting with other, fellow hikers. It looks a lot like that in real life as well in that we need to meet both our physical and emotional needs. The relationships we cultivate with ourselves and others, whether business or personal, create the ultimate supporting structure upon which we build our dreams.

If you incorporate these 10 key success factors into your life one small step at a time, you can rest assured that the faraway summits of your wildest dreams will get closer with each passing day. Feel the fear and do it anyway.

ABOUT THE AUTHOR

Paula Gregorowicz, owner of The Paula G Company, partners with women who are sick and tired of spending their days doing work they do not enjoy to help them blow the lid off their wildest dreams. You can learn more and subscribe to the free e-zine "Beyond the Daily Grind" at http://www.thepaulagcompany.com.

77

Romancing the Woman You Love

Karonne Mazier

Have you ever seen a woman who has received a romantic gesture or gift that is so spectacular, so powerful, it actually moves her to tears? Tears of joy. Tears of love. Tears of being overwhelmed with a man's complete thoughtfulness.

Even if only in the movies, have you seen that woman?

That is exactly what we are going to create together. And in the future, when you offer a gesture or a gift, that moment will transcend time. That moment will last through the next day . . . the next month . . . and through the next 10 years, and even longer.

Now, I know a man can show gestures of his affection and buy gifts for the woman he cherishes. But what about finding the perfect gift or creating the perfect romantic experience?

Let us take a moment to think about what a woman deeply desires and wants. It is especially important for a woman to feel treasured—that she is the most important person in the entire world to her man. And to make a woman feel this way is actually quite easy! It comes down to knowing that her man thinks about her. When you make a gesture or give a woman a gift, she wants it to reflect just how much you value her love—that you have thought about it and pondered how it is just perfect for her.

In fact, this is the essence of romance . . . and how you can keep it alive over the years. For a woman, romance is found in the details. Even the smallest attention to detail will make an impression on a woman. Simple gestures like sitting close to her, holding her hand when walking in the park, writing a short love note, or introducing her to friends and colleagues as "the most spectacular woman in the world" will endear you in a woman's heart.

Gentlemen, women do like to be indulged or spoiled occasionally with surprise expressions of your affection, despite any of her protests. Try even an effortless gesture like giving her flowers for no reason and see how she will reward you. What if you went just a little further and gave her a bouquet of flowers—the same arrangement she held on your wedding day or admired in a special restaurant or hotel? Now imagine how she will react when you put in more time and care to surprise her with a grand show of affection. Imagine how your relationship will blossom and how she will radiate sheer joy.

I cannot stress this enough: When you really want to indulge a woman, you need to create the ultimate romantic experience. The ultimate experience encompasses romance, creating a memorable occasion, and anchoring it with a personal and feminine gift. And when you create these experiences for a woman, you will see how her love and appreciation for you only increases with each reflection back to these moments.

To illustrate what I mean, allow me to recount a scenario where my husband got it perfect. I was returning from a business trip to Asia. As I was wandering around JFK searching for the car service I had asked my husband to organize, I finally saw a sign that read "My Royal Treasure." You see, the name of my line of fine jewelry is Royal Treasures Jewelry Collections. In my jet-lagged stupor, I was confused that it should be incorrectly written.

Nevertheless, I started following this man. Just then, my husband leaped out from around a corner! My heart nearly jumped right out of my body! He whisked me outside to a rented limousine, and inside, he had filled it with champagne, cheeses, flowers, and romantic music. As we drove home, my husband held my hand and suggested I take a closer look at the bouquet. Once again, I was confused, but we were having a giggle, so I peered among the petals. Sitting there in the center of a stately calla lily was a stunningly beautiful pair of earrings!

I do not think I could actually breathe for a minute or two. Was I still asleep on the flight and dreaming? And whenever I want a quick reminder of how much my husband truly treasures me, I quickly glance at that airport sign and realize how much he does think of me . . . enough that he should create a play on words with the name of my jewelry collection—something that is important to me.

Let us take a look at some factors that make such a moment unforgettable: the element of surprise; considerable thought, effort, and time; an experience tailored specifically for the woman; shared intimacy; amorous conversation; the spirit of playfulness; and extravagance. Incorporating even a few of these factors into a romantic experience permanently imprints into a woman's mind just how precious she is to her man. Now that is what a woman wants!

A woman wants—needs—to feel special to the man she loves, that he desires her and wants to please her. And when she feels this way, her amorous emotions take over.

Let me explain a bit more of what I am saying. The excitement of my husband's surprise immediately swept me up into a sense of lavishness, splendor, and gaiety. My mind was creating the most powerful love story as it was happening. I was living it . . . right at the moment.

That is right, gentlemen—women create most of the romance story in their heads.

Then to top off the whole experience, I have his earrings as a reminder—as an anchor—of what he did and how he feels about me. All I could think for months was how I was the luckiest woman in the world!

By creating similar moments for the woman you love, you will be memorializing special times. Often men do not realize that this is what women want. But this is exactly what women crave. Years later, you and your love will look back on these experiences as the highlights of your relationship together. You will talk about these times because these are the times you took the effort to create.

A gentleman sets the tone, the place, and the experience. A gentleman's sense of centeredness and peace shines through in the way he cares about those he loves and the world around him. He cares enough to make his woman feel as if she is the most wonderful being in the universe.

Allow me to offer you a bit of insight: Women are emotional beings, and women do love to be swept up in a whirlwind of passion, of enchantment, of frivolity. Every time your dearest love adorns a gift you have given her or glances at a photo of a special time together, the loving emotions connected with it only grow stronger. And that is the power of romance. Romance makes a woman feel desired, appreciated, and loved. It is precisely these feelings that are vital to a woman's happiness and fulfillment.

It is really quite simple. Romance begins with a single action and develops in a woman's head as she is living in the moment. It continues to grow grander and grander over time, with every reflection back to that moment.

So, gentlemen, if you just take the initiative to ignite a spark of romance, the woman you treasure will take it from there and turn it into a flame. A woman appreciates that her man wants to court her for a lifetime. She knows it is not easy . . . but she lives for it!

ABOUT THE AUTHOR

Romantic gift expert Karonne Mazier assists the gentleman in romancing his wife. At http://www.TheGallantGentlemansCommunique.com, sign up to receive unique romantic gift ideas. From now on, you will be able to create memorable experiences for your wife that will have her overcome with such emotion that she will be at a loss for words. She is going to gaze at you and wonder how she was so fortunate to be in your life. You will learn a way of being that will allow you to easily express your deepest feelings—that will always be instantly accessible at the appropriate moments. Are you ready to start?

78

Live Your Dreams by Applying Basic Sales Skills to Your Life

Lisa O'Brien

Have you ever wondered why some people always seem to get everything they want in life? One day an acquaintance tells you that he wants a great job, and the next thing you know, he is on a work assignment in some glamorous location. Then he tells you that he is thinking of buying a new place. Suddenly, you find yourself at the housewarming party of the year at his amazing waterfront home. One minute he is single, and the next, he is blissfully in love. You have to ask yourself, what is it with people like this? Why do they always get all the luck?

Guess what? It's not luck! They *make it happen* by applying basic sales skills to every aspect of their lives. They apply sales skills to their careers to secure career advancement opportunities. They apply sales skills to investment opportunities to build wealth. They apply sales skills to attract a partner.

Following their example, you, too, can apply basic sales skills to the following aspects of your life and make your dreams come true.

Selling in Careers

Career-savvy people can go from one career peak to another by applying basic sales skills in every aspect of their jobs. Career-savvy people know instinctively that to succeed at a fast pace, they must quickly and accurately identify what it is that their employers and industries need the most. For example, Bill Gates has built an amazing career and amassed a fortune by simply identifying and fulfilling the IT needs of millions of corporations and individuals. Career-savvy people do this by using investigative sales skills. They build rapport with colleagues and clients. They take the time to ask questions, listen, and get to know the needs of all stakeholders. They then pinpoint how their own skills and experiences fit in with those needs. Using this knowledge, they proactively approach their employers and demonstrate their industry knowledge, highlighting issues that they know their employers are passionate about. They emphasize how they can use their skills to resolve those issues. Put simply, they realize that no one can say no to something that they need.

Career Selling Dos

- Do identify what matters the most to your employer, clients, and industry.
- Do identify how your skills, education, and experience best fulfil those needs.
- Do approach your employer with your ideas.
- Do sell your ideas to your employer based on what *they* need and want.

Career Selling Don'ts

- Don't ignore the needs of your employer, clients, and industry.
- Don't miss opportunities you have identified by being afraid to take action.
- Don't ever try to gain advancement by promoting how you will benefit and neglecting to highlight the benefits to others.

Selling in Financial Matters

Like most financially wealthy people, you do not need to be the most intelligent, most educated, or highest salaried to become the most financially successful person that you know. How do you do it? By following the lead of other financially successful people. These people secure the investment deals that no one else can secure. Their wealth just grows and grows. While other people work very hard to save and earn money, they just never seem to secure the loans and investment opportunities they need to build wealth.

So what is the secret of building financial success? Financially successful people understand that building wealth is about identifying and maximizing opportunities for financial growth. They understand that to make a lot of money, they need to use their skills to make contact with the right people. They use selling skills to gain the confidence of investors and banking and financial institutions.

First, they use investigative sales skills to research and gain knowledge of the industry. They research every facet of the market that they wish to enter. They take their research a vital step further by investigating what it is that will make investors want to invest in them. When applying for financial backing, they emphasize how investors stand to gain and reassure them with risk minimization strategies.

Financial Selling Dos

- Do look actively for financial investment opportunities.
- Do research what matters to investors.
- Do highlight the benefits to investors.
- Do know the market inside and out and have a risk contingency plan to reassure investors.

Financial Selling Don'ts

- Don't expect financial backing for investments that you have not fully investigated.
- Don't neglect to research what matters the most to investors.

Applying Selling in Love

Have you noticed how some people are only ever single for a very short time? They meet someone, date for a few months, go steady, and the next thing you know, they are married with a child on the way, while others—often the most attractive and most successful people—stay single for many years. They go on date after date but never develop a strong connection. So why is love so much easier for some?

Those people who are lucky in love have an in-built understanding of how to apply sales skills to love. They instinctively understand that winning a heart is not about being the best looking, the smartest, the most successful, and the most perfect person. It is about really getting to the heart of what is important to the people they are dating. When they are on dates, they spend most of the time focused on their dates, listening intently to everything that they say. They ask about the things that matter most to their dates. They share the values and experiences that they have that are most relevant for their dates. These people know instinctively that everyone, no matter who he is, loves to speak his truth, loves to be heard—really heard—and loves to be validated for what matters to him. They do this generously.

Love Selling Dos

- Do listen actively and attentively.
- Do ask questions that show genuine interest.
- Do focus most of your time on your date, not on you.
- Do validate the things that are important to your date.

Love Selling Don'ts

- Don't try to impress with boasting.
- Don't try to convince that your way is the best.
- Don't give too much too soon.
- Don't criticize or condemn.
- Don't blame other people.
- Don't talk constantly about yourself.

By applying basic sales skills to every aspect of your life, you really can achieve your dreams. It is as simple as caring enough to take the time to find out what matters to all stakeholders in any given situation, then matching what you have to offer to those needs.

ABOUT THE AUTHOR

Lisa O'Brien runs CareerCoach, an international online career coaching and career development organization. Lisa is also the author of a number of career development e-books, including *Interview Coach*, *Career Change Coach*, *Goal Setting Coach*, and *Career Crisis Coach*. Lisa's e-books are available for just $19.95 at http://www.onlinecareercoaching.com.

79

SELF APPRECIATION

The Four Temperaments

Randy Rolfe

Why do some people hate to swim and others love it? Why do some people like broad-shouldered, solid physiques and others are drawn to willowy frames? Why do some people explode with anger when others would pout and withdraw? Why do some people become leaders and others are content to follow? Why do some people always get colds and others never? Why does one person want an explanation for everything and another follows his gut with no questions asked? Why does one eat like a horse and stay slim and another can look at food and gain a tummy?

Is it luck, genetics, environment, the stars and planets, parental conditioning, or something else?

With the four temperaments as a key, you will discover a powerful way of understanding better who you are and, even more important, who you want to be. And you can find out how to use this power to help put more balance into your life so that you can feel, think, and act at your best, in harmony with your deepest self and also at peace with those around you.

The four temperaments are four different clusters of characteristics that tend to appear together because of the dominance in each person of one of four distinct *humors*. These four humors were postulated in the ancient Egyptian and Greek world over 2,500 years ago. The humors represent the essence, flow, and force of the universe. They were also called *ethers*, *vapors*, *winds*, or *airs*.

When someone is not behaving like her normal self, do we not still say "she is putting on airs"? Are not the expressions *sense of humor* and *just humor him* still heard? Today, we think of humor as something funny, but that idea evolved when playwrights like Shakespeare created amusing caricatures of the temperaments some 400 years ago.

Before chemistry and the microscope, vapors were believed to influence the body, much like energies that come and go with variations in the environment and the weather. Hippocrates associated them directly with four major liquid substances that had been identified in the body. They also were likened to earth, fire, air, and water and the temperatures and moistures associated with these elements.

The names for the four humors are *choleric*, *melancholic*, *sanguine*, and *phlegmatic*. They sound a bit alien, but we still hear them today, and if we renamed them, we would lose centuries of accumulated wisdom around them.

Here I want to give you immediate tools to put this wisdom to work for you today. I call it training your intuition. Because you probably can already guess certain characteristics that tend to cluster together when you watch your friends, family, or new acquaintances, let your mind play with these concepts as you assess their validity in your life.

People of the melancholic-dominant temperament tend to be tall and willowy, with a fast metabolism in youth but often prone to hyper- or hypothyroid conditions as they age. They store fat in their tummies and backs of the arms and sides of the hips. They are creative, inspiring, passionate people. They like efficiency, value their time, and hate to be bored. They tend toward expressive or analytical careers, as artists, performers, or mathematicians. When angry, they sulk, withdraw, and complain. If this is you, you need to be sure that you are not overdoing sugars and carbs and caffeine, that you have some form of protein within two hours of waking up, and that you get plenty of regular rest. Be sure you get physical exercise and express yourself artistically. Be careful to let others know how you feel. They cannot read your mind, though you think they should. If you are trying to appeal to a melancholic, get to the point quickly, and let him know how you can make his life easier and more exciting.

People of the choleric temperament tend to be squarish of build, with strong jaws and broad shoulders. They will put on weight in the shoulders and chest, never in the legs. They seem to be born leaders, with vision and will and determination to see plans through to execution. They listen to all sides and then move decisively on their gut feelings. When out of humor, they can be aggressive, domineering, and dismissive. They do not worry much about their weight, do not care much for sweets, and think they can operate on little sleep. They usually like beef and simple foods, like baked potatoes. They need to add greens and water to stay balanced. If you are choleric, treat others with patience and forgiveness, and give them time to rest. If you are dealing with a choleric, let him take the lead or appeal to him by showing him how he can achieve the very best in his field.

People of the sanguine-dominant temperament tend to be philosophical and love to share their ideas. They tend to have curvaceous physiques, with well-rounded bottoms in both sexes and hourglass shapes in women. They put on weight on their hips and butts, not much at the waist. They are drawn to teaching and coaching professions. They love to engage people, arrange parties and events, and get together socially. When in bad humor, they become argumentative, bombastic, and sometimes weepy. They are drawn to creamy and spicy—but not particularly hot—foods and need to balance by including lots of vegetables and by avoiding eating too big a breakfast or within two hours of bedtime. If you are sanguine, be sure to stop and listen and give credit to other's opinions. Get regular exercise, particularly walking or swimming. If you are dealing with a sanguine, let him talk until he is finished and appeal to his interest in raising up and empowering others by meaningful communication.

People who are phlegmatic tend to focus on family and relationships. They set a high value on dedication, loyalty, and hard work. They tend to be small of build, with youthful faces and proportions, which keep them looking young for decades. They complain of gaining weight in the knees, if anywhere. They are drawn to helping professions and careers centered around duty and steady effort. They are drawn to dairy products and sweets but do better with more vegetables and good-quality protein foods other than a lot of milk and cheese. They have slow metabolisms and enjoy regular but not too strenuous exercise. If you are phlegmatic, know that you are the best friend anyone could have, and do not be reluctant to express your ideas and desires. If you are dealing with a phlegmatic, give him time to complete his tasks and you will not be disappointed. Appreciate the high value he places on family and friends and applaud his work ethic, skill, and craftsmanship in everything he undertakes.

The take home message from the four temperaments is that we each contribute a unique and essential force to any situation. If you value and appreciate yourself and your gifts and contributions as well as the gifts and contributions of others, your days and your life will be more joyful and effortless.

ABOUT THE AUTHOR

Randy Rolfe, MA, JD, has helped tens of thousands of families for 30 years with her courses, seminars, counseling, coaching, and frequent appearances on national television and radio. Her books have been translated into five languages. Combining her legal background, theology studies, and independent studies in nutrition, addiction, and bioenergetics, she has a unique ability to help you find solutions. Her books include *The Four Temperaments*, *The Seven Secrets of Successful Parents*, *You Can Postpone Anything but Love*, *Adult Children Raising Children*, and *The Affirmations Book for Sharing*. Contact her at Institute for Creative Solutions LLC, http://www.instituteforcreativesolutions.com ((610) 429-5869).

80

The World's Greatest Self-Improvement Superheroes and Their Success Secrets

Michael Lee

Have you ever realized that you have the power to get anything you want and be anything you want to be? If you're still clueless about your abilities, continue reading and learn about the success secrets of the world's greatest self-improvement superheroes.

In a land full of potentials, powerful superheroes live in happiness and fulfillment. But they're not just ordinary superheroes; they belong to the highest breed of the self-improvement clan. They possess the superhuman ability to get anything they want. This article serves as an introduction to these self-improvement superheroes, so below, let us meet them and discover their success secrets.

Assignmentors

These superheroes are able to acquire any quality or ability they desire. They even have the power to instill or "assign" qualities to others, hence contributing to the immense buildup of confidence and happiness.

Success Secret

They use other names perceived to be superior. If they want to encourage someone to write better, they might say, "You're a great writer, Ernest Hemingway. I believe you can always surpass your previous articles."

By assigning the name Ernest Hemingway to the writer, they implant within him, in a subconscious manner, the writing prowess of Hemingway. On the other hand, the writer will try his best to live up to everyone's expectations that he, indeed, possesses the ability of Hemingway.

They also do the bizarre yet highly powerful practice of putting someone else's head into their heads, at least in their minds. If they want to be as intelligent as Einstein, they go to a quiet place where they can relax and concentrate. Then they imagine wearing Einstein's head over them. They absorb his aura, and surprisingly, they will begin to think, act, and feel like Einstein.

Goal Masters

Goal masters are positively mad scientists who meticulously prepare well-laid plans and goals that allow them to conquer their futures.

Success Secret

They write down their goals and break them into tiny, bite-sized chunks. They know the importance of doing it step by step, little by little, to get to their destination. They have the power of flexibility—no, not the power of elasticity, but the power to adjust to the circumstances, prepare new goals, and continue pursuing them bit by bit. They are master motivators, with the discipline to stick to their objectives. They enjoy the journey in the attainment of their goals.
Goal masters know their limits. They know that if their goals are irrational, they will get results that will further prevent them from attaining their objectives. For example, if they set a goal to make a million dollars in a month (unless they are one of those financial geniuses), their subconscious will command them to sacrifice sleep, ignore stress, work endlessly, and so on. And when they actually do what their subconscious minds tell them, they will fail, get frustrated, and give up, thinking that nothing works, no matter how hard they try.

Therefore goal masters set their goals to achievable mode. Their goals can be difficult to achieve, but they make sure they are possible to attain. Instead of the above scenario, they set something like earning $20,000 a month. After they achieve that feat, they set a higher goal of, say, $40,000 a month. They know the value of patience and working systematically.

316

Hocus Focus

These magicians can tackle any task at lightning-fast speeds and with laser-like accuracy.

Success Secret

They focus their energies on one thing at a time and give it all they got. All their attention is concentrated on the particular task at hand. They are able to endure and withstand outside distractions because they have developed the discipline, willpower, and determination to continue pushing until their purposes have been accomplished.

Time Commanders

These superheroes are able to make time submit to their will. They have the power to summon all the time in the world to do whatever they please.
Success Secret

They are extremely organized in everything that they do. They put labels on bottles, place similar files in one folder, and prepare in advance a list of things they have to do for the next day.
They can also use their minds to organize things they have to remember. Studies have shown that people can only retain information that fits between five and nine categories at a time. This is the 7 ± 2 rule of neurolinguistic programming.

Time commanders are aware of this rule; hence they have devised a strategy known as "categorization." If they have many things to do, they group related tasks together. They combine activities such as reading books, listening to educational tapes, and watching training videos into a category like "education." They group swimming, playing basketball, and paying fees for the gym into a category called "fitness." They do this for all their other tasks.

Their greatest strategy is known as "delegation." They know the incomparable power of leverage. They delegate trivial and repetitive tasks to other people who can do them satisfactorily so that they can concentrate on becoming more productive with their most valued possession—time.

Visualizers

The visualizers can bring into reality anything that their powerful minds can conceive.

Success Secret

Every day, they keenly visualize what they want to become or what they want to achieve. They envisage the events so clearly that they can actually feel and experience the happiness, excitement, and other strong emotions accompanied by their visualizations. The Universe interprets the pictures unleashed by their subconscious minds and transforms them into reality.

Affirmationaries

These superheroes use the power of words to get anything they like and be anything they want to be.

Success Secret

They loudly chant the mantras of success (known as affirmations) every day with passion and the belief that they are already getting and experiencing what they are chanting. They do not say "I will be a great doctor" or whatever they want to be. They say "I am the greatest doctor in the world." And they believe it with all their hearts; that is why they succeed.

Abundance Attractors

They attract fortunes, luck, blessings, or the so-called good things in life.

Success Secret

They cut off any negative thoughts or problems from their minds and count their blessings. They thank God, the Universe, and people around them for all the wonderful things they are receiving, have received, and will be receiving.

By doing this, they are acknowledging that they are indeed blessed and flowing with abundance. And by showing gratitude and giving thanks, they are befriending the Universe to give them more.

They give generously. If they want more money, they give money to those who need it more. If they want to have lots of friends, they become trusted friends to everyone they meet.

But they do not expect anything in return. They give because they want to and because it makes them happy, not because they have a hidden agenda in mind.

They also know how to receive gratefully, aside from being great givers. If someone compliments them, they do not say "no, I'm not that good." Instead, they say "thank you." By being grateful and appreciative of those who have given something to them, they are attracting more blessings and abundance into their lives.

Attitude Shifters

They remain positive and composed, despite all obstacles and challenges.

Success Secret

They never allow any negative thoughts to enter their minds. Whenever something negative tries to evade their minds, they just quickly shift their thoughts to something positive.

And the most powerful of them all . . .

You!

You have the combined powers of all of the above superheroes and can do anything!

Success Secret

As long as you apply the success secrets above, you are invincible and unstoppable in anything that you do.

ABOUT THE AUTHOR

Michael Lee is the author of *How to Be a Red Hot Persuasion Wizard . . . in 20 Days or Less*, an e-book that reveals mind-altering persuasion techniques on how to tremendously enhance your relationships, create unlimited wealth, and get anything you want . . . just like magic. Get a sample chapter, plus super success secrets and highly stimulating "Get What You Want" advice, at http://www.20daypersuasion.com. He is also the cofounder of http://www.self-improvement-millionaires.com and is licensed as a certified public accountant.

81

How to Successfully Create a Long-Lasting Love Relationship

Eva Dahlberg

Love relationships start as the biggest thing in life, but relationships change as time goes by. Suddenly, when you find your partner has become strong and dominating and you are weak and inferior, you ask yourself, how do I successfully create the long-lasting love relationship that I am worth and really want to achieve?

You feel that you have become unsure about what you like and what your partner thinks. You do not believe that you can achieve what you want. The big question is, where did your great relationship go, and how do you find your way back?

To find the answer, we must concentrate on *you!*

Now you cry, what about my partner? Why do we not talk about him or her? The answer is that only *you* can take responsibility for yourself and your life. Trust me—*you* can successfully find your answers and create what you want.

When you want to successfully achieve a long-lasting love relationship, the most powerful and simple tool is the What-Why-How-Where-When (WWHWW™) model, which I will introduce to you.

What

Many things change over time, and we all grow and learn every day from what we experience in our lives. How you maintain your love relationship depends on your values together with your experiences. Values are the beliefs and self-instructions that you have committed to. To be explicit, most of your values were subconsciously committed to a long time ago, and they run everything you do.

Take Bill as an example: He has been consciously seeking love, but he subconsciously feels unworthy. He never managed to have a long relationship until he became aware of these subconscious values. After working his values through, Bill created his new values and has now had a successful relationship for the past 10 years.

Begin your process by asking the following:

- What do I want in my relationship?
- What do I dislike?
- What has changed since I first met my partner?
- Who was I when we met?
- What is the worst thing that can happen? Is it not better to know that than to live in unhappiness?

You can and must decide what is true for you—you have the right and the responsibility to choose how you want to live your life. Remember, no one else can do that for you.

Why

The truth is that we all learn how to live and run a love relationship when we grow up and see our parents. Sometimes it can help you to look back on their relationship. Remember to do this with a grown-up way of looking instead of going back to the young you. How would you describe your parents' relationship today? Can you see similarities between their behavior and your behavior in your relationship?

Why is it that the values you committed to when you were young still run your life after you have grown up? Because those values subconsciously follow you all the time until you create and commit to new, true values. Let us look at how subconscious values can impact your life when they do not fit with your grown-up life.

The most common effect is anger, which has three common faces. The first is depression, being the face of anger that turns against you—you reject, hate, and blame yourself. The second face is passive aggression, when you do not take responsibility for the aggression and blame others for what you have set in motion. Finally, the third face is when you are angry but smile and pretend to be someone you are not—you are fooling others. When you do this, you lose your self-respect.

To get rid of this anger, you must become aware of it. Ask yourself the following:

- Why do you not like yourself?
- Why do you blame others?
- Why do you feel anger?
- Why do you want to change?

How

You must create new values when you feel stuck on old ones. Remember that we do not want to change—it is hard work and uncomfortable, but worth everything.

Now it is time to find out how everything has become what it is and how you can create the successful change you really want. Take three different sheets of paper and label them "Me in the Beginning" (describe the person you were when your relationship began), "Me Today" (describe the person you are today), and "Me in My Dreams" (describe how you want to be).

Begin your creative process by observing yourself for a few weeks. Look for feelings and thoughts like the following:

- In the beginning . . .
- You make me . . .
- You do not . . .
- It is your . . .
- I do not like . . .
- I want . . .

No matter what you think, I guarantee that thoughts like those above are controlling you all the time. The subconscious values that create those thoughts continuously sabotage you in your relationship. Every time you notice these thoughts and feelings, write them down on the correct paper. Describe what you feel, think, and the images you might see. Take your time, and be *honest* with yourself.

When you feel ready, take your papers with you and go to a place where you can be totally undisturbed. Read, think, and feel through everything you have written. Look for patterns. Use this thinking loop: Why do I feel this—what can I change—what if that happens—what happens then? Peel down layer after layer, like an onion, until you find your true, core values. Now you understand your subconscious values, and it is time to create and commit to new values that fit with your life today.

One of the greatest ways to find new values is to look for the polar opposite value of the old one. Also, create as many different perspectives as you can around each old value. Think, feel, and trust yourself in the process of truly developing the new right values for you! To help yourself achieve the new values, write them down on small cards and carry them with you always.

Where

If you create many new values, where do you begin? The answer is to prioritize and choose the three most important ones. In your heart, commit to begin living from these. To change and live a new value takes time and consistent practice, so overcome your personal challenges by stepping out of your comfort zone and taking action. Remember to focus on sharing your good qualities with others.

When

Now, when you are truly committed to your new values, start taking action immediately! Be aware of procrastination, and if you think to yourself "this will not work," remember that this is also a value. To motivate you, I would like to ask, how long did it take you to learn how to drive? Ask yourself, how long am I going to work to make my dreams come true? The given answer is, of course, as long as it takes.

You are unique!

You are, in every moment, as perfect as you can be based on the knowledge and experience you have. You can only become better. You are unique! No one else can be better at being you than *you!*

ABOUT THE AUTHOR

Eva Dahlberg is President of Your Coach Company and a professional personal coach. "When you want to trust yourself" is the motto of her coaching business. She has coached many persons and has helped them to create and achieve successful change in their lives.

It does not matter what you want to change—we are all human. You can successfully change everything from your private life to your business management by following the WWHWW™ model created by Eva Dahlberg. Contact her at eva@yourcoachcompany.com for a *free* trial session, or visit her Web site at http://www.yourcoachcompany.com.

82

Stress and Stones

John Mehrmann

"Why do you have a pile of rocks on your desk?"

"Those aren't just rocks," I replied. "These small stones are gifts, remnants from great bridges that people built to cross over troubled waters. I keep them here to remind me. Take one, as my gift to you, and remember."

Everyone faces periods of stress, disappointment, loss, or personal challenge. The most significant differences are the frequency and severity of the personal challenges. How we cope with these periods influences personal contentment and is reflected in our words and actions.

In times of stress, disappointment is exaggerated and obstacles are magnified. Even though the root cause of the stress might be associated with a specific issue, concerns can begin to have an impact on other seemingly minor activities or decisions. This can lead to mental and emotional duress, resulting in physical fatigue. Like a snowball rapidly descending a mountain, it gathers speed, consuming, combining, and colliding with our other daily activities until we are overwhelmed by an avalanche of issues.

Rather than ignore thoughts or take them all at once, focus on each concern one at a time. Visualize each problem as a stone. The size of the stone grows and takes shape based on the intensity and complexity of the challenge. As you contemplate the nuances and the implications of each issue, imagine the shape of the stone adjusting until it is complete. Consider every potential result of your obstacle. Every potential variation is a different perspective of the stone. Like your stone, the issue may appear jagged or pitted. Perceived from different angles, the issue may appear easier to handle.

That stone represents the stress, fear, and frustration associated with that issue or challenge. It may appear unyielding, solid, and formidable. The stone that you have created may be difficult to manage or to change. When you have defined the problem, then your stone is complete.

Imagine rolling the stone down the grassy hillside and placing it on the bank beside a wide river. When that stone that represents your obstacle is firmly in place at the edge of the river, it is time to leave it and to start thinking about the details of challenges that will define your next stone.

Close your eyes and imagine using these stones to build the beginning of an impressive bridge across the river. You may have seen pictures of an old stone bridge that spanned a wide river. Use the stones created from your challenges to construct a similar bridge. Sometimes the chasm is deep. Sometimes the water runs cold and fast beneath your feet. Some bridges are long and narrow, while others are low and wide. The stones and the chasm determine the size and shape of the bridge that needs to be crossed. It takes many stones to build a bridge, large and small.

It requires patience and skill to fit the stones in place and build a great bridge. Once a stone has been set in place, it does not change and is used only once. If you start to think about that challenge again, then remember where you placed that stone, and stop dwelling on the issue. Use these stones to build one side of the bridge, the side that comes from your current dilemma. This side of the river may be bleak and stormy, but the skies on the other side of the river are blue, clear, and bright.

Just as there are times of stress and conflict, there are also moments of serenity. If you are experiencing stress, then you must surely also remember periods when it did not exist. Those moments of peace, calm, and joy will return. Perhaps you will find yourself enjoying a sunset, listening to the ocean, sitting on the front-porch swing with your children, or relaxing in your favorite chair with a good book. Take a moment to pause and reflect on the many things that you have to be grateful for in your life at that moment. Remember these things in detail, and shape these into the stones in your imagination. It is time to complete the other half of your bridge.

When you realize how fortunate you are, you are standing on the clear and sunny side of the river. With time you will discover that there are far more stones that represent thoughts of happiness than that represent conflict. When you reflect during moments of contentment, your appreciation will increase with recognition of the challenges that you have overcome on the path to building and crossing that bridge.

Minor inconveniences can easily become distractions. How often do little things like traffic lights or inconveniences in our schedules create an undue amount of stress? Is it because some other stress has magnified a minor inconvenience, or does a lack of conflict amplify the temporary inconvenience by comparison? Will you allow a minor inconvenience to have a negative impact on your mood or reflect in your interaction with others? A minor inconvenience is something that you will forget about in a day or a week, but the impact of expressing your irritation may have much longer-lasting effects. It is better to treat delays, mistakes, and minor issues like small pebbles and drop them on the roadway to fill the small crevices in your bridge. Walk over and past these small issues on your journey to the bright side of your life.

What shore are you standing on today? Are you looking for a way to overcome your challenges and strive for serenity? If you recognize the blessings in your life, have you taken a few moments to reflect on the obstacles that you overcame to reach this point in your journey? How is your current position reflected in the words and actions that you share with others? Your relationships are more than stones. Your relationships are the precious gems that make your bridge sparkle and shine.

Schedule a very specific time at the end of each day to close your eyes for five minutes to contemplate your current position. Hold a small stone in your hand and think about where you would place it in the section of the bridge that you are building today.

ABOUT THE AUTHOR

John Mehrmann is an authority on emotional intelligence, talent management, and organizational development. He is a consultant, coach, trainer, and speaker with Executive Blueprints, Inc., an organization devoted to improving business practices and developing human capital. ExecutiveBlueprints.com is an online resource with self-paced tutorials, tools, exercises, and educational and inspirational articles contributed from experienced professionals. Additional materials are available from http://www.InstituteForAdvancedLeadership.com.

83

Who Are You, Really?: On Finding Your Soul

Piercarla Garusi

Do you know who you are?

Have you ever taken the time to think about who you are, seriously? Have you ever taken the time to think about why you are here on this planet? Do you realize that there is not, there never has been, and there never, *ever* will be another you? You are unique, and there is a reason why you are on this planet: You have a mission to accomplish.

If you are not going to be the real you, the rest of us, the whole of humanity, are going to miss out; and if you do not accomplish your mission, nobody else will.

How do you feel about that? Excited or terrified?

You are not here by chance; there is a plan behind your birth. You are, truly and simply, a wonder. But have you ever taken the time to think about or, better still, write down your unique qualities, characteristics, talents, gifts, and treasures? Why do you not start doing it now? This will help you to start developing knowledge of yourself.

Now let me ask you a question or two: Who is the most important person in your life, right now? Which is the most important relationship in your life? I am sure you know the answer . . . the answer is *you*. Was that your answer? Do not hide yourself! I can see you!

Once I did a survey in one of my workshops, and I asked these questions. Only 2 percent of the people answered in this way, but we need to change that to at least 98 percent!

Let me tell you very clearly: *You are the most important person in your life, and the most important relationship is the one with yourself.*

I know you are going to ask me, "Isn't this selfish?" The answer is *no*.

Let me ask you another question: Who is the person with whom you will spend your entire life, *guaranteed*? So it is worth having a good relationship with that person, is it not?

In order to develop the relationship with yourself, you need to take time, just you, alone, and ask yourself questions. Here is an exercise to help you develop a relationship with yourself and get more centered.

Sit down in a quiet place, preferably on the floor, for about 20 minutes. Close your eyes, and start asking yourself questions. Do not try to answer consciously—just ask questions to yourself, and you will simply feel the answers inside. If you do not feel anything, do not worry—it will come. Just keep asking questions, such as the following.

- Am I being the real me?
- Am I welcoming, embracing, accepting, approving, and supporting myself?
- Am I encouraging, forgiving, and justifying myself, saying "I always do the best I can"?
- Do I love myself unconditionally and constantly?
- Am I cherishing and celebrating myself for who I am?
- Am I giving myself the worth I deserve?
- Am I respecting myself and my needs?
- Am I treating myself well?
- Do I thank myself?
- Am I giving myself the permission to be myself?
- Am I giving myself the permission to be happy?
- Am I giving myself the permission to create and live the life that would make me happy?

Once you have finished these 20 minutes of meditation with yourself, thank yourself and come out of it. Repeat this time with yourself every day, when it suits you best, and you will develop a meaningful relationship with yourself.

Now you will start knowing who you are and developing a relationship with yourself, but *you are much more than that*. What about your soul? Have you ever taken the time to connect with your soul? Connecting with your soul will give you depth, will help you develop your philosophy on the world and on life, and will help you get clarity on your values, code of conduct, and morals; it will give you your spirituality and enable you to find true meaning and fulfillment.

In order to connect with your soul, you need to meditate: spend time with yourself in silence, ask yourself philosophical questions, look with wonder at the simple things in life—nature, the smile of a child, human warmth. Savor things, take time to discover; ask yourself which are your true values, morals, and what you stand for, and keep searching for a deep meaning in things and life. *Look beyond, go beyond, and go inside yourself: Your inner life is there.*

Then find ways to express your inner self, your inner life, by writing, by painting, by playing an instrument, by creating something with your hands, or by simply being and loving.

You can also decide to connect with Someone Higher than you, God or a Higher Power.

Believing in Someone Higher will enable you
- to overcome depression and loneliness, by knowing that the Higher Presence is continuous and thus feeling a connection
- to overcome hopelessness and despair by knowing you are continuously supported and helped and encouraged by the Higher Presence
- to overcome feelings of unworthiness and feeling unloved by knowing that the Higher Presence loves you unconditionally, immensely, and constantly.

Thus you will be able to find your true peace of heart in all things and at every moment.

When are you going to give yourself this wonderful gift you totally deserve?

<u>ABOUT THE AUTHOR</u>

Piercarla Garusi is a life coach and NLP practitioner, the director of PG Coaching Ltd. She is passionate about helping people unleash their power, overcome depression, anxiety, social anxiety, fear, anger, traumas, and emotional abuse, and just be well and feel good. She is also passionate about helping people connect with their souls and be the extraordinary people they truly are, developing their spirituality and creating lives that make them truly happy. For more information, please visit http://www.pgcoaching.co.uk or e-mail info@pgcoaching.co.uk. Thank you and be blessed.

84

STRESS

From Distress to Success:
Practical Ways to Transform Your
Distress into Success

George Grant

In my 30 years of professional experience as an analytical chemist, toxicologist, microbiologist, professor, speaker, specialist in natural medicine, and consultant for large companies, I decided to complete my doctoral degree specializing in stress management at the University of Toronto, Canada, in 1995. Since I was working at the time as a professor, it was a stressful event, but as I look back 11 years ago, I managed to complete all the degree requirements in less than three years on a part-time basis, which is a record at the university. In a rapidly changing, fast-paced world and competitive environment, thriving under pressure is vital for wellness and success. I am going to share with you useful, practical ways to transform your distress into success.

Stress is a neutral term that can mean *eustress*, "good stress," or *distress*, "bad stress." The goal of stress management should be to achieve "balance wellness," which means to reduce distress while increasing eustress.

A stressor is any demand on our minds or bodies, positive or negative. A distressor is any demand resulting in harm to our minds and bodies. Distressors may be too much or too little arousal in harm to mind and body. These are common examples of distressors in our modern, fast-paced society:

1. psychological distressors due to work, family, work commute, social relationships, changes, decisions, emotional issues, anger, and guilt
2. physical distressors due to chemical or environmental factors, pain, disease, aging, and daily wear and tear.

It is important to note that awareness of stressors can itself be a deterrent to turning them into distressors, according to Dr. Hans Selye, a Canadian pioneer in stress research. Knowing what hurts us and how we perceive it has an inherent curative value.

The practical way to minimize psychological distressors is to anticipate, monitor, and regulate common distressors and be aware of interpretations and perceptions of distressors. Examples of signs of distressors are headaches, depression, anxiety, edginess, irritability, a churning stomach, trembling hands, fuzzy thinking, poor concentration, poor memory, tight shoulders, back problems, panic attacks, high blood pressure, dizzy spells, heart problems, arthritis, ulcers, low energy, increased conflict at home and work, feelings of joylessness, low self-esteem, feeling stuck in a career, and a loss of interest in sex. Escaping from distress through alcohol, drug use, gambling, overeating, and smoking can have serious psychological and/or physical consequences.

We can transform distress habits that cause "imbalance illness" into wellness habits to achieve total balance.

- *Time management wellness habits:* Maintain control over one's time to minimize hurry; balance work, play, and solitude; and minimize boredom and stagnation.
- *Physical wellness habits:* Sound nutritional practices; regular exercise; adequate sleep; proper eating habits (reduce caffeine, soft drinks, alcohol, and food additives); drinking plenty of water daily; deep breathing; and maintaining a saliva pH of 7.4 (since alkalinity correlates with balance, while acidity correlates with imbalance).
- *Environmental wellness habits:* Awareness of the state of the environment at work and home as well as the global environment as related to indoor air, exposure to toxins, and social responsibility to protect the environment.
- *Emotional wellness habits:* Laugh often; smile more; give and receive hugs daily; do not sweat the small stuff; experience being more proactive rather than reactive; practice meditation and daily relaxation; learn Neuro-Linguistic Programming; try biofeedback; practice self-hypnosis; learn

progressive muscle relaxation; perform visualization and the ability to experience the preponderance of positive over negative emotional states.

- *Social wellness habits:* Practice empathy, active listening, caring, and compassion for others; enthusiasm; share intimacy; friendships; be a servant heart; set realistic goals and expectations from family and friends and accept criticism gracefully; live in the moment and achieve permanent inner peace by focusing on your deep breathing and mediation daily. The more acts of kindness you give, the more you will receive and feel fulfilled.
- *Intellectual wellness habits:* The ability to think clearly and independently; unquenchable curiosity; and lifelong learning. Stay away from the news on the radio or TV, particularly the first 10 minutes after rising and 10 minutes before going to bed.

When you reach the wellness zone, you will feel self-actualized, intuitive, full of humor, competent under pressure, and a sense of serendipity and synergy. You will be at peak performance and feel optimistic about the future.

Having the ABCs (a positive mental *attitude*, proper *belief*, and a solid *commitment*) is essential to transforming any distress into success. Create your own life since you are the master of your own destiny.

ABOUT THE AUTHOR

Dr. George Grant is a renowned, multitalented scientist and former professor who specializes in nutritional and environmental medicine. He is the coauthor of seven books, several published research articles, book reviews, international conference presentations, and hundreds of public speaking engagements across North America. Dr. George Grant is an active professional member of seven professional organizations in Canada and the United States. He is a licensed analytical chemist, food/nutrition scientist, toxicologist, and microbiologist and is a consultant for several international firms. Dr. Grant recently received the Leading World Intellectual award from the International Congress on Natural Medicine in Nassau, Bahamas. Dr. George Grant participated in several studies, including ADD, fibromyalgia, prevention of heart disease, stress management, multiple chemical sensitivity, and indoor air quality problems. He is listed in the *International Who's Who of Professionals*. Please visit http://www.academyofwellness.com.

85

Strengthen Your Relationship and Strengthen Yourself

Wendy Bridger & Margrit Harris

Do you remember all those fun science experiments as a kid? How about the one with the magnet and the iron shavings? Was it not amazing to see how powerfully two magnets would oppose each other when they were faced the wrong way? It was incredible how strongly they connected and how much more power they had when they faced the right way.

Our relationships with our significant others are very similar to those magnets. We either can spend our time and energy making sure we are turned the way we feel is best for us, or we can take that same energy, turn toward each other, and unleash more energy, creative power, and productivity than we have ever known.

So often, people view self-improvement as a quest involving only the individual. However, when we have committed to share our lives with someone else, it is imperative that we get them on board as well. It is kind of like two horses pulling a cart side by side. One horse can become stronger than the other, but ultimately, it can only pull the cart as fast as the weaker animal. In a committed relationship, it is the same way. Let me give you a personal example from my own life that happened this very morning.

My husband, Chris, is fulfilling his dreams by getting his law degree, which means very long hours studying very tedious material. I am also living my dreams staying at home with our daughter while running a successful Internet business. We have learned that one important part of pursuing those dreams is strengthening each other. For example, I woke up this morning to the sounds of our baby daughter crying and ready to eat. I stumbled out of bed as quietly as possible as my husband did not need to be up for another hour.

When it was time for Chris to get up, I gently woke him with a kiss and told him it was time to get up. He thanked me for the dinner I had left him before taking off to my meeting the night before as he rolled out of bed. I headed for the kitchen to make him a lunch and noticed the mound of dishes we both had been too busy to tackle yesterday and possibly the day before. Before I had finished washing the second dish, my husband was at my side and offered to finish them up. I thanked him and proceeded to make him an extra special lunch and get to work on my business.

After he was done in the kitchen, I heard one of our songs playing from the stereo, and I looked to see my husband dancing in the living room with our daughter. He asked me to join him. With her nestled in between us, we took a few minutes to dance together. Chris then went and put on my favorite shirt of his before having a quick breakfast and going our separate ways for the day. Although both of us had a busy, stressful, hectic day ahead of us, each of us was ready to take on the world because of the energy and love we had found in each other.

Sounds like a made-up fairy tale, does it not? What is the secret? Actually, it is the result of constant, vigilant hard work and conscious effort on both our parts. Instead of improving and progressing completely on our own, we have learned to share the load and strengthen the other. Think back on the two horses pulling the cart side by side. The stronger horse can only go as fast as its weaker counterpart. Pulling the cart harder will only make him tired and will not get him down the road any faster. In contrast, strengthening his partner will not only get him to his destination faster, it will lighten his load as well.

Another key thing to strengthening your partner and, in turn, building yourself is knowing what makes a difference to your partner. What is meaningful to your partner? For example, this morning, my husband and I danced in the living room. Many would assume he did that for me. In reality, he is the romantic in our relationship. Although I enjoyed the dance, I did it for him because it means so much to him. In turn, he knows it means the world to me when he spends time with our daughter, so dancing as a threesome was uplifting for everyone.

Are you ready to begin strengthening your partner and reaping the benefits of growing together? Here are some ways to get started.

- Recognize that strengthening each other takes time and effort. When you want to be successful in your career, you put time, thought, and effort into your job and make it a priority. It is no different with making a relationship successful and meaningful. Try to do at least one small thing each day to strengthen your partner.
- Find out what strengthens your partner. This is different with everyone. A great way to do this is by asking him what means a lot to him. Sometimes people do not really know. A great tool to help discover more about yourself and your partner is through assessment tools and personality tests. Through assessment tools you can discover what makes your partner tick and what is meaningful to him.
- Once you know what strengthens your partner, make a conscious effort to do those things for him, not what you like to do to help. If your spouse loves it when you join him in his hobbies, learn to sit through that football game without grumbling or run that 5K with him. He, in turn, will be more willing to help around the house if he knows that is what means most to you.
- Be careful not to keep score on who is giving more up for the other. There will be times in your partnership where one will provide more support as the other needs more. Remember, the point is to grow together, not compete against each other.

As you begin strengthening each other, your power and ability to accomplish much in this life will increase in ways you have never imagined. Remember, just as magnets, we have two choices on how to spend our energy in our relationships. We can either work hard to keep things the way we want it, or we can turn toward each other and, in turn, strengthen each other and become a powerful force for everyone: our families, our community, our coworkers, and especially ourselves.

ABOUT THE AUTHOR

Wendy Bridger, LMSW, and her partner Margrit Harris, MSSW, are cocreators of the Right Relationship Real Happiness Series. In this program series, people truly discover themselves and their partners. Included in each series are four Awareness Tools that provide valuable insight into creating meaningful relationships and real happiness. This mother-daughter team has over 25 years of experience helping people better their relationships. They have worked throughout the United States and the Philippines. Each is happily married and practices what she teaches. For more information, go to http://www.rightrelationshiprealhappiness.com.

86

Dude, You've Succeeded Before . . .
What Makes You Think You'll Fail Now?

Kevin Gianni

The only way you have achieved any success you have had in your life is by making commitments. When you make a commitment to anyone, including yourself, you have set your goal, and you can then start achieving it.

I am sure you, just like everyone else, have many different successes to date—maybe you have gotten a degree, started your own business, just got a raise, or wrote a book. Many different people have different views on what is successful and what is not—for some, success is raising a wonderful child or making a 15-layer chocolate cake; for others, it is completing a 20-story apartment building or flying around the world in a hot air balloon!

It is not important how others view your successes; what is important is that you view them as successes and know how you succeeded. Of the people I work with as a trainer in the health and fitness industry, 99.9 percent have succeeded in the past. Only about 10 percent consciously know they have. If you can recognize and point out your successes, you will be wildly successful.

I was working with a client who needed to lose a substantial amount of weight—about 80 pounds. She was a young and motivated business owner who started her own private practice in her mid-twenties—a real strong young woman. Her challenge was that she was afraid of starting to lose the weight because she thought she was going to fail. Sound familiar? Just about everyone can understand this at some level in fitness or in business. So I had her list her past successes in her workbook.

Surprisingly (not to me, but to her), since high school, she has been a success at *everything* she has done. There was not a year unaccounted for that she was not successful in something that she started. I pointed this pattern out, and she recognized it. Then I asked her, "You've been a success since high school, so what makes you think that you're going to fail now? You haven't failed at anything in 8 years!"

She understood.

Too many times, we can base our emotions and feelings on unfounded principles. What have you thought that you could not do before but then realized you were just making your own roadblocks?

Your past success can be the framework for your future success. Why? Because with each past success you have had, there have been ups and downs, times you wished you could quit and times you felt great. When you look at what you have done before, you can use that as a reference point for what you are doing now or a present goal.

Here is an example.

My college graduation was a big deal for me. I label it as one of my big successes. In those four years, there were times I wanted to quit, there were times when I had a blast, and then there were times when I questioned what I was doing in school in the first place.

Each one of those things I felt along the way toward graduation was all part of the larger picture or goal, which was the college diploma I received when I finished or accomplished my goal.

You see, every path to reach a goal is different because different things and emotions and circumstances come up when you are striving to achieve it.

But listen to this . . .

Every path to reach a goal is *similar* because the *same types* of things, emotions, and circumstances come up when you are striving to achieve it.

On the path to reaching any goal, everyone feels doubt, excitement, fear, and questioning. It is natural. So when you think about reaching your goals, you have to build in the structure—or know that these things will happen and that you can overcome them easily.

That is why looking at your own past successes is so important. By taking a past framework or structure of a goal that you achieved, you can actually see the times that you wavered, and when you waver while you are attempting this new and present goal, you will not get too discouraged because it is part of the process.

I apply my past success in college to many things. When I set a goal to run a race and two months before the race, I do not feel like I want to continue training, I will just think about the time I finished college and that there were plenty of times that I did not want to go to class anymore. Eventually, I got back on track in college, and with the knowledge of that, I know that eventually, I will get back on track with my training schedule and run the race that I set my sights on.

How can you apply this to your success? Think about what you have succeeded in and write down examples. It can be in business, with your family, with your personal finances, and so on. Break down each into a timeline, and highlight the high and low points. You will be surprised at how many difficulties you had that you did not remember.

You then can use this structure to be assured that you will continue to succeed in the future because you understand the anatomy of the path toward any goal.

ABOUT THE AUTHOR

Kevin Gianni is the author of *The Busy Person's Fitness Solution*. He is on a personal mission to demystify health and fitness and demonstrate how easy it is for busy people to be in great shape. He conducts seminars, writes articles, has been quoted in the national press, and is the creator of the revolutionary "50-Second Fitness Quick Fix Video-zine"—the only video fitness newsletter that gives you the skinny on everything health and fitness related in quick, easy-to-digest bites. Visit http://www.LiveAwesome.com to see it for yourself for free!

87

Picking through the Landscape of Success

Nancy Heimstra

If one advances confidently in the direction of his dreams, and endeavors to live the life which he has imagined, he will meet with success unexpected in common hours.

—Henry David Thoreau

Grains of Sand

How does one advance confidently in the direction of his dreams? One way to do this is to check in with yourself about your actions. Are you taking actions that are supporting your dreams? Just ask yourself a few times a day, "Did I take action that is moving me in the right direction?" It may be as simple as a follow-up phone call or e-mail. It may be the one thing that you have been procrastinating about. Movement in the direction of your goals will create momentum, and as you do more and more, it becomes easier.

I ask myself each day if I have done at least one thing to move my business forward. It does not have to be a huge step, but I find that it keeps me focused on my goals. Just one grain of sand seems so small, but those little grains of effort equal beaches of rewards.

Simple Pebbles

Being confident while moving is a reflection of your belief system. Do you surround yourself with friends who support you? Do you take the time to meditate, read books, or listen to audio programs that inspire and motivate you?

In this increasingly chaotic world it is so important to have resources that encourage you and keep you focused on what is working in your life.

Pay close attention to the quality of your relationships and make sure you are not in the company of complainers or those that bring you down. Sometimes it is important to do a little "housecleaning" of those you interact with. If the relationship is worth keeping, it is worth working on. This may require some heartfelt communication, but the end result is the reward. I love to ask my friends questions about how they perceive me. Sometimes we can be regarded completely differently from how we intend to come across. By doing this, you can gain confidence in your communication skills and have a much deeper understanding of yourself. If you have ever stepped on a simple pebble with a bare foot, funny how something so small can stop you in your tracks. Take a moment to clear the path ahead.

Skipping Rocks

Another way to keep advancing confidently in the direction of your dreams is to do whatever you can, from where you are, with what you have. Do not create stress by reaching so far out of your comfort zone that it causes you to stop moving at all. You always want to reach and grow, but creating goals that are too far from where you are presently can cause a sense of paralysis. Once this occurs, you start to go back to old behaviors and habits. Create a sense of ease with all you do. It is important to maintain that balance.

Part of my dream is to travel around the world speaking. That is not something that I had experience with. For me the way to move in that direction was to join Toastmasters. I am now an officer in my first club, and I have joined a second club. I remember my icebreaker and how nervous I was. Now I look for opportunities to speak whenever I can. It was working my way out of my comfort zone that made it possible to know that my dream is obtainable. To skip a rock takes practice, flow, rhythm, freedom, and enough playfulness to do something just because you want to. What is the next rock you are going to skip, just for the joy of it?

The Boulders

Keep in mind that your goals and dreams are like the horizon: They will always be in the distance. Take time daily to monitor how far you have come.

Congratulate yourself. Really look at all the progress you have made. A journal is an excellent way to keep track of all the steps you have taken. When you take time to celebrate your successes, it will draw even more to you.

I keep a miracle journal. I know that as I am more and more aware of the small miracles that occur on a daily basis in my life, more and more miracles are created, and they become bigger and bigger. Find your way of keeping tangible evidence of your progress.

You are then on your way to the success unexpected in common hours. You will be amazed at how easy it is when you keep on the path and focused on your dreams, all the while enjoying every moment along the way.

Majestic Mountains

No matter what your dreams and goals are, the end result you are always seeking is happiness, in one form or another. It may be peace, contentment, love, or success. All of these elements can be condensed down into happiness on some level. If you remain true to your path and make happiness in each moment important, as you move forward toward your goal, you will know the true success in common hours. Eliminate the thoughts of being happy "when": when you are more prosperous, successful, weigh less, or any of the other dreams you have. Take the shortcut and be happy now, in each moment, and unexpected success will be yours to savor as a bonus.

What if I told you that there was nowhere to go today, nothing to fix today, nothing to do today? What if I told you that this is it, this is what the top of your mountain looks like—today, if you do not like the view, turn around. You might be missing the entire vista.

ABOUT THE AUTHOR

Nancy Heimstra, a certified comprehensive coach, mentors women who are tired of living someone else's version of their lives. She helps them discover their true passions and supports and encourages them to live authentic lives through a process of deep self-discovery and taking bold action. Are you ready to color your life "outside the lines"? Sign up for her newsletter at http://www.authenticlivingnow.com.

88

The Architect of Destiny

Kevin Lankford

One should have an excuse-ectemy and remove them all from life!
—Kevin Lankford

Dare mighty things!
—Teddy Roosevelt

This chapter is one I find to be quite a challenge because the only architect of destiny there can be for *you* is *you!* So in this chapter you will be required to write your own destiny. Oh sure, I will provide fodder to stimulate your thought processes; all you have to do is seriously reflect on the direction these mental vitamins will take you.

Success is not random or a matter of luck. It requires a formula, which provides the desired outcome. Ever since I was a kid, I have always loved a product called Kool-Aid. It has been around for what seems like forever (talk about marketing), and kids still seem to love it just as much today. The greatest thing about Kool-Aid is that it is a powdered drink beverage: You simply add water and some sugar, stir, and you have two quarts of a delicious drink to quench any thirst. It is the *formula.* You cannot do it any other way than that.

The formula is tested, tried, and proven to work consistently the same way every time. It is so simple that even a child can do it. The man who invented it created success in a pack. It is a formula that is successful. In this chapter we will create your personal formula.

346

Those with the *formula* for success are the ones who win. Are you not ready to become a winner? Say it: "I'm a winner!" Well, stay with me now while we examine some of the questions put forth by a great thinker of our time who believed that one could shape one's own destiny:

For to what purpose is all the toil and bustle of this world? What is the end of avarice and ambition, of the pursuit of wealth, of power, and preeminence? . . . From whence, then, arises that emulation which runs through all the different ranks of men, and what are the advantages which we propose by that great purpose of human life which we call bettering our position?
—Adam Smith

Adam Smith was a man who lived from 1723 to 1790. He is known for being a great Scot economist and one of the forward thinkers of his time. He was an author who was an inspiration to such notables as Thomas Jefferson.

Adam Smith asked some good questions, huh? Questions are designed to improve your effectiveness. Suppose he was sitting before you after having traveled through time and asked you this question: "For to what purpose is all the toil and bustle of this world?" We could say that labor exists and the activity and commotion of this world are here for progress. The toil that exists has truly been valuable to us here in the twenty-first century and has allowed civilization to continue progressing!

"What is the end of avarice and ambition, of the pursuit of wealth, of power, and preeminence?" *Avarice* means to have too great a desire to have wealth or greed for riches. *Ambition* is its cousin, meaning a drive to succeed and to be enterprising enough to take risks in undertaking new challenges to succeed. The preeminent longing to excel forward and surpass the ordinary also refers to success. Its conclusion is found in your purpose.

In order to be a millionaire, your purpose has to be far more than the money. You seek a million dollars for who you become, and then you can give away a million dollars!

"From whence, then, arises that emulation which runs through all the different ranks of men, and what are the advantages which we propose by that great purpose of human life which we call bettering our position?" I like this part of the question because it reinforces *bettering your best*. *Emulation* is the desire or ambition to equal or surpass. We seek to *do* better, not to *be* better than others.

The true growth comes when we dare to challenge the best—when we look for the best. I believe that yearning, that aspiration for greatness, is an innate quality in us all. Even the forefathers said, "We are endowed by our creator to have life, liberty and the pursuit of happiness!"

Your value system can be a great tool in being the architect of your destiny. Values are the social principles, goals, or standards held or accepted by you and the society in which you live. Try listing your values and keeping them nearby, for example:

- peace of mind
- wealth
- good health
- a loving relationship
- family
- happiness
- free time
- spiritual fulfillment
- friendships
- retirement
- living to old age
- own business
- respect from others
- sense of accomplishment.

And of course, the list could go on and on.

Next list the destructive values you wish to eliminate or avoid participation in, such as:

- cheating or stealing
- gambling
- false sense of superiority or inferiority
- gossip, prejudice, bigotry, blame, criticism
- overindulgence in food, alcohol
- drugs
- smoking.

Are your values consistent with your behavior? Accept no excuses. *Excuses are an explanation for a disappointment.* Instead of explaining why you could not do something, ask yourself *how* you can do it. Have an "excuse-ectemy!" In other words, remove the ability to come up with reasons why you did not do something. Get rid of excuses.

Do you have a formula? Now go out and design your destiny. Remember, everything that was ever accomplished was at first nothing more than a thought held in the mind of the architect. Get all the tools, get all the materials, get all the support, and be who you have to be to do what you have to do, to have what others may never have! Develop a blueprint.

1. Determine your own best approach to setting your goals.
2. Do not confuse wishful thinking with goals.
3. Approach goals as a process, not as a destination, and ignore old programming that stops your forward progress.

ABOUT THE AUTHOR

If you want to leave your family a legacy with a better future, you must take massive visionary action. *Bettering Your Best: Using Your Strengths to Springboard Success* is a powerful process of self-inventory and creativity. Kevin truly wants you to succeed and recognize that the things you have done on your part are a result of the thoughts and actions that produced your outcomes. You can climb higher when you choose better ladders. Visit Kevin online at http://www.lulu.com/Kevin2.

89

The Work of Byron Katie:
Four Questions That Can Change Your Life

Byron Katie

Meeting Your Thoughts with Understanding

The Work is a simple yet powerful process of inquiry that teaches you to identify and question the stressful thoughts that cause all the suffering in the world. It consists of four questions that you apply to a stressful thought. It's a way to understand what's hurting you, a way to end all your stress and suffering. It works for everyone who is open to it, and it has a profound effect on your whole life. It will affect not only your own life, but your partner's life and the lives of your children and your children's children.

A thought is harmless unless we believe it. It's not our thoughts, but the *attachment* to our thoughts, that causes suffering. Attaching to a thought means believing that it's true, without inquiring. A belief is a thought that we've been attaching to, often for years.

Most people think that they are what their thoughts tell them they are. One day I noticed that I wasn't breathing—I was being breathed. Then I also noticed, to my amazement, that I wasn't thinking—that I was actually being thought and that thinking isn't personal. Do you wake up in the morning and say to yourself, "I think I won't think today"? It's too late: You're already thinking! Thoughts just appear. They come out of nothing and go back to nothing, like clouds moving across the empty sky. They come to pass, not to stay. There is no harm in them until we attach to them as if they were true.

No one has ever been able to control his thinking, although people may tell the story of how they have. I don't let go of my thoughts—I meet them with understanding, then *they* let go of *me*.

Putting the Mind on Paper

The first step in The Work is to write down your stressful thoughts about any situation in your life, past, present, or future—about a person you dislike or a situation with someone who angers or frightens or saddens you. (There's a sample Worksheet in *Loving What* Is, or you can go to www.TheWork.com and download and print a Judge-Your-Neighbor Worksheet.)

For thousands of years, we have been taught not to judge—but let's face it, we still do it all the time. The truth is that we all have judgments running in our heads. Through The Work we finally have permission to let those judgments speak out, or even scream out, on paper. We may find that even the most unpleasant thoughts can be met with unconditional love.

I encourage you to write about someone whom you haven't yet totally forgiven. This is the most powerful place to begin. Even if you've forgiven that person 99 percent, you aren't free until your forgiveness is complete. The 1 percent you haven't forgiven them is the very place where you're stuck in all your other relationships (including your relationship with yourself).

If you are new to The Work, I strongly suggest that you not write about yourself at first. If you start by judging yourself, your answers often come with old motives and with answers that don't work. Judging someone else, then inquiring and turning it around, is the direct path to freedom. You can judge yourself later, when you have been doing inquiry long enough to trust the power of your own truths.

If you begin by pointing the finger of blame outward, then the focus isn't on you. You can just let loose and be uncensored. We're often quite sure about what other people need to do, how they should live, whom they should be with. We have 20/20 vision about others, but not about ourselves.

When you do The Work, you see who you are by seeing who you think other people are. Eventually you come to see that everything outside you is a reflection

351

of your own thinking. You are the storyteller, the projector of all stories, and the world is the projected image of your thoughts.

Since the beginning of time, people have been trying to change the world so that they can be happy. This hasn't ever worked, because it approaches the problem backward. What The Work gives us is a way to change the projector—mind— rather than the projected. It's like when there's a piece of lint on a projector's lens. We think there's a flaw on the screen, and we try to change this person and that person, whomever the flaw appears to be on next. But it's futile to try to change the projected images. Once we realize where the lint is, we can clear the lens itself. This is the end of suffering, and the beginning of a little joy in paradise.

The Work: Four Questions and a Turnaround

The Work can be applied to any thought that causes you anger, fear, sadness, or frustration—any thought that keeps you from living in peace. Thoughts such as "My mother doesn't love me," "My boss doesn't appreciate me," "I'm too fat," "I need to be healthier," "My children should obey me," or "My brother should stop drinking" pass through our minds many times a day. When you believe these thoughts, you suffer; but when you question them, you can discover what is really hurting you. Once you realize the difference between what is real and what is not, you naturally begin to act with clarity and efficiency and to live the life you always wanted to live.

After you have filled in the blanks on the Judge-Your-Neighbor Worksheet, you question each of your statements with the four questions of The Work and then you turn the statement around. (The turnaround is a way of experiencing the opposite of what you believe.)

Stressful thought: "My husband doesn't listen to me."

The four questions:

1. Is it true?
2. Can you absolutely know that it's true?
3. How do you react when you believe that thought?
4. Who would you be without the thought?

Apply each of these four questions in turn to the stressful thought. Ask yourself the question, sit still, wait, and allow your answer to surface from deep within.

Once you have walked yourself through the four questions, turn the thought around by finding opposites to the statement you wrote. "My husband doesn't listen to me." One turnaround is "My husband does listen to me." Find three genuine examples of how that statement is true in your life. There are other possible turnarounds, such as "I don't listen to me" and "I don't listen to my husband." Find three examples for each turnaround.

When you question your stressful thoughts, you come to see that everything that has been troubling you is just a misunderstanding. You realize that what you believe isn't necessarily so. This is the beginning of freedom. The Work always leaves you as a kinder, clearer, happier human being.

ABOUT THE AUTHOR

Byron Katie is an internationally renowned speaker and author. Over the past twenty years, she has introduced The Work to hundreds of thousands of people throughout the world, at free public events, in corporations, universities, schools, churches, prisons, hospitals, in weekend intensives, and at her nine-day School for The Work. "Katie's events are riveting to watch," the *Times* of London reported, "and not just because people are baring their souls. Katie's laser-like tough love burns away all illusions." Eckhart Tolle, the best-selling author of *The Power of Now* said, "Byron Katie's Work is a blessing for our planet." And *Time* magazine named Katie a "spiritual innovator for the new millennium." She has written three best-selling books: *Loving What Is, I Need Your Love—Is That True?,* and *A Thousand Names for Joy.* Her website is www.TheWork.com, where you will find her blog, her schedule, a network of facilitators of The Work, a free hotline, audio and video clips, articles, and basic information about The Work.

90

Emotionally Intelligent Time Management: Why There Is No Such Thing as Time Management and What to Do about It

Michael Erwin

After many years of attempting to "manage time," I have come to the realization that it is not time that needs management!

Time moves on—a second, a minute, an hour comes and goes. It never stops—it is very consistent. In one day, 86,400 seconds. So what is all this about time management then? Well, it is really about *self-management*. Let us get clear—we are really talking about how we manage what we do, while time moves on.

What Does This Mean?

First, by getting clear that the focus is on self-management, we accept responsibility. We can then recognize that we cannot manage time, but we can manage ourselves! This is a challenging thought. When we think from a framework of managing time, it is like thinking about training a dog. We do it *to* something else, and if the results do not come, well, "the dog" was hard to train.

Time Is Impossible to Manage: It Will Not Stop

Once we have "reframed" our thinking from time management to self-management, we can truly become responsible for being more productive and improving our outcomes. I believe there are two key self-management factors that impact your outcomes. They are *clarity* and *desire*. When you are really clear about what you want to achieve *and* you have the desire, your actions will be more productive.

So how do you get clarity and desire? Developing clarity and desire uses emotional intelligence skills and abilities. Relying on purely rational, logical thinking processes will only get you part of the way.

Let us talk a little more about these.

Clarity

Clarity is about knowing exactly what outcome you want. The clearer you are about your outcome, the more productive you are. When you know exactly what outcome you want to achieve, you are much more focused. You become aware of all the possible actions to move you toward your desired outcome.

Truly knowing what you want your outcome to be *includes* how you want to *feel*. In fact, how you want to feel is usually *the* most important outcome you need to be clear about. Clearly knowing how you want to feel uses your skills of emotional self-awareness.

There are two key ways clarity impacts outcomes. The first is knowing whether an activity is productive or unproductive. I define *productive* in terms of moving me closer to a desired outcome (*unproductive* is *not* moving closer to a desired outcome). When planning or starting a task, ask yourself if the activity will help you progress toward achieving your goal. Lack of clarity makes answering this question hard and therefore decreases productivity.

Once we are able to determine whether an activity moves us toward our outcomes, then we look which of the possible actions will be the *most* productive. For example, if my desired outcome was to travel to New York from London, the following travel methods would move me closer to my destination— walking, taking a boat, driving, and getting a flight.

The most productive of these in terms of time used would be to fly. To develop ways to improve self-management and become more personally productive, here are some questions I suggest you could ask yourself.

- If I were going on a vacation tomorrow for two or more weeks, what would I want to complete today?
- What is the highest value-added action I can do?
- What can I, and only I, do?
- Why am I on the payroll? What is my purpose here?

355

To know if a task *is* productive or the *most* productive, you need to clearly know your outcome.

The cloudy confusion that descends on most of us when we lack clarity comes from how we feel. This is where we need to be skilled in emotional self-awareness, emotional self-expression, and emotional awareness of others. To clear the fog, we need to know how we really feel and be prepared to express that in an appropriate way. We also need to recognize the emotions (or potential emotions) of others and how much impact they are having on us.

Desire

When we are clear about the outcome and the activities that will generate the outcome, then the only thing that can stop us is a lack of desire. In simple terms, if you do not do the actions, then you do not want it enough. You *let* something get in the way. You decide (consciously or subconsciously) that something else is more desirable at that point in time.

This is where many of us get caught up in the day-to-day. Often, you do not consciously decide something else is more important, but you might as well have. In fact, I suggest you would be better off if you did consciously decide not to do something—at least that way you would be clearer about which direction you are heading.

Do you get caught in the day-to-day? Do you find yourself busy reacting to things, rather than consciously choosing the actions and direction you want to move in? If you were a ship, would you stay on your charted course, or are you sailing without a rudder, at the mercy of every change of wind and tide?

A lack of desire is usually associated with a lack of connection to the goal. The connection comes from within and is heavily influenced by how you feel. Do you lack passion because it is not really your goal ("it's what *Dad* wanted me to do")? Do you feel more fear than excitement? Maybe you feel like you *should* have the goal rather than feeling inspired by your goal.

An emotionally intelligent individual is usually more aware of how he feels about his goals. This enables him to create goals he is emotionally connected to, and this increases the action, progress, and success. You achieve more in less time with what seems like less effort.

356

In summary, there is no such thing as time management because time rolls on exactly the same for everyone. So you must take responsibility for self-management. A key part of self-management is knowing how you, and others, feel—the skills of emotional intelligence. Becoming more emotionally intelligent will help you develop *clarity* about your outcomes and will help you to really connect to the goals with great *desire*. When you apply these, I guarantee you will achieve more in less time with less effort.

ABOUT THE AUTHOR

Michael Erwin is a transformational coach and coaching director of DIY LifeCoach. DIY LifeCoach enables you to *coach yourself* to greater success in life. DIY LifeCoach uses a unique, purpose-designed approach to coaching that enables you to "achieve more in less time with less effort." Contact Michael at michael@diylifecoach.com.

91

Leadership Tips from My Dad, A Real Wise Guy: Lee (L. B.) Weiss (September 21, 1925–April 30, 1982)

Nicki Weiss

My dad has been dead for almost half of my life, yet I think about him every day. I am grateful to have had a funny, loving, and wonderful dad, who left a legacy of decency and wisdom.

L. B. had a saying for almost any situation. Something about his style made these sayings stick—perhaps a combination of his humor, timing, cheeriness, and innate common sense. After he died, many friends wrote our family, saying they will always remember L. B. for saying such-and-such. My mother compiled these snippets of wisdom, and when I reviewed them recently, I realized how much my dad had taught me about leadership and leading a life of common sense.

If any of the following touch you, please feel free to quote them as "L. B.'isms."

"There are more horses' asses in this world than there are horses."

This saying works for me on many levels, especially in work relationships. If I am dealing with someone who is acting badly, being rude or inconsiderate or demanding, I try not to stay in their sphere. Following my dad's advice, I give myself permission to only deal with people I like and respect.

This saying also reminds me not to be a horse's ass myself (not always so obvious to me). A client who I adore recently canceled a seminar on the day it was to run. He had a number of good reasons for canceling, however, our agreement stated that he pay me the full fee in this situation. As I was writing up the invoice, I felt uncomfortable, and my father's saying popped into my head. I could have rightly charged the full fee and felt like an ass for being petty when this client has given me so much business. Or I could do something different. I charged him half.

"The last chapter has not been written on Nicki."

As I was misspending my youth (dropped out of university, lived in a teepee on one of western Canada's most beautiful gulf islands, picked apples and oysters), my father continuously reassured my mother that I would turn out okay.

I am grateful for my father's confidence in me. He was able to see my potential when others could not, and his assurance that I could do anything I wanted and be successful still resonates through me.

My father was a coach in the truest sense of the word. He saw his children, and our friends, bigger than we saw ourselves. He could clearly see a path for us and told us what he saw. He saw that my kind sister, who was good with her hands, could be a wonderful occupational therapist and that my brilliant sister-in-law could be an ace accountant. He told me to go into sales.

I was completely offended. Sales? He told me that when I was 20 years old. At the time, I thought sales was anti-intellectual, manipulative, and boring. L. B. saw it differently. He told me I was a noodge and a noodnik (translation: a persistent pest). He told me I was a hard worker, smart, a good generalist, persuasive, talented with people, had people's best interests in my heart, and liked variety. He told me that I would be wildly successful. After university (yes, I went back and finished), I remembered what he had said. I got my first sales job and loved it.

"Different is easy. Good is hard."

L. B. had great instincts. He had an uncanny sense about new products that would not fly, a process that was too complicated, people who were a little too full of themselves, or a wheel that did not need reinvention.

He was a stickler for quality and competence. My father was a corporate accountant who always had a business on the side. One was a Baskin-Robbins ice cream parlor. He was constantly hiring and training teenagers to scoop ice cream that was exactly two ounces, to treat customers well, to not rip him off, to be able to count back change, and to work hard. Regularly, at the dinner table, he talked about what constituted good work and what incompetence looked like.

He taught me that there are no shortcuts to good; the only route is through repeated practice.

"Neither a borrower nor a lender be."

As kids, we were always running out of money. Our eyes were always bigger than our wallets. (I know lots of big kids today who have the same problem.) My father taught us the art of leading a balanced life and the lesson that living debt-free would give us choices. He taught us that borrowing money from friends could wreck a friendship.

In this age of instant gratification, where bigger and more is better, I bless the wisdom he left me. It has never steered me wrong.

"What's a nickel or a dime when you're out for a good time?"

My father the accountant was always careful with money. Some may have called him cheap. Yet whenever we were on vacation, he loved to live it up. He did not spend money in an extravagant way (he was a product of the Great Depression and World War II), but in a cheery, life-affirming, and fun way. He always said to be generous to yourself and to others, particularly if you are down on your luck.

"I wish she had the courtesy to treat me like a stranger."

My father would say this about his problematic mother-in-law. Apparently, my grandmother was not always so nice to him.

This leadership principle is so amazingly simple. It says, "If you don't like me, you can be indifferent to me, but mean is unacceptable." I notice a fair amount of meanness in the workplace that takes the form of passive aggression. We have all seen it but maybe not put a name to it: gossip, withholding or not fully sharing information, criticizing management, and not supporting colleagues. We would not treat strangers like this.

"The best things in life aren't things."

This saying taught me to value my relationships above everything else, to depend on myself and to be accountable to others, to be decent, and to have fun.

I do not want you to think I was not given tons of things by my parents because I was. However, I was conditioned from a very young age to believe that the world did not owe me a living. I was given a serious work ethic that I will always carry with me. If I want something, I go after it. I will not step on people to get whatever it is, and I will not cheat or steal, but I will work until I get it or do not want it anymore.

What's this got to do with leadership and improving your life, Nicki?

I am hoping that you see some value in my dad's teachings and sayings and that when you work, live, and lead, you are a good example to those around you.

My dad lived with a spring in his step, integrity in his heart, and his own brand of humor. Your living example will be what ultimately makes you great as a leader and as a human being.

Thanks, Dad.

Love,
Nud-nicki

ABOUT THE AUTHOR

Nicki Weiss is an internationally recognized certified professional management coach, Master Trainer, and workshop leader. Nicki has trained and coached over 6,000 business and sales executives. Her company provides classroom training, distance learning, and individual and group coaching. Nicki combines her powerful coaching abilities and strong facilitation skills to help managers become more effective leaders and to help salespeople sell more—sanely and humanely. Nicki's style is fun, challenging, warm, and results focused. Check out her award-winning monthly e-zine, "Something for Nothing™," at http://www.saleswise.ca. It is full of ideas for retaining, developing, and motivating your team. Contact her at nicki@saleswise.ca or by phone at (416) 778–4145.

This article may be reprinted in its entirety with express written permission from Nicki Weiss. The reprint must include the section "About the Author."

92

VALIDATION

Validation of Food for Thought

Patricia T. Watkins

Let us not deceive ourselves here . . . if any of us think ourselves to be wise based on popular standards of this age, think again. But we can be smart. Oh, we can be *real* smart about what it takes to bring our bodies to a state of good and even great health!

We already know to give our bodies sufficient to abundant rest every day. Okay, sometimes we play a little catch-up with this on a five-day work schedule, but overall, we need to gift six to eight hours of the rest/sleep combo to ourselves every day. Regarding exercise, oh boy, let us make it really simple here. You *know* to do it, and if you are honest, you know about *what* you should do and *how much* your body requires. If not, grab a couple exercise books and stop by your local gym for some quick advice. It will only take a few minutes, and you will be well on your way to a new looking you within weeks.

Now for the most enjoyable—food! Whether by whole food nutrition or whole food supplements, anyone can benefit. Consider these three food validations before eating or drinking and smart healthy choices will become second nature to your eating habits.

Food Validation #1: Think about *how* you think about food and drink

Is the character of our food so unthinkably bad, or are we allowing our human nature to be duped to the saturation point of fraudulence? Who is in control of what you think? Who is in control of what you put into your mouth? You should be! Are you?

Just because you can chew or swallow something that fits into your mouth and gullet does not make it food, does it? Consider whole food as something edible that requires little or no processing before ingesting and is truly beneficial.

What you ingest should actually be food. Your health depends on it.

Take action: Sheer logic says that good food and drink *in* results in good health *out*, while bad, fake, or overprocessed food *in* results in poor health *out*.

Make a decision *now* that will affect you for the rest of your life. Choose health. Good, whole food is grown in good soil with clean water and free of harmful chemicals. It contains 100 percent value because nature provides far more nutrition and gives far more support than anything man can isolate and reproduce in a laboratory. Whole food is a nutritional treasure from nature. Enjoy!

How old must one be to understand this food validation point? The sooner the better. My son learned this at age three. He stopped cold atop a midwest airport viewing tower one hot, smoldering afternoon with me in tow. He was not interested in watching his daddy fly off into the clouds. But he was interested (mesmerized, in fact) as to why a vanilla ice cream cone was not melting on top the roof in the blazing heat of day. He vocalized his choice in one simple phrase: "Acky. It no melt." Wow! It was a good observation indeed!

Food Validation #2: Think about *why* and *what* you consume and are able to digest

We often tend to choose products that offer us the least benefit or actually hinder our health and performance. Why? What do we actually believe about food in its purest form? The purpose of food is for nutrition—to grow, energize, and sustain.

Giving thought to honest characteristics of food can be more than just an eye-opener. It truly can be a life-changing experience. For some, even life saving! Just the very process of thinking about food gives us the necessary time for searching and validating. Thus we make better choices.

Take Action: Choose smart, healthy, real, whole foods with the least amount of processing and containing a balance of protein and carbohydrates, raw milks and fermentation, whole food supplements and probiotics. Just say no to preservatives and most additives. Drink pure, clean water without the enzyme inhibitor fluoride, or a tea, juice, or smoothie without sweeteners are best. If you have the good fortune of acquiring clean, fresh, raw Jersey milk or goat's milk, consider yourself gifted indeed. In all you eat and drink, do so for the sake of nutrition.

Food Validation #3: Think about *when* and *where* you eat and drink

What could be so basic and vital and yet so misrepresented even to the point of fraud? Food, of course. Stop believing all the advertising hype when selecting food and drink away from home. Making poor choices over years may cause you to miss out on a lifetime of good health. But you can still benefit with a turn in the right direction to whole foods now!

History and science tell us that whole food groups of every color supply us with maximum health benefits. Having trouble finding quality food? Not to worry. Food and supplement manufacturers of noble character have proven that specific cold-pressed and low-temperature methods of drying and preparing their pure, raw materials ensure the highest integrity as sources of nutrition.

Take Action: The simpler the meal, the more nutritious it is likely to be. Try these choices when eating on the go and packing your food is not an option.

1. Choose whole foods that are as fresh and in season as possible.
2. For early meals, enjoy eggs, fruit, lean meats, and fish. Go light, or avoid nutritionally dead carbohydrates.
3. In the afternoon, try colorful salads with cold-pressed virgin olive or grape seed oil, lean meats and fish, fruit, and nuts.
4. When evening comes, partake of meats, fish, raw or lightly steamed vegetables, or salad.
5. For dessert, treat yourself to an organic, dark chocolate and say, "I truly deserve this!"

When fresh, whole foods are not easily obtainable or when you need the extra support of supplements, choose those that are labeled "whole food." And when probiotics become necessary or important to you, choose them as whole food, too.

Start looking at the noble character of pure foods. Whoever thought it would become necessary to validate seeds, soil, and the water supply before consuming food? Until you really know what is in all that, you cannot know what is safe to ingest, digest, and surround yourself with on this great planet earth . . . even if the FDA and national dieticians give their blessing. Just how serious are you about your health? That of your children? That of their children?

Hmmm . . . and why sit *you* there until you die? Why not get on your feet and begin making good decisions based upon information that is overwhelmingly available for anyone at the click of a mouse? Think about your food issues from the perspective of truth. Make your daily food selections based upon what you have learned and what you know to be honest and of a good report, not on what some companies want you to buy, whose purpose is only to profit their stockholders. Why not give yourself a do-over by making today the beginning of the rest of your healthy life? Good health is not just about you. It is for your children and all those you care about who will have the early benefits of learning from you.

ABOUT THE AUTHOR

Patricia Travis Watkins, a distant cousin of Colonel William Barrett Travis, famed at the Alamo, is a writer, editor, children's author, production-partnered in fine design stationery, and a longtime health advocate for all families and their domesticated pets. She has a broad, working knowledge of whole foods and quality products for healthy, natural lifestyles as vice president of sales of Watkins and Watkins Artisans, Inc. In addition, Patricia writes the monthly blog for her book's Web site (http://www.boydfriend.com); *BOYD-FRIEND: His "Yippie-Skippie" Journey to a Forever Home* is available from the Web site or Amazon.com.

93

Who Is Wearing Your Pants?
Living Your Dreams . . . Not Your Hopes

Wanda Lee MacPhee

> A solitary fantasy can transform a million realities.
> —Maya Angelou

Who is "wearing the pants" in your life? Who determines your destiny and success?

One aspect to wearing your pants is creating your present and future. You are the creator of your destiny . . . so what does that look like for you?

Often we use the words *hopes* and *dreams* interchangeably as we plan our lives and future successes. When we stop to consider the differences between hopes and dreams, we see that this is not accurate. In fact, this is a limiting factor in creating our reality of success.

A hope implies that you are not in control of your destiny. A hope is something that you leave to others to create . . . and someone else will wear the pants. A hope is a wish that is often seen as an unlikely possibility, and your deep inner self does not truly believe that it is going to be a reality.

A dream is something quite different. It is created by you and forms the template for your own life. A dream contains the vision and the action that are required to create reality. A dream is your vision—a prediction of what is to come. A dream is fully owned and believed by your inner self . . . and you are wearing the pants!

Where Is Your Dream Taking You?

Creating your best reality requires a complete and vivid vision of what your life will actually look and feel like—your dream of the future. The foundation of your future and the road map that you will follow to success is determined by the completed vision that you have for your life. Those areas that you do not create in your dreams become voids in the plan that someone else will determine.

Workshop:
1. Take some time to reflect on your vision of success. Consider all the areas of your life—family, career, spiritual, community, financial, recreational, and so on. Let your mind consciously and unconsciously travel to your deepest dreams.
2. Now consciously add additional layers of detail to your vision of success. Be vivid in your vision . . . make it so real so that it is as if you are already there.

Those who want to wear the pants in their lives leave nothing to chance, luck, or hope. They create the master plan as completely and in such detail that they are the only ones wearing the pants. Your dream becomes your inspiration and the road to fulfilling the grand purpose of your life.

There are many examples of incredibly successful people who started their journey without the benefit of a privileged birth. They were from financially impoverished, emotionally unsupportive, intellectually undernurturing, or spiritually lost backgrounds but rose to create fabulous lives of spiritual peace, wisdom, love, and wealth. One of the best examples of that in our current society is Oprah Winfrey. Her biography is a perfect illustration of manifesting a dream to make a significant contribution to the world, despite growing up in poverty, a woman, and an African American.

Why her? Why not you, too?

Some may say that this is just good luck and bad luck, a random chance, a fairy godmother's intervention, or a magic trick. I suggest that there is nothing chance or luck has to do with it! In looking at the lives of those who grew so successfully, they have certain characteristics in common. One of these is a strong and vivid vision of their future success. If the child and teenaged Oprah had not seen herself in a place beyond her current reality, then there is no way that she would have ended up as she is today – a successful businesswoman, a leader for the black community, a multimillionaire, and a generous contributor to many charities and projects around the world.

Author Jim Collins discusses this in relation to corporate success in his book *Good to Great*. The BHAG, or "big hairy audacious goal," is a key component to the success of those companies who outperform their peers substantially over time. Success and motivational expert Mark Victor Hansen refers to this phenomenon as "beginning with the end in mind."

If you do not know what success looks like for you, how will you know when you find it? Will you be like the emperor who had no clothes, relying on what others tell you, even though you cannot see the pants yourself?

From Dreams to Reality

As lovely as that vision in your head is, it needs to be brought into reality and acted on to create successful results. In the words of Frederick Faust, "There is a giant asleep within every person. When that giant awakes, miracles happen."

The stepping-stones to move your present life toward the life of your dreams are your goals. These are the signposts to mark your way from "now" to "then" in achieving your vision. The dream may be perfect but needs actions to make it manifest. By setting your goals and taking action on them, you wear the pants in creating your dreams in the world.

There are many experts on goal setting that will help you move forward in the creation of your dream plan. I would like to share with you just a couple of things that have been revolutionary in my experience with goals and living toward my dream.

First, there is no wrong answer.

For those of us who are perfectionists and those who may be afraid of committing to the unknown future, this is a reassuring thought! Many of us find goal setting to be incredibly intimidating. We get caught up in the voices in our heads that feed our fears:

- What if I do not achieve it? Am I a failure?
- Who am I to think I can do that?
- What if the pants do not really look as good as I think they will?

So set realistic and achievable goals. In today's fast-paced society, there is often little patience for steady growth. We may be attempting to create our success in such a short period of time that we are overzealous in our goals and timelines for attaining them. Then, when we predictably fail to achieve the goal on schedule, we feed the fear monster and the negative messages in our heads get louder and more insistent. Give yourself permission to be dedicated and yet flexible. Goals are not meant to be rigid and unchanging, but living and real.

Second, write them down. So simple . . . and yet so powerful!

Workshop
1. Set your goals . . . and keep going. Write down at least 100 goals that will be part of your dream.
2. Choose the first goal to achieve.
3. List the top three actions that you can start doing today to make that goal happen. If it does not take three, then use the other two to take action on the second goal, and so on.

A written goal is many hundreds of times more likely to be achieved than one that merely stays inside your head. I have found this to be one of the most phenomenal tools in my own life. I started the process of writing goals, cutting out pictures to represent my dreams, and even displaying them on a "dream board" in my office. It was shocking that keeping these tangible pieces of my vision in view had such a powerful influence on reaching these goals. I would love for you to do the same!

Third, do something to move that goal toward reality. By doing just three things to move toward my goals each day, I have accomplished 21 actions in only one week—and 1,095 in the first year alone. That momentum has now enabled me to increase to five actions per day. Now even more goals are being accomplished and at a faster rate. Accomplished entrepreneur and businesswoman Mary Kay Ashe is often quoted as saying that this was her key to success. She chose the seven key things to do each day to accomplish her dream, and before long, it became reality.

This is your pattern for creating and wearing the pants of your life. Now, make them real . . . and make them yours!

ABOUT THE AUTHOR

Dr. Wanda Lee MacPhee is a successful chiropractor and professional leader. She speaks to groups across Canada and facilitates workshops for professional groups. She is now completing her first book project entitled *Who Is Wearing Your Pants? The Authentic Guide for Finding Your Unique Success in Life*. Dr. Wanda has a passion for helping others to discover their paths to fulfillment and live their purpose, with a particular focus on young professional women. She believes everyone can decide to wear the pants in her life and make her dreams a reality. Please visit her Web site for more information: http://www.whoiswearingyourpants.com or http://www.whoiswearingyourpants.ca.

94

WINNING IN LIFE

Learn to Be a Winner

Les Brown

I believe there are three kinds of people. There are winners, who know what they want and understand their potential and the possibilities. They take life on. Next are losers, who do not have a clue as to who they are. They allow circumstances to shape their lives and their self-image.

I believe there is a third group as well. This consists of potential winners whose lives are just slightly out of alignment. I call them wayward winners. It may be that they just need to learn how to be real winners. Perhaps they have hit a bump or two that has knocked them off course and they are temporarily befuddled. A failed relationship, a lost job, financial problems, unformed goals, a lack of parental support, illness, many things can send us off course temporarily.

Wayward winners are not lost souls; they just need some tweaking and coaching and nudging to get them back on course. A map might be nice. Many of these wayward winners are easily identifiable because they are always searching.

Right now, there are many wayward winners out there braving rain, sleet, and snow because they, too, still believe that they have untapped talents. They attend motivational seminars and listen to inspirational tapes, and they plunge onward, believing that sooner or later, they will find their way again.

Other wayward winners have temporarily given up. They are damaged and disoriented, their confidence badly eroded. They tend to drift through life numbly. The friends and relatives and loved ones of wayward winners see that they are out of sync and wonder why they cannot be satisfied, why they do not settle down. They wonder how people who have such obvious abilities and great potential can be so disoriented and unsure.

It is difficult for others to understand the rawness of a broken heart or the aching emptiness of an unguided spirit. You and I know. We have been there. Wayward winners know that there are possibilities out there, but too often, they feel locked out from them. Some are afraid to risk any more because of what they have risked and lost already.

I know now that as difficult as it may be for you wayward winners to do, it is necessary to continue to test yourselves. Even though you have been hurt before, it is the only way to grow. We all have the capacity to change, to lead meaningful and productive lives by awakening our consciousness.

You know there are going to be tough times as you go about changing your life, so brace yourself, and you will be able to handle them. When you get into your seat on an airplane, what is the first thing they tell you to do? Fasten your seat belt. Brace yourself for the turbulence.

When you decide to move your life to the next level of accomplishment, you must fasten your mental and spiritual seat belts because it is going to be a while before you reach that comfortable level again. You will reach it, but you must endure the turbulence of change in order to grow.

Try this technique to help you through the difficult times of change and growth. Find four reasons why you cannot succumb to your fears and your troubles. Find those deep sources of motivation that can lift you out of the turbulence and above the clouds. You must change your life because, for example:

- you have not yet tapped the talents given you
- you want to leave something more for your children
- you want to live life rather than letting life live you
- you want to do what makes you happy.

It is in these rocky early moments of bringing change to your life that you discover who you are. In the prosperous times you build what is in your pocket. In the tough times you strengthen what is in your heart. And that is when you gain insight into yourself, insight that leads to self-mastery and an expansion of your consciousness as a life force in both your personal and professional lives.

ABOUT THE AUTHOR

Les Brown is a world-renowned speaker, successful entrepreneur, best-selling author, radio and television celebrity, and nine-year cancer survivor. As a renowned professional speaker, author, and television personality, Les Brown has risen to national prominence by delivering a high-energy message that tells people how to shake off mediocrity and live up to their greatness. Les has had no formal education beyond high school, but with persistence and determination, he has initiated and continued a process of unending self-education that has distinguished him as an authority on harnessing human potential. In 1989, Les Brown was the recipient of the National Speakers Association's highest honor: the Council of Peers Award of Excellence (CPAE). In addition, he was selected one of the World's Top Five Speakers for 1992 by Toastmasters International and was a recipient of the Golden Gavel Award. In 1990, Les recorded his first in a series of speech presentations entitled "You Deserve," which was awarded a Chicago-area Emmy and became the leading fundraising program of its kind for pledges to PBS stations nationwide. Les Brown is an internationally recognized speaker and CEO of Les Brown Enterprises, Inc. He is also the author of the highly acclaimed and successful books *Live Your Dreams* and the newly released *It's Not Over Until You Win*. Les is the former host of *The Les Brown Show*, a nationally syndicated daily television talk show that focused on solutions rather than on problems. For information on Les's speaking schedule, books, and tapes, visit http://www.lesbrown.com.

95

WISDOM

Profound Words of Wisdom to Fire Your Life from Within

Kunbi Korostensky

During the 20 years in which I worked with various people helping them to overcome numerous health problems, one question I was frequently asked by my patients and clients was "once I have regained better health, what can I do to keep it?" Reaching a healthful state is only half the journey. Knowing how to live consciously will enable you to enjoy long-lasting health and balance. This article will give you some idea of what it means to practice conscious living.

Primarily, try to refrain from getting agitated over situations or people. Fretting about others is an indication of resistance. The more you resist what others do or say, the unhappier you will be, thereby disrupting your inner peace.

Instead, learn to accept what you cannot change and direct your inner strength to things that invigorate and motivate you to become a better person. Very soon, you will notice how people and situations around you begin to change.

I have also found applying the following set of principles to be very helpful in maintaining a healthy, happy, and harmonious life.

1. When you wake up in the morning, take a few minutes to be conscious of how precious the gift of life is. Give thanks for a new day and for being alive, and before closing your eyes at night, once again give thanks for having been granted the day to experience, to learn, and to grow. Nothing is more precious than the gift of life, so be grateful for each single day you have.

2. Give your body daily that which it requires to regenerate itself and to stay healthy and strong.
- Eat holistic foods with less animal protein.
- Drink up to six glasses of clear, still, fresh water daily to cleanse your body.
- Consciously breathe in often through the nose while raising the abdomen, and breathe out through the mouth by gently lowering the abdomen.
- Eat slowly, and chew your food particles very well before swallowing to aid digestion.
- Take a good multimineral product, vitamin C, essential amino acids, and enzymes daily to supplement your food intake. There are a lot of free radicals in the atmosphere, which are partly responsible for many chronic diseases.
- Eat daily some sort of raw diet ("life") food, such as fruits, nuts, grains, seeds, or fresh salads, to enhance your metabolism.

3. Break through your limitations and concentrate your energy on what you know you can do best.

4. Be consequent and disciplined in whatever you do, and give your full, undivided attention to the matter at present.

5. Find the time to go into seclusion at least once a day for about 10–15 minutes. During this time, sit still, relax, and turn your attention inward. Be quiet, and observe what is happening inside of you. This way you will gradually enhance your intuitive perception and attain inner clarity, thus strengthening your soul.

While you sit still, imagine the eternal life force passing through your whole being, like a wave of the gentle breeze of energy right to the very core of your soul. As you open yourself fully to this energy, allow deep gratitude to arise from within you for all the blessings and love you constantly receive.

6. Learn to put a leash on rampant and chaotic thoughts, and try to cultivate more harmonious, loving, and positive thoughts, for the thought forms you give life to can either enhance your life and your whole being or encumber your entire existence.

7. Let joy and gratitude fill your heart daily and radiate this to the people you meet. Show consideration not only to fellow humans, but also to other living beings. Have patience with those who might not be as fortunate as you.

8. Learn to show genuine concern, kindness, and understanding to others. Encourage others where it is necessary, and try to see the good side of people by bringing out the best in them. Be respectful to others, and be helpful where it is required, but do not act imposingly and in a pushy manner.

9. Avoid loud outbursts and anger because these are detrimental to your health. They also create tension in your energy field. Endeavor to remain focused and peaceful, even in the heat of a discussion, and do not let anger take control.

10. Let enthusiasm and appreciation rule your heart. Smile often, and no matter what might go wrong, remember that you are lucky to be alive and that each passing day presents you with new opportunities to make amendments; treasure this awareness.

11. Most of what we run after depletes our energy reserves. Take the time to rid yourself of excessive baggage, and make more time for your loved ones and for the things that give meaning to your life.

12. Every now and again, turn your gaze inward. Should you still find therein any disturbing feelings, like ghosts from the past, let go of them by picturing yourself standing under a full, cascading waterfall. While the waterfall washes over you, imagine its sparkling, pure, and clear waters cleansing you, washing you anew and removing all the turmoil from your soul until all old wounds have been salvaged and you feel new, pulsating strength arising from within.

13. Forgive yourself and others for whatever might have been, for the present is all you have. Leave the past where it belongs. It is gone, and you cannot wish it back.

14. Try to keep a sense of balance in all you do: work and play, eating and drinking. A life of equilibrium and discipline helps you remain in harmony with the natural law of balance, which keeps everything in regulation.

15. Do not waste your energy on chatty talks and excessive sports. Instead, try to channel your energy into creative thinking and resourceful ideas.

16. Have a creative mind and not a competitive mind, for a creative mind taps into the ever-flowing life force from a higher source, and a competitive mind uses borrowed energy, which is congested and short-lived.

17. Listen within. Use your intuition, your inner tutor, and your voice of wisdom. Avoid anger, frustration, or fear. These short circuit your energy and thus diminish the power of your intuition

The essence of life is to be conscious of the laws in creation, which encompass everything in our lives and beyond, and to live conscientiously within these laws bodily, mindfully, and spiritually, for that which we call life is just an insignificant remnant of the ever-emanating, pulsating, and replenishing power surging forth from the highest source beyond our comprehension.

I wish you the inner strength to be able to turn your gaze inward and upward daily for the task that needs to be undertaken and accomplished, that is, for you to live each day and each moment in the full consciousness of *your being* for the full maturity of your *inner self!* Conscious living is exuberant joy, and radiating that joy is your natural ability to demonstrate the state of your inner self. Even after you have attained intact health, it is essential to continue to nurture your inner self and keep on a path of conscious living.

ABOUT THE AUTHOR

Olakunbi (Kunbi) Korostensky, ND/MA, a psychotherapist, is a Life Changer Coach™ specializing in helping people struggling with new changes in their lives. She is also a spiritual teacher for women who want to attain feminine excellence in their lives and businesses through their intrinsic spiritual power. She is the founder of the Awaken Women International, a community providing women worldwide with spiritual tools to expand their scopes and attain feminine excellence. As president of Stiftung Attitudinal Healing, a nonprofit organization founded by her in Switzerland, she is dedicated to embracing love instead of fear. Visit http://www.embracingchanges.com and http://www.awakenwomen.com.

96

The Scientific Process Behind Making Wishes Come True

Mark Victor Hansen

I have told people thousands of times that they have just got to ask for what they want. And I find that most people only have one problem with this directive: They do not *know* what they want!

You Cannot Ask for What You Want Unless You Know What It Is!

In this exercise I am going to start you on a wonderful path of painting your dreams into reality. I am going to teach you the secrets behind setting—and achieving—your greatest ambitions.

Before we set off on this path together, let me make one thing very clear: The word *goals* can be intimidating—it can feel so overbearing that it keeps people from even beginning the process. So let us instead think of goals as a "to-do list with deadlines."

Do the deadlines have to be tomorrow? Next week? Of course not. This is your to-do list for the rest of your life. Goals can be added to, subtracted from, and—most importantly—scratched off the list as you move through your life.

Here is a checklist to ensure you are using a successful framework to set your to-do list:

- **Your most important goals must be yours.** Not your spouse's. Not your child's. Not your employer's. Yours. When you let other people determine your definition of success, you are sabotaging your own future.
- **Your goals must mean something to you.** When you write your goals, you must ask yourself, "What's really important to me? What am I prepared to give up to make this happen?" Your reasons for charting a new course of action give you the drive and energy to get up every morning.
- **Your goals must be specific and measurable.**
- **Vague generalizations and wishy-washy statements are not good enough.** Be very specific!
- **Your goals must be flexible.** A flexible plan keeps you from feeling suffocated and allows you to take advantage of genuine opportunities that walk in your future door.
- **Your goals must be challenging and exciting.** Force yourself to jump out of your comfort zone to acquire that energy and edge.
- **Your goals must be in alignment with your values.** Pay attention to your intuition, your gut. When you set a goal that contradicts your values, something inside will twinge. Pay attention.
- **Your goals must be well balanced.** Make sure you include areas that allow time to relax, have fun, and enjoy people in your closest circle.
- **Your goals must be realistic.** Be expansive, but do not be ridiculous. If you are four feet tall, you will probably never play in the NBA. Also, be sure to allow yourself time to get there.
- **Your goals must include contribution.** Unfortunately, many people get so wrapped up in pursuing their goals that they do not have time in their lives to give something back to society. Build this into your goals program.
- **Your goals need to be supported.** Either selectively share a few of your dreams with a number of people, or share all of your dreams with a select few people. In either case you are creating a web of support and accountability for yourself.

Go for the Gusto—101 Goals!

It is time to get started on your master plan. Give yourself some quiet time, put on some relaxing music . . . and write down 101 goals.

Open your mind to *all* the possibilities. Start each goal with "I am" or "I will." Do not even *think* about restricting yourself! To help you with this process, here are some key questions to ask yourself:

380

- What do I want to do?
- What do I want to have?
- Where do I want to go?
- What contribution do I want to make?
- What do I want to learn?
- Who do I want to meet and spend my time with?
- How much do I want to earn, save, and invest?
- What will I do for fun and optimum health?

This process may take two hours. It may take two weeks. Do not stop until you have 101 goals. Remember, you are building your better life here—it is the only life you have.

ABOUT THE AUTHOR

In the area of human potential, no one is more respected than Mark Victor Hansen. With his business partner, Jack Canfield, Mark created the *Chicken Soup for the Soul* series. With over 100 million *Chicken Soup for the Soul* books sold around the world, it is one of the most successful publishing franchises in the world today. He serves as chairman of M. V. Hansen & Associates, Inc. The *Chicken Soup* idea was just one of many that has propelled Mark into the worldwide spotlight as a sought-after keynote speaker, best-selling author, and marketing maven. For more on Mark Victor Hansen, please visit http://www.markvictorhansen.com.

Copyright © 2001, Mark Victor Hansen, America's Leading Expert on Human Potential

97

WORK AND LIFE BALANCE

Tipping the Scales:
How Is Your Work-Life Balance?

Marc de Bruin

Recently, I did a Google search on the key words "life balance"; it yielded me 10.1 million hits. The key words "work life balance" got me almost eight million hits. Work, life, and balance between the two are quite hot topics!

Balance = 50-50?

Is there something objective that we can call "work-life balance," a state we can achieve and know we have it? In other words, can work-life balance be defined for each and every one of us?

I do not think so. Balance is always *perceived* balance, which is an individual matter. Work-life balance means that we are happy with all aspects of our lives, physically, mentally, and emotionally, and this is different for each person. We have control. We can do everything we feel *needs* to be done at work, but we also have a private life next to it and participate in the community. We set goals, make plans, and stick with them.

Out of Whack

In my life I always sense that there *is* actually something like work-life balance when the balance is thrown off! I am doing okay up until a certain point, and then life starts to feel out of whack—there is no time to do what I *need* to do, let alone what I *want* to do. Family, social activities, and work all start to encroach upon me; everything needs to be juggled, relationships seem to get tighter and tighter, work becomes even *more* demanding, I start to cross out weekends to at least have two days to myself, and so on . . . it is all too much.

Technology does not make it any easier: e-mails, (mobile) phones, beepers, pagers, sms, video messaging or conferencing, voicemails, Web sites, magazines, newspapers . . . we can hardly run from it all.

Moreover, bosses nowadays expect us to take on more work every day, work longer hours and more days; it is not surprising that the World Health Organization calls work-related stress a "worldwide epidemic." It makes us want to run and hide in the woods!

The Issue

What is the issue? It is not that we do not know the answer to the problem. Everyone can come up with good ideas to bring back the balance: more exercise, delegating tasks, letting go of burdens, prioritizing, working fewer hours and fewer days, sharing jobs, varying the work week, learning to say no, and so on. So why is there still so much perceived lack of balance among many of us?

It is because of a *values* conflict.

Values

Values are huge drivers for our behavior. They are the attributes in life that are most important to us as individuals; they are the answer we give to the question "what is really important to you?" The answer can concern any life area, be it work, family, relationships, money, health, personal development, and so on.

Values are private, personal beliefs about good and bad, right and wrong. They are the foundation on which we base our judgments in life. Values can be words like *honesty, integrity, love, balance, rest, fun, fear, worry,* and *doubt* or sentences like "the world is a good place to live," "my work fulfils me," "chocolate is bad for my health," and so on.

Values are formed within us from the day we are born, mostly by our parents ("you shouldn't be doing that; that is *bad*"; "you are so beautiful; you will be famous"), but also by peers, teachers, colleagues, and events in our lives. Values are stored not in our conscious, reasoning minds, but in our subconscious, creative minds, so mostly we are not aware of what our values are—unless we start to consciously look at them and think about them.

As it is suggested that 95 percent of what we think and do is dictated by our *subconscious* beliefs, values determine our behavior—and emotions—greatly, without us noticing much of them. In the work-life balance example, we feel out of whack but have not got a clue why *exactly*. Our perception of not being balanced means that there is inner (value) conflict: Our inner values are not reflected in our outer behavior. We desire *this* but do and get *the other*.

The Solution

We need to find out what we want our lives to look like, create a life vision, and assess what work-life balance means to us as individuals. Most people do not do that. They live by default, forever getting what they always got and perpetuating the vicious cycle. Life happens *to* them rather than *from* them. And exactly there is where we can start to make a difference.

We need to realize that life is a product of our minds—we create our experiences through our thoughts, and we assess what has happened through our thoughts again. Realizing this makes us able to consciously *respond* to our present outcomes and to *change* our future outcomes. Life is no longer something that happened to us one day and in which we now seem to be stuck.

Be fair: There will always be times when life gets thrown off-balance—a sudden holiday comes up, a baby is born, a huge storm blows the house down, you are involved in a car accident, suddenly you are "promoted" to a foreign country, you fall ill, you win the lottery, you receive an invitation for a wedding next day, and so on. Generally, though, it is about striking equilibrium in all aspects of our lives, as far as this lies within our power.

Tips

Let me give you some tips that will help you to get more balance in your life.

- Improve your current state of mind. How do you feel *right now* regarding your work and life? If you feel off-balance, identify which values are infringed upon, and resolve to align yourself with those values from now on.

384

- Set some easy-to-achieve, short-term goals. Pursuing goals usually will create more balance immediately as you are creating a vision.
- Protect your private time from your work time. There is a huge gray field, and if you let it, your life *and* work become more and more gray and blurry.
- Know that there is always an alternative. Ask for support, whether from family, friends, colleagues, your community, or your boss. Tell them you are feeling off-balance and want to improve the situation. Honesty is nearly always appreciated.
- Improve your lifestyle. Your working conditions may be fantastic, but if you eat and drink too much (or unhealthily), sleep too little, exercise too little, smoke, use drugs, and think negatively most of the time, you will feel lack of balance regardless.
- Hire a life or business coach (but that is quite self-explanatory); a coach will get you on track and keep you there. I can guarantee you that (if you choose to commit).

Rest assured that life will not be dull ever; there will be times you are challenged and the scales are tipped. It is on *you* to restore the balance by looking at what is really important to you in your life. That will require action. Action will get you results.

The system works. Are you willing to work the system?

About the Author

Marc is a certified life and business coach, master NLP practitioner, author, and speaker in Queensland, Australia. He specializes in coaching professionals and small business owners worldwide who are at critical junctions in their lives. Having been an attorney for nearly six years in his "previous life" in the Netherlands, Marc knows how daunting taking steps in a new direction can seem to be, yet how rewarding it is when one does. Marc can be contacted through his Web sites http://www.designyourdestinycoaching.com and http://www.landmarc.info.

98

The Power of a Positive Workplace

Ken Blanchard

In an organization where empowerment is the watchword, all things are possible.

No magic elixir, no one-time effort, no management fad will make people gung-ho about the company they work for. Creating a positive environment is an ongoing commitment. I have often said that profit is the applause you get for taking care of your customers. That starts with building an organization that motivates and empowers the people who work there.

In *Gung Ho!*, a book I wrote with Sheldon Bowles, we present three lessons for building a positive work environment. The first lesson centers on the power of worthwhile work. People feel real joy from doing something they believe is meaningful. When Walt Disney started his theme park, he told his cast members (employees) that they were in the happiness business, which sounds a lot more exciting than the theme park business. Those in the financial services sector are really in the peace of mind business, which is a lot more appealing than financial services. In the same vein, many real estate salespeople talk about the value of helping people "reach the American dream."

When you create an inspiring vision for your business, it can create excitement for everyone in your organization, which in turn can make customers excited about what you do.

BYOB (Bring Your Own Brain)

But creating the vision gets you only partway there. The second lesson of *Gung Ho!* is that positive organizations put their people in charge of achieving the goal.

They train and develop people to *bring their brains to work* and take responsibility for making decisions.

At too many organizations, people are encouraged to leave their brains at home. The culture at these companies, either overt or implicit, is that work decisions are made from the top down.

Wayne Dyer, the great personal growth teacher, said years ago that there are two kinds of people in life: ducks and eagles. Ducks act like victims and go, "Quack! Quack! Quack!" Eagles take initiative and soar above the crowd. As a customer, you can always identify a bureaucracy if you have a problem and are confronted by ducks who quack, "It's our policy. I didn't make the rules—I just work here. Do you want to talk to my supervisor? Quack! Quack! Quack!"

Most of us have had experiences in which our requests for service have resulted in a lot of quacking and our needs not being met. More often than not, this kind of customer experience results from a failure on the part of organizational leaders to put their people in charge of achieving the goal.

Great service does not happen by accident. You have to train your people to take initiative and responsibility for solving customer problems. At the Ritz-Carlton, all new associates go through a six-week training program before they are ready to be full-time associates. Why does the program take so long? Because after the six-week training, a new associate is given a $2,000 discretionary fund that they can use to solve a customer's problem without consulting anybody, including their boss. That makes gung-ho employees.

The third and final lesson is that people working together in an organization need to cheer each other on. Of all the things I have taught over the years, the most important is the power of catching people doing things right and accentuating the positive. So often in organizations, the leadership engages in what I call "sea gull management." Managers are not around until people make a mistake. Then they fly in, make a lot of noise, dump on everybody, and fly out. This does not make for a very motivating work environment.

People need to be recognized. They need to be caught doing something right and publicly acknowledged for it. Offering kudos for genuine good work makes people's spirits soar.

Share the Pain and the Joy

I grew up with a mom who accentuated the positive. She told everybody that I sang before I talked, I danced before I walked, and I smiled before I frowned. Yet the concept really came alive for me later in life, when I had a wonderful opportunity to work with Norman Vincent Peale, author of *The Power of Positive Thinking*. Larry Hughes, president of William Morrow, called me in 1985 and said, "Ken, would you consider writing a book with Norman Vincent Peale?"

"Is he still alive?" I asked. My mom and dad had gone to his church before I was born.

Larry replied, "Not only is he alive—he's the most incredible guy you'll ever want to meet."

So I went to New York and had wonderful three-hour lunch with Norman and his wife, Ruth, Larry, my agent, Margret McBride, and our editor, Pat Golbitz. The book was *The Power of Ethical Management* (William Morrow, 1988).

Working with Norman and Ruth Peale sold me forever on the importance of positive thinking. They taught me that people like to be around positive thinkers because they exude positive energy. Norman and Ruth also convinced me that positive thinking is a choice and that choice keeps people from getting down on themselves or others. Positive thinkers always seem to take to the high road and get positive results. I have always tried to apply positive thinking, particularly in our own organization. In fact, when things are going badly, people look to me to turn lemons into lemonade.

For example, in 1992, when the economy was struggling and our company was getting hit hard, our CEO, Tom McKee—my wife's brother—gave the bad news, reporting that our finances were less than rosy. Everybody was a little down, so I got up and said, "Don't worry—someday we're going to own this whole block!" We always look back on that story and laugh because now we *do* own most of the block.

The tragic events on September 11, 2001, were another serious setback for our business. On that day we had trainers all over the country whose events were canceled. In one month we lost $1.5 million. Because the cancellations were not the trainers' fault, we felt they should be paid and brought home. But that decision sent us limping into our year-end. If we hoped to stay in the black, we had to cut $350,000 to $400,000 a month in expenses for the next three months.

The quickest way to cut expenses would have been to cut people, but that is not the kind of company we wanted to be. We asked the three "Ethics Check" questions that Norman Vincent Peale and I had developed in *The Power of Ethical Management*:

1. **Is it legal?** Of course it was legal to get rid of people if we could not pay them.
2. **Is it fair to all involved?** We thought, no, it was not fair to throw people out in the street when the country had been attacked and the economy was in bad shape.
3. **If you choose to do this, how will it make you feel about yourself? Would you like it published in the local newspaper? Would you like your grandchildren to know?** The answers to the last questions were anything but positive. Getting rid of people was not the answer to our financial woes.

Instead, we opened our books, as we normally do, sharing our financial condition with everybody on our staff of over 275 people. We formed task forces to look at how to increase revenues and a task force on how to cut expenses. Everybody pulled together and agreed to take salary cuts, although we decided not to cut salaries of people who were making less than $50,000 a year because it is tough enough living in San Diego. We agreed that if people left, we would not replace them. We stopped matching 401(k) contributions.

In the midst of these tough times I said, "When we pull out of this, we're all going to Hawaii."

Our CEO, Tom McKee, just about dropped his teeth. "Tijuana, maybe," he said, "but not Hawaii."

Our belt tightening continued for 2002 and 2003. In 2004, things started to turn around, and by November we had accomplished our financial goal for the year. We had budgeted for $38 million in revenue for the year and came in at $44 million at the end of the year. Sure enough, the following February, we took more than 300 people to Hawaii for a three-and-a-half-day celebration. Some of our people had never flown before, and well over half of them had never been to

Hawaii. People said they could not sleep at night because their faces hurt from smiling so much.

Positive thinking really works. Negative thinking never has and never will.

A Positive Difference

A couple of years ago, I had a customer service experience that really highlights the difference between a positive work environment and a negative one. I was heading to the airport for a trip that was going to take me to four different cities. As I approached the terminal, I realized that I had forgotten my driver's license and did not have a passport with me, either. Not having time to go back home to get them and make the flight, I had to be creative.

One of my books has my picture on the cover: *Everyone's a Coach*, which I wrote with the legendary football coach Don Shula. When I got to the airport, I ran into the bookstore and, luckily, there was a copy of our book. Fortunately, my first flight was on Southwest Airlines. As I was checking my bag, the porter asked to see my identification.

I said, "I feel bad. I don't have a driver's license or a passport. But will this do?" I showed him the cover of the book.

He shouted out, "The man knows Shula! Put him in first class!" Of course, Southwest does not have first class. Everybody by the check-in started to high-five me. I was like a hero.

Herb Kelleher, who founded Southwest, not only wanted to give his customers the lowest possible price, he also wanted to give them the best possible service. He set the organization up in a way that empowered everyone—including the front line baggage check folks—to soar like eagles. He gave them power to make decisions, use their brains, and create raving fans. Kelleher—who recently retired, turning over the reins to his long-time colleague, Colleen Barrett—felt that people could use their brains in interpreting policies. Why do airlines ask for identification? To make sure the person getting on the plane is the person with the name on the ticket. That was an easy call for the Southwest Airlines' front line person.

The next airline I had to go to before my office could overnight my driver's license was an airline that is in financial trouble. The ducks were quacking everywhere. The curbside attendant looked at my book and said, "You've got to be kidding me. You'd better go to the ticket counter. Quack! Quack!" When I showed the book to the woman at the ticket counter, she said, "You'd better talk to my supervisor. Quack! Quack!" I had to talk to four different levels of management before I could board the flight.

In the troubled airline the hierarchy was alive and well. All the energy was moving away from pleasing customers and moving toward serving the hierarchy—following the policies, procedures, rules, and regulations to the letter. That is no way to create positive experiences for customers. It just produces a duck pond.

The secret to positive leadership is to create an inspiring vision that gives people worthwhile work. Then let people use their brains, so they can soar like eagles. Most important, you need to cheer each other on. This not only motivates people, but also puts smiles on customers' faces—and makes your cash register go *ca-ching*.

ABOUT THE AUTHOR

Ken Blanchard is an award-winning speaker with a PhD in educational administration and leadership from Cornell University. He has been a guest on *Good Morning America* and *The Today Show* and has been featured in *Time*, *People*, *U.S. News & World Report*, and other popular publications. Blanchard is also cofounder of Lead Like Jesus, a nonprofit ministry dedicated to inspiring and equipping people to walk their faith in business and in life. He and his wife, Margie, live in San Diego.

Ken Blanchard is the chairman and chief spiritual officer of The Ken Blanchard Companies (http://www.kenblanchard.com), a global leader in workplace learning, employee productivity, and leadership and team effectiveness. He has written more than 40 books, including *The One Minute Manager*, *Raving Fans*, *Gung Ho!*, and *Whale Done!* He was recently inducted into the Amazon Hall of Fame as one of their top 25 best-selling authors of all time. His books have combined sales of more than 18 million copies in more than 25 languages.

99

Where There Is Smoke, There Is Fire

Ed Drozda

Every manager and almost every employee has tended his share of workplace fires. From smoldering embers to raging infernos, they hamper our ability to manage the routine events upon which our operations depend. The world is not a perfect place, and we should be proud of our ability to multitask, to resolve issues, and to maintain control, whether in crisis or otherwise. But how often have you said (or heard) "I spend too much time putting out fires?" Perhaps much more than you would like.

When it comes to workplace fires, there are three core ideas to keep in mind: identify and manage the real fires; dispatch the false alarms (that is, distinguish them from the real deal); and prevent fires whenever possible.

I spent the first 20 years of my professional life in the field of transfusion medicine and therapy. I saw my share of major fires, such as trauma victims and surgical cases with complications. Despite the fact that these fires occurred without warning, I was trained and conditioned in such a way that enabled me to aid in putting out these fires. The experience improved my fire-fighting skills as well as my ability to differentiate the real fires from the false alarms.

Dial 911

The assembly line halts because components are out of stock, the already irate customer is handled inappropriately—no matter what your industry, a real fire is an immediate concern. These situations are not difficult to recognize: They interrupt the typical work flow and demand prompt resolution.

Managing these situations is a matter of responsiveness and preparedness. Once a fire occurs, it is essential to take immediate action; a small fire has the potential to grow larger. Do not let it! Everyone should have a role in fire management, whether it is recognizing or extinguishing the blaze. Staff must be prepared either to take action or to communicate quickly to those who will take action.

Not all fires can be prevented. Whether or not a fire can be prevented, every fire should be viewed as an opportunity to prepare for future occurrences. Learn from past events, and take steps to prepare for future occurrences.

Oops! Just Kidding

Rumors, misunderstandings, hearsay . . . suffice it to say, a false alarm is very intrusive and often more time consuming than the real deal. A false alarm is an event (often a personal account of something happening in the workplace) that is neither urgent nor of considerable importance and generally of little to no concern for the business. However, though false alarms can distract us from the things that matter most, it does not mean they can always be ignored. Discretion must be applied when deciding upon the proper way to dispatch false alarms. For example, the ramblings of a chronic complainer are very time consuming. This is not an urgent matter, and the level of importance is probably suspect as well, however, these ramblings may have a considerable impact upon fellow employees and could result in more serious consequences at some point in time. A false alarm—well, yes, but important all the same. On the other hand, an unsubstantiated rumor can effectively be discredited and ignored, without considerable effort.

Regardless of the origin, it is important to be able to discern the false alarms from the real thing. True fires demand a timely and thorough response; false alarms may require further attention, but they are not urgent, and so you need to learn to prioritize them so that they do not interfere with your ability to manage the important things in a timely manner.

More important, staff must be encouraged to deal with false alarms before rallying the troops to support them. A false alarm often becomes a multialarm fire because others are drawn into the fray. Encourage staff to interpret and act upon the false alarms rather than fanning the flames.

Since false alarms do occur, learn to distinguish them from the real fires, and promptly dispatch those which require no further action. In those cases where further action is required, allocate time when matters of greater priority will not be compromised. In the meantime, it is a good idea that you do not let the false alarms discourage you—after all, they are as much a part of life as death and taxes.

An Ounce of Prevention

An important workplace goal is to reduce the incidence of real fires and to manage the intrusion of false alarms. This effort is the responsibility of all members of the workplace team. It is also a formidable task that should be put into perspective.

Reducing the incidence of fires is an achievable goal, as is the ability to speed your response time and to improve your fire management skills. But outright prevention? Let's be realistic about this. There are matters that are under your control and some that are not. Outright prevention is, like perfection, a goal to *strive* for, but it is beyond your grasp. Besides, if you prevented all of the fires, what would become of your crisis management skills?

Make every effort to reduce the incidence of fires, and prepare your teams to manage fires when they do occur. In an effort to accomplish these goals, encourage staff to be vigilant for smoldering fires that can be managed before they spread. Define processes through which fires are managed and ensure that staff are fully aware of and actively engaged in these processes. Furthermore, provide clear expectations so that all staff are able to take steps to prevent the formation of uncontrolled fires. Finally, acknowledge those whose vigilance has paid off, and learn from their achievements.

Managing workplace alarms and fires is critical to maintaining a smooth and efficient work environment. Learning to distinguish false from true alarms, effectively managing real fires, and, where possible, preventing fires is the responsibility of every manager and staff member.

ABOUT THE AUTHOR

Since 1996, Ed Drozda has facilitated the success of businesses of all sizes through effective management of comprehensive projects and strategically delivered business/executive coaching. As a project manager, he has worked with major pharmaceutical, medical device manufacturing, and blood collection companies. As a business/executive coach, Ed enjoys working with dynamic executives and business owners who seek to develop and grow their businesses. Ed partners with clients to negotiate the tortuous path to success by focusing on clarity, strategy, and synergy. He challenges and leads his clients to bring their goals to fruition while discovering and exploiting their inherent strengths. Visit him on the Web at http://www.4eandd.com.

100

Do You Dream of Being a Full-Time Writer?

Suzanne Lieurance

If your dream is to become a full-time writer who works in the comfort of her own home, sitting at the computer in cozy pjs or a sweat suit all day, then you need to make sure you are ready for the writer's life. Mainly, you need to ask yourself this question: *Do I really like to write?*

Understand the Writer's Life

As a freelance writer myself, and a writing teacher and writing coach, I am always surprised at the people I meet who say that I am living their dream. They would give anything to be able to quit their day jobs and write all day, just like I do. Yet when I ask them about their writing, they do not really write very much. Not only that, many of them hate to rewrite, and they do not like to read. Yikes! To me, that is like a professional basketball player saying he does not like to practice and he hates wearing athletic shoes. Reading, writing, and certainly rewriting are just part of the game for those of us who make our living as freelance writers. If you do not enjoy those parts of the game, then maybe you need to find another game and certainly another dream. The writer's life could turn out to be more of a nightmare for you.

The writer's life is much more than signing books in bookstores or appearing on *Oprah* to promote your latest novel. Most of the time, a writer sits alone at the keyboard. When the writing is not going well, this "dream life" can be frustrating and agonizing. But when the writing is going well (as it usually does after a period of agony for each project), there is nothing else the true writer would rather be doing than reworking a story or article until the whole thing starts to come together.

Find Time to Write

Maybe you really do like to write, rewrite, and read, but your personal life and work schedule do not allow you unlimited time for writing. Do not let that stand in the way of your dream. Make a commitment to yourself that writing is going to be a priority. Even if all you can manage is 15 minutes of writing a day, stick to that. If you do, it will not be long until you somehow find additional time to write.

Try These Other Tips

Here are other tips I give my writing and coaching students who are serious about one day living their dream of being a full-time writer.

1. **Do not make excuses.** Once you start working with editors, they will not want to hear excuses for work not being completed on time.

Treat yourself as an editor would. Do not accept excuses from yourself for not writing. Just find the time and do it. Write! Many writers who are now best-selling authors got up at 5:00 A.M. to write their first novel or they stayed up to write long after the rest of their families went to bed each night.

2. **Stick to only a few small projects at first.** Do not try to write a novel if you have never even managed to finish a short nonfiction article or a short story. You will overwhelm yourself from the start. Instead, write in a journal each day for a few weeks until you get in the habit of writing regularly. Once you have done that, set other writing goals for yourself, like finishing a nonfiction article.

3. **Do not attempt to write for the glossy magazine markets right off the bat.** Competition is fierce for publication in those big glossy magazines you see in the bookstores. Learn to write for smaller, local publications first. You will have more immediate success, which will inspire you to keep writing.

4. **Take a writing course, or find a writing coach or mentor who can help you improve your writing.** A mentor or writing coach can also keep you on track with your writing goals.

Once you have been writing regularly for a few months, you will know for sure if full-time writing really is the "dream life" you always thought it would be.

ABOUT THE AUTHOR

Suzanne Lieurance is a full-time freelance writer and the "working writer's coach." She helps people who love to write become "working" freelance writers. Lieurance is also a master teacher at http://www.universityofmasters.com, offering a course called Freelance Writing: How to Jump-Start Your Career. Lieurance is the author of 12 published books and is currently under contract for two more. Visit http://www.the-working-writers-coach.blogspot.com for more information about her intensive 8-week Working Writer's Coaching Program, or visit her Web sites at http://www.suzannelieurance.com and http://www.workingwriterscoach.com for information about her books and other writing services. E-mail her at workingwriterscoach@hotmail.com.

101

YOU AND YOUR MIND

Developing the Correct Mind-Set for Stepping Outside the Box

Adrian McMaster

Stepping outside the box is a term used to describe the creativity and innovation of entrepreneurs from all professional fields. Outside-the-box thinking often provides solutions to complex problems or allows entrepreneurs to develop new methods of doing business that can increase profits, reduce expenses, increase employee retention, or reduce negative incidents in the workplace. If you want to be able to step outside the box and think creatively, you will need to develop the correct mind-set for being innovative and learning how to move away from traditional methods of thinking that have become stagnant and underproductive. There are many ways to ease yourself into this mind-set if you are willing to take the initiative and put in the effort.

One of the first steps to developing the mind-set needed for outside-the-box thinking is to alter your thinking so that it coincides with the principles of this concept. If you have been solving problems with traditional problem-solving methods and have not seen good results, you may be ready to try stepping outside the box to come up with more creative solutions to your business problems. Most of the time, we think it is good to work hard or work smart. The key to outside-the-box thinking is to play smart. It is important to remove all judgment from the process. While generating new ideas, consider everything during the creative process. There are literally no "bad" ideas. Develop an understanding of how stepping outside the box can benefit your business, and work toward using this type of thinking when you face business problems. Many books and Web sites can give information on this type of thinking if you need more information on what stepping outside the box can do for you. An example is our Web page www.lead-a-powerful-life.com/innovation.htm. You can also consult with a business or personal development coach who specializes in motivation and creativity. The coach will ask you pointed questions that will change your perspective on the subject so that you can find new ideas. Working with this type of professional can give you a clear picture of how to step outside the box and the type of results you can expect to see once you do so. A good creative coach can also teach you various methods to arrive at new solutions to a problem. There are many established techniques for innovating, and a good Web search on the keywords "creativity" and "innovation" can lead you to hours of results.

The next step in developing the mind-set needed for outside-the-box thinking is to immerse yourself in activities that encourage creativity and innovative thinking. You can simply look at things in new and different ways. Imagine your problem solved. What does it look like? Imagine it bigger, smaller, faster, slower, more expensive, and less expensive. You might consider taking seminars or workshops dedicated to helping you find your creative self. There are many noncredit courses at community colleges that can help you to develop your creativity. You can also consider taking a course in a creative discipline, such as art or music. You can ask the question to people who would not normally be concerned with it. You may be surprised at how well that works. Look at what other industries do to solve similar problems. Can their solutions be adapted to your situation? The relaxation and sense of accomplishment that accompany working in a creative setting can often trigger innovative business ideas. Immersing yourself in creativity-boosting surroundings will help you on your way to developing the correct mind-set needed for stepping outside the box and solving problems in new and exciting ways. Many creative professionals surround their work spaces with bright colors, or even toys, to stimulate their imaginations. Try playing different styles of music. Sometimes varying your routine or familiar patterns can stir things loose.

Stepping outside the box to think creatively and implement innovative solutions to problems is not an easy task to accomplish. In order to develop the correct mind-set for this type of thinking, you need to understand that being innovative and creative in terms of problem solving can be very difficult if you do not loosen up. One key to your mind-set will be to understand that you will have to put a great deal of time and effort into your initial attempts at stepping outside the box. You should try to go back to a childlike viewpoint. Reach beyond the point of thinking where you mind starts saying that what you are thinking is fantasy. This means that you may have some initial difficulty in moving away from previous ways of thinking and moving toward being able to use outside-the-box thinking on a more permanent basis. Most of us have been raised by well-meaning parents and teachers who tell us things like "stop daydreaming!" Certainly this plays a part in our difficulty in stretching our imaginations. A good, stimulating practice is to insist on at least three answers to any question. Our minds tend to work in binary. If we go beyond the either/or process of thinking, we often find the solution we have been looking for. The sooner you can commit yourself to putting the required effort into developing your mind-set, the sooner you can use the principles of thinking outside the box to benefit your business. If you commit yourself to smart play and perseverance, you can develop the mind-set needed to step outside the box and develop creative solutions for your organization.

ABOUT THE AUTHOR

Adrian McMaster is one of Australia's top innovation and mind-set coaches and the director of Creative Attitudes, PTY LTD. His techniques will unlock your creativity and help you transform your life and business. Adrian has a powerful collection of e-books to assist you in developing your mind-set, and Adrian will give you a free, 10-minute Innovation Assessment by quickly going to http://www.lead-a-powerful-life.com.

ABOUT SELFGROWTH.COM

SelfGrowth.com is an Internet super-site for self-improvement and personal growth. It is part of a network of Web sites owned and operated by Self Improvement Online, Inc., a privately held New Jersey–based Internet company.

Our company's mission is to provide our Web site guests with high-quality self improvement and natural health information, with the one simple goal in mind: making their lives better. We provide information on topics ranging from goal setting and stress management to natural health and alternative medicine.

If you want to get a sense for our Web site's visibility on the Internet, you can start by going to Google, Yahoo, America Online, Lycos, or just about any search engine on the World Wide Web and typing the words "self-improvement." SelfGrowth.com consistently comes up as the top or one of the top Web sites for self-improvement.

OTHER FACTS ABOUT THE SITE

SelfGrowth.com offers a wealth of information on self-improvement. Our site:

- Publishes nine informative newsletters on self-improvement, personal growth, and natural health that go out to over 950,000 subscribers.
- Offers over 4,000 unique articles from more than 1,100 experts.
- Links to over 5,000 Web sites in an organized directory.
- Features an updated self-improvement store and event calendar.
- Gets visitors from over 100 countries.

CONTACT INFORMATION

ADDRESS:	Self Improvement Online, Inc.
	20 Arie Drive
	Marlboro, New Jersey 07746
PHONE:	(732) 761–9930
E-MAIL:	webmaster@selfgrowth.com
WEB SITE:	www.selfgrowth.com

Author Index

Author Index

AUTHOR INDEX

AUTHOR INDEX

A

Allen, Jeff, 162-165
Andersen, Sten M., 232-235
Antares, Kiernan, 17-21
Apollon, Susan Barbara, 225-228
Arste, Dolores, 216-220

B

Belceto, Shane, 267-270
Blanchard, Ken, 386-391
Bridger, Wendy, 337-339
Brown, Les, 372-374
Brown, Sheryl R., 292-295
Bungay Stanier, Michael, 49-52

C

Campanelli, Jeannie, 30-32
Carey, Peggy, 97-100
Carter, Wendy Y., 5-8
Cavaleri, Steve, 125-128, 199-202
Cordero, Lesley, 26-29
Corrigan, Stacy, 93-96

D

Dahlberg, Eva, 321-325
de Bruin, Marc, 382-385
Dicks, Sheila, 74-76
Doherty, Wesley, 9-12
Donaldson, Ken, 287-291
Drozda, Ed, 392-395

E

Ellis, John, 275-278
Erickson, Earl D., 229-231
Erwin, Michael, 354-357
Eubanks, Barbara, 42-44

F

Fiset, Nathalie, 150-153

G

Gail, Leslie, 257-259
Galt, Melissa, 209-211
Garusi, Piercarla, 330-333
Gianni, Kevin, 340-342
Giovanni, Katharine C., 248-252
Grant, George, 334-336
Gregorowicz, Paula, 299-302
Griffin, Jeanette, 133-136

H

Hall, Karen Wheeler, 260-263
Hansen, Mark Victor, 379-381
Harris, George, 113-116
Harris, Margrit, 337-339
Hayes, Laurie, 57-59
Heimstra, Nancy, 343-345
Hepperle, Barb, 38-41
Herkes, Carl, 71-73

K

Kahler, Joe, 89-92
Katie, Byron, 350-353
Keetch, Paul, 212-215
King-Meyer, Halette M., 129-132
Knight, Christopher M., 13-16
Korostensky, Kunbi, 375-378

L

Lankford, Kevin, 346-349
Lee, Michael, 315-320
Lieurance, Suzanne, 396-398
Loomis, Lynette M., 177-180
Louden, Rod, 240-243
Luckett, Doni, 203-205

405

ABOUT DAVID RIKLAN

David Riklan is the president and founder of Self Improvement Online, Inc., the leading provider of self-improvement and personal growth information on the Internet.

His company was founded in 1998 and now maintains four websites on self-improvement and natural health, including:

1. www.SelfGrowth.com
2. www.SelfImprovementNewsletters.com
3. www.NaturalHealthNewsletters.com
4. www.NaturalHealthWeb.com

His company also publishes nine e-mail newsletters going out to over 950,000 weekly subscribers on the topics of self improvement, natural health, personal growth, relationships, home business, sales skills, and brain improvement.

David's first book—*Self Improvement: The Top 101 Experts Who Help Us Improve Our Lives*—has been praised by leading industry experts as the "Encyclopedia of Self Improvement." That book's success motivated him to continue publishing books which, like the one you're reading now, seek to improve the lives of others.

He has a degree in chemical engineering from the State University of New York at Buffalo and has 20 years of experience in sales, marketing, management, and training for companies such as Hewlett-Packard and The Memory Training Institute.

His interest in self-improvement and personal growth began over 20 years ago and was best defined through his work as an instructor for Dale Carnegie Training, a performance-based training company.

David is a self-professed self-improvement junkie – and proud of it. His house is full of self-improvement books and tapes. He took his first self-improvement class, an Evelyn Wood speed-reading course, when he was 16 years old, and his interest hasn't ceased yet.

He lives and works in New Jersey with his wife and business partner, Michelle Riklan. Together, they run Self Improvement Online, Inc. and are raising three wonderful children: Joshua, Jonathan, and Rachel.